RICHARD G. JENKIN
A GREAT SON OF CORNWALL
MAP DYVROETH
MAB MEUR A GERNOW

RICHARD G. JENKIN
A GREAT SON OF CORNWALL
MAP DYVROETH
MAB MEUR A GERNOW

Edited by Derek R. Williams

Francis Boutle Publishers

First published by Francis Boutle Publishers
272 Alexandra Park Road
London N22 7BG
Tel/Fax: (020) 8889 7744
Email: info@francisboutle.co.uk
www.francisboutle.co.uk

Richard Jenkin: A Great Son of Cornwall © Contributors, 2013
All rights reserved.
No part of this book may be reproduced, stored
in a retrieval system, or transmitted, in any form
or by any means, electronic, mechanical
photocopying or otherwise without the prior permission of the publishers.

ISBN 978 1 90342785 9

Gwas gwyr an Arluth
Gwas gwyr an Eglos
Gwas gwyr an Yeth Kernewek:
Mab mur a Gernow

Ken MacKinnon

Richard Jenkin

Contents

9	List of illustrations
11	Acknowledgements
13	Foreword – *Maureen Fuller, Grand Bard of Gorsedh Kernow*
15	Preface – *Julyan Holmes*
19	Introduction – *Conan James Trevenen Jenkin*
25	My Cornwall – *Richard G. Jenkin*
37	Homecoming – *Richard G. Jenkin*
41	Following the rays of the Awen: Richard Jenkin and Gorsedh Kernow – *Peter W. Thomas*
80	Celtic Cornwall lives on – *Richard G. Jenkin*
83	'Years of dreaming and scheming...': Esedhvos Kernow – *Derek R. Williams*
100	Sermon: Saint James/Pregoth: Synt Jamys – *Richard G. Jenkin*
107	A voice heard all over the parish: Richard Jenkin, Helston and Old Cornwall – *Ann Trevenen Jenkin*
124	'Michael Joseph was a man...' – *Richard G. Jenkin*
125	'Breathing the fire of Cornish patriotism': *New Cornwall* Derek R. Williams
165	Election Impressions – *Richard G. Jenkin*
168	Vote Mebyon Kernow, vote Jenkin – *Dick Cole*
192	The first UK European Election of 1979 – *Colin Murley*
194	'Wales' – *Richard G. Jenkin*
195	Whegh Bro Un Enef/Six Countries One Soul – *Ann Trevenen Jenkin*
224	'Cusk lemmyn, cuf-colon'/'Sleep now, sweetheart' – *Richard G. Jenkin*

227	'Bedhen Breder Warbarth': Richard Jenkin and the Cornish Language – *Jori Ansell*
241	Modernising Vocabulary – *Richard G. Jenkin*
244	The Cornish-language Poetry of Richard Jenkin: a short survey – *Donald R. Rawe*
254	Cornish Literature in the 20th century – *Richard G. Jenkin*
263	The Haunting Voice: the English-language poetry of Richard Jenkin – *Bert Biscoe*
279	Reminiscences
294	Tributes
303	Freedom – *Richard G. Jenkin*
306	Richard G. Jenkin: a chronology – *Derek R. Williams*
317	Select bibliography of the writings of Richard G. Jenkin – *Ann Trevenen Jenkin* and *Derek R. Williams*
320	Notes on contributors

List of Illustrations

6	Richard Jenkin
18	Richard outside his home 'An Gernyk', Leedstown, September 1982
24	Richard at Trethevy Quoit, St Cleer, 2002
30	Richard at Furry Day, Helston, May 1966, with Loveday, Gawen and Morwenna
35	Richard 'Crying the Neck'
40	Richard and Ann Jenkin with Archdruid Dafydd Rowlands, Welsh National Eisteddfod, 1996
44	Letter, dated 15 July 1947, from Edwin Chirgwin, informing Jenkin of his election to Gorsedh Kernow
49	Richard Jenkin, newly-elected Grand Bard, with Hugh Miners, newly-elected Deputy Grand Bard, 1976
54	Richard welcoming his daughter Morwenna as a Cornish bard, Bodmin, 1979
89	Richard addressing the Welsh National Eisteddfod, Flint, 1969 (?)
92	Poster for Esedhvos Kernow, 1983
94	Letter card for Esedhvos Kernow, 1983
110	Richard as the dragon in Helston's Hal an Tow, Furry Day, May 1965
115	Richard 'Crying the Neck', Crowan
119	Crowan Parish Council, November 1994
129	Cover for *New Cornwall*, August-September 1958
134	Cover design for *New Cornwall* by Mary Mills, used from January 1964
136	Page from Richard Jenkin's notebook showing rough outline of con-

	tents of *New Cornwall*
166	Mebyon Kernow flyer for a meeting during the 1970 General Election
178	Mebyon Kernow leaflet for the European Assembly Elections, 7 June 1979
182	Mebyon Kernow flyer, General Election, 9 June 1983, when Richard stood in Falmouth-Camborne
184	Richard Jenkin leads the memorial service to Cornish martyrs at St Keverne, 8 July 1983
200	Rev (sic) Richard Jenkin's ticket for the Celtic Congress, Truro, August-September 1950
202	Cover of Celtic International Youth Camp brochure, August-September 1956
204	Celtic Congress delegates, Ramsey, Isle of Man, 1952
207	Ticket for Grand St Piran's Day draw, Celtic Congress, March 1963
213	Cover of booklet to commemorate visit of Celtic Congress to Newquay, April 1988
214	Cover of booklet for Celtic Congress, Lesneven, Brittany, July 1989
217	Richard and Ann Jenkin, Celtic Congress, Carmarthen, July 2002
233	Cover of the first issue of *Delyow Derow*, Winter 1988
265	Manuscript of Richard's poem 'Cornish Harbour' or 'Past and Present'
287	Advertisement and order form for *Cornwall: The Hidden Land*, *New Cornwall*, July 1963
300	Crowan church tower flying the Cornish flag purchased from the Richard Jenkin memorial fund
304	Richard Jenkin's gravestone in Crowan churchyard

Acknowledgements

The breadth and depth of Richard Jenkin's activities and friendships in Cornwall, the other Celtic territories, and beyond mean that a great number of individuals and organisations have helped in the preparation of this book – too many, in fact, to mention by name, although some are acknowledged in the footnotes to the articles.

However, I feel duty-bound to thank the following in particular.

Ann Trevenen Jenkin, who has done so much to encourage her late husband's friends and colleagues to share their memories of him, has gone out of her way to make the family archive available to one and all, and has always been there to advise, guide, and – where necessary – cajole.

Fellow contributors for giving so freely of their time in researching and writing about aspects of Richard Jenkin's life and work.

Maureen Fuller for her foreword and Julyan Holmes for his preface

Those who have shared their memories of Richard Jenkin.

The following organisations for providing funding: Cornwall Heritage Trust, The Federation of Old Cornwall Societies, Gorsedh Kernow, An Guntelles Keltek – Kernow (The Celtic Congress – Cornwall), Kesva an Taves Kernewek (Cornish Language Board), Mebyon Kernow – The Party for Cornwall, and the Sir Arthur Quiller-Couch Memorial Fund.

Clive Boutle of Francis Boutle Publishers for his guidance along the way.

Editor's note
Except where a contributor indicated a different preference, I have used the Standard Written Form of Cornish for the word 'gorsedd' in both Cornish and English contexts, so 'Gorsedh Kernow' and 'Cornish Gorsedh'. In Welsh,

Breton or generally Celtic contexts, the Welsh word 'gorsedd' or its plural 'gorseddau' is used. The spelling of the word in quotations is in the form of the original.

Derek R. Williams
September 2013

Foreword

As I look at the titles of the chapters from the contributors to this book, I can see that the reader is in for a treat. The diversity of the subjects reflects the man Richard was, a man who was fully involved in the Cornish scene, a passionate patriot. From being a Cornish speaker, a poet, a magazine editor, a guiding light of the Esedhvos and the Celtic Congress, twice Grand Bard of Gorsedh Kernow to entering the political world as a candidate for Mebyon Kernow, one can see that Richard was a multi-faceted man with an abiding love of Cornwall. At the same time, Richard was a devoted family man and cherished by his family.

From a personal point of view, Richard was the first person I heard speaking Cornish, which engendered a need in me to become a Cornish speaker. As *Map Dyvroeth*, he received me into the bardic circle with the name of *Steren Mor* at Nine Maidens, St Columb in 1977. Eventually, like him, I became the Gorsedh Marshal, in charge of all the Gorsedh ceremonies and I now follow in his wake as Grand Bard.

Enjoy this miscellany of writings, a veritable Crowdy Crawn about a man who embraced the Cornish scene and enhanced it.

Maureen Fuller
Grand Bard Gorsedh Kernow

Pan wrav vy mires orth titlow an chapters a'n gevriysi dhe'n lyver-ma, y hallav vy gweles an redyor dhe vos leun a lowena. Diverseth an destennow a dhastewyn bos an den, Richard, nebonan o omvyskys yn tien y'n wel gernewek, gwlaskarer gans passhyon. Dhyworth bos kerneweger, prydydh, pennskrifer lyver-termyn, golow ow kidya an Esedhvos ha Kuntelles Keltek, Bardh Meur Gorsedh Kernow diwweyth, dhe entra an bys politek avel ombrofyer rag Mebyon Kernow, y hyllir gweles Richard dhe vos den liesenebik gans kerensa orth Kernow heb fin. Yn kettermyn, Richard o den leun a lel wonis rag y deylu hag ev o chershyes gans y deylu.

Dhyworth an welva bersonel, Richard o an kynsa den a glewis vy ow kewsel yn Kernewek, ha hemma a wrug edhomm dhymm a vos ha bos kerneweger. Avel Map Dyvroeth, *ev a'm kemeras y'n kylgh bardhek gans hanow* Steren Mor *y'n Naw Moren, Sen Colum, y'n vlydhen mil naw kans seytek ha tri-ugens. Wostiwedh, avello, my eth ha bos kaslewydh an Orsedh, yn charj a solempnitys an Orsedh oll, ha lemmyn yth ov-vy holyer yn y gammow avel Bardh Meur.*

Omlowenha ow redya an kemmysk a skrifow-ma, Kroder Krohen yn hwir a-dro dhe dhen neb a vyrlas an welva gernewek, orth hy gwellhe.

Steren Mor
Bardh Meur Gorsedh Kernow

Preface

Julyan Holmes

For us learning Cornish in the 1970s, there was hardly anywhere to go and try out our mastery of the language, except for church services that were organised occasionally in churches all over Cornwall. There would be found a group of people of whom we were, rightly, in awe. One of this group was Richard Jenkin, *Map Dyvroeth*. No doubt that was where I saw him for the first time. Or it could have been at a meeting of some other organisation – the Celtic Congress, maybe, or Mebyon Kernow – for Richard was active in them all.

    A trace of northern English in his voice immediately reminded listeners of his upbringing in Derbyshire, followed by education in Manchester. Clearly, however, he never forgot he was, through his family, a Son of Cornwall.

    Richard's life's works on behalf of Cornwall are an unparalleled example of what can be achieved by somebody returning from the Cornish diaspora.

    A member of Mebyon Kernow from its formation in 1951, he became Vice-Chairman in 1968. Standing for Falmouth-Camborne in the Westminster election of 1970, he achieved the highest vote ever for that party: over 960 votes. A feat he repeated – with 10,000 votes – at the European Election, when he demanded the provision of a single constituency for Kernow.

    At the local level he was a member for several years of his parish council at Crowan and also its chairman.

    When he became a Bard at the age of twenty-two in 1947, in recognition of his studies in the Cornish language, he took the name *Map Dyvroeth* – 'Son of Exile'.

Apart from academic studies in Kernewek, he continued to write poetry throughout his life, including some in a little self-published magazine, *Delyow Derow*, which he signed as Garfield Richardson.

No matter where he was, he found time to strengthen the Cornish cause. This included, sometimes, giving speeches in both Cornish and English. Nor did he let his teaching post at Helston School distract him from the struggle.

Richard had a strong influence on many people, and, given this, and not forgetting the enthusiasm of his wife, Ann Trevenen, it is no surprise to find his children continuing his efforts in various parts of the Cornish revival. No great surprise, but greatly to his credit.

A quiet man, not one for boasting or self-congratulation, his reputation will last a long time, here in Kernow.

Dhyn ni dhyskoryon Kernewek adro dhe 1970, skant nyns esa chons dhe omvetya hag omassaya y'n taves saw unsel orth gonisyow eglos a vedha ornys oll adro dhe'n vro. Ena y fedha bagas a dus, an dus hen, o ewn dhyn omglewes pur uvel sevel y'ga mysk. Onan anedha o Richard Jenkin, Map Dyvroeth. Heb mar y feu yndella ma'n gwelis dhe'n kynsa prys. Saw y hallas bos yn herwydh neb kowethas aral drefen bos Richard gweythresek yn pub gwedh a'n dasserghyans, mar pe an Guntelles Keltek po Mebyon Kernow.

Orth y glewes, ton y lev a dhiskevras y vos genys ha megys yn Derbyshire ha, wosa henna, re'n kavsa y dhyskans yn Mankonion (Manchester). Byttegyns efan yw na vynna byskweth ankevi y vos, dre y deylu, mab a Gernow.

Oberow y vewnans a-barth y vammvro yw patron heb par a'n pyth a allo bos gwrys dre dhen a dhehwel a'n diaspora.

Esel a Vebyon Kernow dhyworth an dalleth yn 1951, y teuth dhe vos Is-Kaderyer yn 1968. Ev yth o neb a dhrehedhas an moyha sewena a-barth MK yn dewisyansow Westminster, ow kuntel moy es 960 lev pan sevis rag Aberfala-Kammbronn yn 1970, ha moy es 10,000 a-barth Kernow oll pan ledyas an gorholedh rag sedh unnik rag Kernow yn Senedh Europa.

War vynk isella yth o lies bledhen esel konsel y bluw e'ev, Pluwgrewen, (Crowan), ha 'y gaderyer magata.

Pan veu va gwrys Bardh yn 1947, dhe'n oos a 22 vloodh, y feu avel 'Bardh an Yeth'.

Preface

Richard a besya ow skrifa bardhonogow a hys y vewnans. Rag ensampel, omdhiskwedhes a russons yn lyvrigow Delyow Derow, sinys treweythyow: Garfield Richardson.

Ny vern ple'th esa, yn Kernow po Pow Sows, y kavas termyn dhe grevhe an omsav.

Ny wrug y soodh avel dyskader yn Hellys y lettya unn tamm rag gwruthyl a-barth enev Kernow, ow ri arethyow yn Kernewek keffrys ha Sowsnek.

Gwres ha nerth y golon yn kever puptra Kernewek a borthas roweth war veur a bobel. Rag henna hag yn unn berthi kov a dangolon y wreg, Ann Trevenen, nyns yw marth kavos eseli y deylu ow pesya y ober yn diblans leow a vri. Nyns yw marth, mes meur dh'y wormola.

Den kosel, heb na bost na fasow, y vri a wra durya hirneth omma yn Kernow.

Richard outside his home 'An Gernyk', Leedstown, September 1982

Introduction

Conan James Trevenen Jenkin

It is now over a decade since the death on 29 October 2002 of Richard Garfield Jenkin who held the bardic name *Map Dyvroeth* – Son of Exile. Like many family members who have lost a close relation, I still feel a sense of grief and loss even after all this time. It would be honest to admit I miss my father very much, not just because I am his son, but also because I admired him in so many ways. All of his children held him in great regard, not least because of his kindness as a father, but also because we felt he had many other qualities which we all learned from and hoped to emulate. This volume will seek to depict many of the attributes which we so valued as children and which father bought to all the many range of activities that he was so engaged in to promote his Cornwall and his Cornish identity.

I certainly still miss the opportunity to discuss a wide variety of Cornish issues with him. He was very much a polymath; a Cornish renaissance man who could turn his hand to carving, wood working, art and craftwork. His hand built dining-room table has outlasted him. His knowledge in all sorts of fields amazed us all. His interests spanned the sciences, literature, arts, history, language, geography, politics and archaeology. One could be sure that if you wanted to know something about almost anything then he would be able to draw on his wealth of knowledge and experience to give you good counsel. So even ten years on I still miss the opportunity to discuss issues of Cornish language, Cornish politics, Cornish culture and Cornish identity. I sincerely hope that readers of this volume will begin to understand the man and appreciate his life's work in much the same way that his family do.

However, it was not a given that my father would contribute to the Cornish revival in so many ways. He had to choose, like Henry Jenner, to be Cornish and could easily have lost his Cornish identity and heritage in exile in England. Many people, even those who knew him well, may only have a hazy understanding of his background, formative years in England and why, even until his death, one could still detect a slight Mancunian tinge in his speech. So, as part of this introduction to the volume, I have included some background information about my father's heritage and roots and how they influenced him throughout his whole life and activities within the Cornish Revival.

In September 1947, at the Gorsedh ceremony in Launceston led by Grand Bard Robert Morton Nance, Richard Garfield Jenkin, at the age of just 22, was elected to the College of Bards of the Cornish Gorsedh through qualification in the Cornish language. In keeping with Richard's chosen name 'Son of Exile', he was not there, but was still in 'exile' far away from Cornwall in the Middle East where he was concluding his war-time service in the Royal Signals. So, it was not until the following year that he was able to attend his first Gorsedh ceremony at Carwynnen near Camborne. It was this sense of being an exiled Cornishman and his great love of the Cornish language which informed much of his subsequent activities. But these concerns had deep roots both in his psyche and the heritage and culture he received from his family.

Richard's journey of life began in 1925 in Ilkeston, Derbyshire, far from Cornwall. He was born to Richard Jenkin (1895-1952) and Emily Winifrid Veda Hebbes (1893-1983). 'Winnie' came from an old Bedfordshire family that had a keen sense of duty and public service; two generations of them had served in the local constabulary and some had even worked at Windsor Castle for England's royalty. She fell for Richard, my grandfather, during the First World War when she saw him playing in the church army band. They were married on 19 November 1917 and eleven months later produced a daughter Pamela Vida Jenkin (1918-1992). Seven years later Richard Garfield Jenkin was born and named after father (Richard) and Uncle Garfield (1892-1951), Richard's slightly older brother who had emigrated to America. He was known amongst his family as Garfield, something that continued at least until the death of his father in 1952. This followed the tradition of using the second name as the distinguishing name of the family – a common practice amongst west Cornwall families.

In fact, Richard senior, my father's father, came from the parish of Paul next to Penzance. The Jenkin family had been fishermen out of both Newlyn and Mousehole for generations and had a strong relationship with the sea. Father's cousins continued this vocation up to the end of the 20th century. Richard senior, in contrast, went out on a fishing boat once and was so violently sick he never took to the fishing business and never properly learnt to swim. This led him to working as an agricultural worker – he is listed as such, aged 16, in the census of 1911 – and in local quarries, including those in the Lamorna valley and later around St Keverne. When war broke out in 1914, Richard senior joined up and, surprisingly, despite his inability to swim, was allocated to the Royal Navy where his musical skills allowed him to join the military band. The family story had him being dragged on a leash to get him through the swimming test and nearly drowning in the process. My father certainly inherited the lack of interest in swimming, but loved rowing and kept a rowing boat for many years.

Richard's ancestry linked him to many of the local Paul parish families including the Harveys and the Bodinnars. In later years my father made great efforts as a family historian to investigate both his ancestry and his wife Ann Trevenen's ancestry. On the Jenkin side of the family, he was able to trace the paternal line through generations of Paul fishermen and market gardeners to yeoman farmers from the neighbouring Madron parish. By the early 1600s the Jenkin family were tilling the soils of Great Bosullow Farm near to Chun Castle and Men-an-Tol, and high on the Penwith moorland. There was little doubt in his mind that they would have been part of Penwith's community of Cornish-language speakers. It was this sense of continuity and longevity that inspired Richard in his work to support and promote the Cornish language.

Richard's own interest in the Cornish language was sparked as a young man by the discovery of a book about the Cornish language in Manchester civic library. He at once set about learning the language and communicating with Robert Morton Nance amongst others in order to re-connect himself with what he considered to be his ancestral homeland. Far away in Manchester, he felt very keenly the sense of exile of many people with Cornish heritage who had been forced into emigration as part of the great Cornish Diaspora from the 1880s onwards.

My father's family from Mousehole were not immune to the pre and post-war paralysis that has been so well described by modern Cornish historians. Richard was only too aware that his father was the only one of eight brothers who had not become an economic migrant to America, and was only in exile in England. Some of the family later returned and my father valued meeting all his many cousins in Mousehole during long summer holidays and connecting with his Cornish roots and heritage. By that time Richard senior had completed his training as a vicar in the Church of England and had a post in the parish of Middleton, Manchester. His son was brought up with a strong sense of morality – Christianity along with a sense of the importance of family and his Cornish roots. So, my father and his father would make the long journey down from Manchester on bicycles. On one such occasion, when father was aged almost fourteen, they returned early to Manchester by train in order to reach the family home before the outbreak of war with Germany in September 1939.

In 1944, aged 18, he completed his studies at the William Hulme Grammar School, Manchester and was admitted to Oxford University to study chemistry. Richard threw himself into university life meeting fellow students who were interested in Cornwall and making life-long friends, such as David Balhatchet (*Map Frynkes*) and Nina Mabey (Nina Bawden the novelist). Other famous fellow students included Richard Burton who was briefly there at the same time, and a certain Margaret Roberts who later married a Dennis Thatcher, but the less said about that the better. A.L. Rowse (*Lef a Gernow*) was also an important figure at Oxford at the time, adding to the heady mix that Richard was exposed to. After not completing his first year with high enough marks – perhaps because of all his Cornish activities – he was called up to join the army.

In 1945 my father began his basic training in the Royal Signals, but by the time that this had finished, the war was largely over. And for the next few years he was sent to a number of trouble spots including Greece, Palestine and Iraq. Whilst in the army he had communicated in Cornish with other language enthusiasts and had managed to get these messages through the army censor.

Around the same time, Richard's father managed to end his period of exile by returning to Cornwall to take up the post of Vicar of St Gennys in north

Cornwall, not far from Bude. Richard visited him there whilst on leave and was perhaps inspired by the beauty and Cornishness of this borderland to suggest Morwenna as an appropriate name for his first child in 1957. Richard senior moved in 1950 to the parish of St Mewan near St Austell where he passed away in 1953 from a heart attack after digging a grave in the churchyard. His grave can be found near to the church and is notable for its use of the Cornish language on the headstone. From that point onwards my father became increasingly concerned about his own mortality and spiritual well-being – something that influenced many of his later concerns.

When his military service concluded, Richard determined to return home to reignite his Cornish roots, train to be a teacher and ultimately – in 1956 – marry Ann Trevenen (*Bryallen*). He would then cease being in 'exile' and return to his ancestral homeland. On his return at the end of 1959, he threw himself into all aspects of the Cornish revival.

It is not the place here to discuss further Richard's contribution to the revival, but after ten years and in the spirit of this season which promises renewal, resurrection and reflection, it seems appropriate for others to bring to a new audience a sense of the continuity and strength of character of a Cornish patriot whom I feel immensely proud to have had as a father. A lot of things have changed in the last ten years, with significant developments in the cultural, linguistic and political front within Cornwall. I feel sure that 'Tas' would be happy with the general direction of travel and the progress made but, like many of us, would be impatient with the need to progress the Cornish revival more quickly. He will not come back to haunt us yet, but his message through his own example is that we should all continue to strive for a 'New Cornwall' and a better and Cornish future for the people of our proud nation. His message would continue to be "Don't ever stop working for Cornwall".

Pask 2013

Richard at Trethevy Quoit, St Cleer, 2002

My Cornwall

Richard G. Jenkin

Everyone has his own Cornwall, the concept that appears in his mind when Cornwall is mentioned. For some it is based on the place where they were born and grew up, though they may have left it long ago; for others who have come to Cornwall late in life, it may be one spot that for them sums up the attraction that brought them here.

These Cornwalls exist in a set of dimensions related to, but not confined by, the three dimensions of the physical reality of Cornwall. Each is individual; they may overlap, but do not coincide.

Each Cornwall is subjective, as perceived by the observer and in My Cornwall there may be as much of me as Cornwall, so I apologise in advance if there seems to be too much 'I'. At any rate, you won't be getting statistics and descriptions of what you know already.

I was not lucky enough to be brought up in Cornwall, though it was ever-present in my consciousness and, by the circumstances of my life, My Cornwall is made up of many images superimposed as in a kaleidoscope.

One of the strongest – perhaps THE strongest – of those images is made up of Mousehole and Paul. My father was born and brought up in Mousehole in The Gurnick – which is why I called my house in Cornwall 'An Gernyk'. My grandmother died early and my grandfather had to bring up a large family on his own. My father left Cornwall as a young man before the First World War and did not return to live in Cornwall until after the Second World War, a few years before his too-early death. However, unlike his six brothers he did not go to

America and over the years he was able to bring his young family home to Cornwall for holidays and to visit his sisters and two brothers who had returned from America.

So, to me in my childhood, Mousehole was the dreamland where the sun always shone and the ever-changing Mount rose out of the waters of the Bay – where we scrambled over the Battery and (great adventure) down by the iron steps and stanchions to the Cave – or over the rocks, by Dicky Daniel's Hole with the tale of a man trapped inside by a huge boulder. A sea-bleached branch under a boulder suggested a bone of a crushed Dick Daniel.

Or again, I remember trying unsuccessfully with a bit of limpet on a bent pin to catch little fishes in a rock pool out the Merlin. I knew who Merlin was from tales of King Arthur and his Knights, but I never identified the actual Merlin Rock nor exactly where Point Spaniard was, though I knew they had killed Jenkin Keigwin at the door of his house.

> Y a-wra tyra war an Men Merlyn
> A-wra lesky Pawl, Pensans ha Newlyn.

Or we would travel to Penzance in Harveys' bus, owned by my father's uncles, to have tea in the Maypole Café, upstairs and through a bead curtain, over the Maypole shop and looking down on Market Jew Street with its two levels and steps up and down, like a pier alongside the traffic in the street.

Then there would be time spent sculling around the harbour in a punt. This confused me as I knew that in regular English a punt was a flat-bottomed boat on a river and I thought that sculls were oars used sitting down. (Actually, I have recently looked this up in the O.E.D. and the definition of a scull as an oar over the stern is the one given first.) Then there was the fun of scrambling down the pier steps or, better, the iron ladder, to jump all over Uncle Tommy's drifter "The Gleaner"; to stand in the little wheelhouse and, for a few minutes, be a steersman on a long ocean voyage, enveloped in the tarry, fishy smell of the nets and the men's clothes.

Many years later, after the war, on the other side of Europe, I wrote:

> Here beside the blue Aegean sea

> The bark-brown nets lie drying in the sun.
> Across the waste of years they bring to me
> A memory of childhood scarce begun
> When by my father's fathers' home I sat
> And saw the nets spread on the old sea wall,
> But oh, how many miles this place from that
> And yet how swift the thought at memory's call.
>
> But truly, I have been so long away
> I must not hope to find the little port
> Unchanged as though the years were yesterday
> And time has passed as quickly as a thought.
> Yet I will go once more to see the place
> Where generations bred my bone and brain
> And, though I find no once-familiar face,
> Beside that sea I'll be at home again.

Or there is the other half of my childhood impressions: Walking up from Mousehole to Paul on a sunny afternoon was very pleasant, but after sunset the tale of the murdered woman by the roadside would be uppermost and one would be very glad to get up the hill and past the churchyard. I remember staying with my aunt in Paul in those days before the war and going with my cousin to fetch water in pails and pitchers, and the Cornish range in the house sparkling and glowing. It was strange to a town child used to mains water and all other services, yet over ten years later, after the war, I found even more old fashioned conditions in North Cornwall, where we even used a cloam oven on occasion.

    I suppose that in one way it was Paul that really determined my future. There is the old cross head on the churchyard wall. That first introduced me to the antiquities of Cornwall and even now it is to me the essential Cornish wheel cross from which all others are deviations – though in fact it is a fairly rare type. There is Dolly Pentreath's memorial with its one sentence of oddly spelt and oddly constructed Cornish. It was from that I first learnt that the Cornish had their own language, which was my language.

It did not take me long to find out that it was related to the other Celtic languages and one of my adolescent hobbies was reading etymological dictionaries to find Celtic words and filling notebooks with parallel columns of words in each language. It left me with an abiding interest in the Celtic languages and linguistics generally. It also encouraged me to read all I could about not only Cornwall but all the Celtic countries, their topography and their histories. I determined that one day I would return to live in Cornwall for I certainly had no roots elsewhere. Before the war we never seemed to stay more than three or four years in any one place in England, and Cornwall was the land to which I turned.

I absorbed all I could of its history and legends, even, at the age of 15, buying myself a copy of Carew's *Survey of Cornwall* which I got in those days for a couple of pounds. After reading the folk tales of Hunt and Bottrell I wrote about Langarrow:

> I see in dreams the long lost land of Langarrow
> Sleeping under silent sandy waves.
> In every house and every roadway narrow
> The dry bones stir in their unquiet graves.
> On sand-soft pillows in a dry, cold kiss
> Skull touches skull as even on that night
> They lay without a thought of aught amiss
> Until the drifting sand blocked out their light.
> The yellowing bones within the tavern cry
> For wine to clear their parching throat of sand;
> And now those bones forever are as dry
> As the dice they rattled in their hand.
> Seven churches stood within the walls –
> Far-famed their slender towers and stately piers –
> Their priests grew fat within the prince's halls,
> Their bells are silent now these many years.
> The merchants' business now no longer thrives,
> The golden sand invades their golden hoards,
> And chokes the mouths that chaffered for men's lives

>   And bartered bodies over counter-boards.
>   The dry bones' rustle fills the sand-sunk town
>   Whispering the tales of shame and lust
>   That brought a rich and powerful kingdom down
>   And closed its people's eyes with yellow dust.

and on another Cornish legend, Tregeagle and the Wind:

>   Behind my back the timid, rain-washed moon
>   Crept slowly through the dark, wind-driven clouds
>   And spread her fearful half-light on the land.
>   My moon-cast shadow crouched before my feet
>   While Tregeagle and the wind howled in the trees.
>
>   I passed the Virgin Mary's lonely lake
>   Where wind-whipt racing waves flung up white arms
>   And broken foam bespattered darkened rocks
>   As Wild Tregeagle tried to bale the pool
>   With Roche the hermit's leaky limpet shell.
>
>   I stood upon the salt-encrusted shore
>   And watched the spray-wet wind hurl sand clouds high
>   As still Tregeagle worked on fruitlessly
>   To spin and splice his fragile ropes of sand
>   That fell in fragments as they left his hand.
>
>   I ran by Roche the hermit's ruined chapel –
>   Through every broken window blowing shrill
>   The wind shrieked like a tortured devil;
>   Tregeagle, caught between hell-flames and heaven,
>   Howled and sobbed and howled again.

During the war I first learnt of the existence of Cornish grammars and dictionaries and set about learning Cornish systematically. From Greece I wrote to

Richard at Furry Day, Helston, May 1966, with (left to right) Loveday, Gawen and Morwenna

Mordon and became a language bard in 1947 while still overseas. My examination piece in Cornish was a series of anecdotes about John Stone as told me by my father.

The next year I was demobbed and found to my delight that my father was returning to Cornwall, to St Gennys, tucked away on the North Coast between Bude and Tintagel – a very different Cornwall, but adding yet another facet to My Cornwall. I was able to make my first visit to Tintagel, formerly just a legendary name; to see my first Midsummer bonfire at St Cleer (organised by Edwin Chirgwin of Newlyn); to seek out Warbstow Barrow, an eerie place with its legend of the buried giant, and to discover the Allen Valley, carpeted with misty bluebells in spring. Stone crosses, ancient inscriptions, hidden in forgotten valleys and lonely lanes. The dark grey slate coast, so different from the granite, was wild in a more frightening way – less accommodating to human presence and human emotion. In one mood it produced this view of Cleave, North Cornwall:

> Here is no soft and rolling countryside:–
> Great cliffs, knife-edged, where bare slate stares like bone
> Protruding from half-vanished carrion flesh;
> Strata straight and tense or, here and there,
> Contorted, cramped like muscles, tetanus-tied –
> Violence persisting after death.
> Here is no calm, death-bed serenity
> But passion choked with passion till it died.
>   To South and West the granite thrusts and bursts
>   Through Cornish earth and, castle-cragged, confronts
>   The heavens, or stands the ceaseless siege of storms
>   And seas, relentless war on every side.
>   A land for heroes, giants, legends, myths.
> But here the Northern rocks writhe yet in pain.
> Reefs run out to rip with stone sharp swords
> The eggshell boats, and human sacrifices
> Lie in lonely churchyards near the cliffs
> That are possessed by older spirits still
> Which vented rage and spite before man came,
> And evil washes in with every tide.

But not all was dark in that forgotten part of Cornwall though modern man seemed there on sufferance only and Newquay and Bude were a world away.

From there – after a few years – we went to St Mewan near St Austell, on the edge of the lunar landscape of the china-clay country: from a distance the tents of the Israelites, but close to, the bone heaps of dead and decayed granite. In a fertile crescent around the wasteland were the farmlands between the moors and the sea – yet another facet of My Cornwall; from the beach at Caerhayes to the Trystan Stone and Castle Dor a land of history and mystery underlying the workaday world.

After the death of my father, my mother moved to Camborne and though I was now working outside Cornwall and only home for the holidays, it became another Cornwall to explore and assimilate. Camborne-Redruth, an industrial centre in Cornwall, has its own significance and character. Things happened there. The early history of Mebyon Kernow began there and it is mainly people I remember from that time. Acquaintances I had already made ripened into friends: Talek and Gunwyn (future Grand Bards), Charles Thomas, Helena Charles, Lambert Truran, and my wife-to-be, Ann Trevenen.

The post-war period had its stresses for Cornwall and I now noticed these more; the endemic unemployment in a supposed era of full employment; the constant emigration and the rapid growth of the tourist industry which threatened to swamp what was left of Cornish Cornwall. Contemplation of St Ives in summer produced a Hurrah for the Tourist Trade:

> Down in the land of the piskey-shops
> Taking in tourists pays more than the crops.
> Fishers don't fish and farmers don't farm,
> They sell the mugs a piskey charm,
> A sail round the bay, or a real cream tea,
> And feather their nests with L.S.D.
> Down by the quay in their oil-stained jeans
> The artists are painting their seascape scenes.
> Out in the sun, where the customers can watch
> They cover canvas with squiggle and blotch,
>   "Sell it you cheap for ten quid down –
>   Cost you fifteen guineas when I show in Town."
> Go to the Hotel, five star grade:
> "No room at all, sir, I'm afraid,
> Put you in the annexe just down the road."
> But the little bedroom is cold as a toad.
> Here's a little café in simple Tudor style –
> Head-cracking oak-beams and table-tops of tile –
> Queue twenty minutes for a table by the door,
> Order the tea and wait twenty more,
> Baked beans on toast, or fried fish and chips,

All else is off, and the teapot drips.
Outside, the town is bursting at the seams
As traffic tries to enter in ever-growing streams.
Here in the centre they meet and stagnate.
"They also swear who only sit and wait."

Eventually we returned to Cornwall for good, my wife and I and two baby daughters, for whom I had written a lullaby in Cornish. Certainly it had a great deal of use in the first few years. It brought in the Sea and the Stars and the Guardian Angel to bring sleep.

Cusk yn-ta, Cuf-colon,
Clew whystra tros an don.
Yn hunrosow hanas mor
Dhys a-dhoro cuscas clor.

Kemer 'wyth, Elyk glan,
Anedhy-hy, Cares splan.
Mowes whecca ages-sy
Nefra yn bys-ma ny welta-jy.

Ster ebren whath a-splan,
Kentrow nen a'n nef efan.
Gwrens dewynya dres an nos
Bys yn bore pan wrons-y mos.

[*Sleep well, Sweetheart,*
Hear whispering the surge of the wave.
May the murmur of the sea in dreams
Bring to you gentle sleep.

Pure little Angel, take care
Of her, bright Love.
A sweeter girl than she is

In this world you will never see.

Stars of the sky still shine,
Roof-nails of the wide heavens.
Let them shine throughout the night
Until the dawn when they will go.]

For the past twenty years we have lived, as some might say, in the middle of nowhere. Neither in Camborne, nor Helston, nor Hayle nor Marazion, but in between in a little village surrounded by small farms and derelict mine waste rapidly returning to patches of wild moor. From here I can survey all My Cornwalls and bring them into one many-facetted crystal such as my son finds on the mine dumps – unregarded beauty – but the oldest, deepest layer is still strong:

> Where I live now I look towards the Mount
> Whose castled crag o'ertops the land between,
> Though nothing of its watery foot is seen,
> And often on fine days the higher ground
> Beyond the bay lies like a fairy land
> Whose church towers stand out black against the sky.
> Always the tower at Paul attracts my eye
> As if in answer to the blood's command
> To turn towards its fountain-head once more.
> For in that parish my fore-fathers dwelt
> Before the Saxon speech betrayed the Celt
> And stole from him his history and his lore.
> Four hundred years ago, the church books say,
> A little girl was christened there at Paul –
> The fading ink has lost beyond recall
> The name they gave her on that far-off day,
> But still her father's name stands written clear –
> Richard Jenkin – my father's was the same
> And I also was christened with this name.

Richard 'Crying the Neck', n.d. (copyright Green Lane Studio, Redruth)

> So as I stand before the window here,
> My daughters each asleep in her own cot,
> I often think of him whose name I bear,
> Whose ancestral blood perhaps I share,
> And wonder how his life was lived, and what
> He hoped and planned for her, his little one,
> Baptised that day, four centuries ago,
> But never now in this world shall I know
> For other records of them all are gone.

And My Cornwall has gone on expanding: I have danced in the 12 o'clock Dance on Furry Day; I have been part of the Hal-an-Tow; I have Cried the Neck and recited the Cornish at the Midsummer Bonfire on Wendron Beacon. I have seen the Padstow Obby Oss and the Hurling at St Columb and St Ives. I have crawled through the Men an Tol and the fougou at Pendeen. I have been at every Gorsedd but three in the last 35 years.

I have not only loved Cornwall and its past but I have tried to work for its survival into the future as recognisably Cornish, a Celtic country.

This is My Cornwall, a quartz crystal from the rock, fractured, imperfect, but shining from its many facets.

[This autobiographical fragment, written – almost certainly for a talk – circa 1980, is to be found in the Jenkin family archive.]

Homecoming

Richard G. Jenkin

The old man nodded.

It was New Year 1948 that we disembarked and went through the demobilisation centre in an unfamiliar London. I collected a blue suit that soon became too tight and shiny, and my first trilby hat that had too narrow a brim. Then, with a railway warrant for the North in my pocket, I was off home to celebrate the tail-end of Christmas and a combined disembarkation and demobilisation leave.

Up in the mill country of Lancashire Dad and Mother were waiting surrounded by packing cases, for Dad had just been given a new post back in Cornwall. At last we were returning "home", back to the land he had left thirty years before. Until now Cornwall had been the place for summer holidays, visiting aunts and uncles and cousins whose lives had been so different from ours. Now it was to be our permanent home.

Dad had been longing to get back to Cornwall; now, at last, we were going. It was not to his birthplace in the West; in fact, it was about as far away as it could be and still be on the right side of the Tamar, up in unknown North Cornwall. Still, it was "home".

Dad went on ahead to get the house ready for occupation. A few days later, having cleared up the last details, Mother and I followed. The night train from Manchester trundled down the length of England till dawn found us in Exeter, changing to the unfamiliar Southern Region line. On we went to Launceston and a completely new Cornwall, changing at the tiny Halwill Junction, so different from Middleton Junction in the midst of cotton mills. Finally the little train puffed into Otterham Station – no town, no village, just a couple of houses.

No buses, no taxis either – how were we to get the last ten miles home? The station porter rang for a car for us. "Perhaps you and your husband would like to wait by the fire till he comes?" This offended my susceptibilities. Though Mother was a striking woman of fifty-five I did not think that, still in my twenties, I looked old enough to be her husband, even after three years overseas!

Eventually, after a long drive through green fields and by isolated farms, we arrived at the rambling old house tucked away on its own, not far from the cliffs. There are wilder places in Cornwall and the land there is all cultivated farm land, but there are very few people to be seen. Instead of the hurrying throngs of the city now it was an event to be noted when we saw a distant figure walking the cliff path.

We took some time to adjust to the new life. Candles and oil-lamps needed more thought and preparation than clicking an electric switch. Tilley lamps and Aladdin lamps gave a beautiful bright light but somehow it didn't penetrate to the corners of the rooms like electricity. A candle going out in a draughty corridor could be upsetting to the nerves and the dancing shadows excited the imagination.

The oil-stove smelt and didn't cook like gas. Making a cup of tea took twice as long. In the linhay we found a cloam oven built into the wall, and with only theoretical knowledge of its use we tried it out a couple of times. The cake was pretty good, slightly soft in the centre and one edge scorched, but eatable.

The water stopped running in the taps. Our neighbouring farmer explained that there must be an air-lock in the pipe between the house and the spring two fields away. He showed us how to use the semi-rotary pump fixed to the side of the house and half an hour's pumping restored the syphon action and got the water running again.

It was fortunate we could get our milk and eggs from the farm and the grocer called once a week and dealt with our rations, for the nearest town was twelve miles away – one bus there in the morning and another back in the middle of the afternoon. There was no chance now to run down to the shop at the corner of the street or spend an evening in the cinema, and we had to remember to keep charged accumulators for the wireless, as we had not had to do for fifteen years in the North.

Dad had returned home, not only to the land of his birth but also to the conditions of his childhood. He didn't have long to enjoy it, however. Within five years he was buried in Cornish soil, though still miles from his native parish. Mother, the English girl he had married during the First World War, lived another thirty years, but further West in Cornwall where Dad would have loved to be.

As for me, I had to leave home again to find work and it wasn't until ten years later that I was able to return home permanently – but that is another story, said the old man.

[Entered under the pen-name Gwythy Segh in the 1986 Esedhvos Kernow English Short Story category]

Richard and Ann Jenkin with Archdruid Dafydd Rowlands, Welsh National Eisteddfod, 1996

Following the rays of the Awen: Richard Jenkin and Gorsedh Kernow

Peter W. Thomas

Introduction
Richard Jenkin was a Bard of Gorsedh Kernow (the Cornish Gorsedd)[1] for fifty-five years, holding office as Bardh Meur (Grand Bard) for nine of those years. Apart from the exceptional case of Robert Morton Nance (*Mordon*), no other person has served as Grand Bard for a longer period. Richard Jenkin's extended tenure came about because he was re-elected three years after stepping down following two successive terms in office, and he is (so far) the only person to have been called upon to serve again in that way. He had already been a bard for twenty-nine years before becoming Grand Bard for the first time in 1976. Indeed, his wealth of experience and reliability as leader were the qualities which led to his election to a third term, at the darkest time in the history of the Gorsedd. Throughout his association with Gorsedh Kernow he worked tirelessly and unstintingly to promote the organisation as a means of enhancing all aspects of Cornish life and culture. Since he was also working so hard for Cornwall in many other fields, his record of service is a truly outstanding one.

Beginnings
At the meeting of the Council of Gorsedh Kernow held on 28 June 1947, the members decided the names of those who were to be initiated as new bards at that year's Gorsedd ceremony. One of those who had been elected by examina-

tion in the Cornish language was the 21-year-old 'Sigmn. R.G. Jenkin. Signal Troop. British Instructional Team ... Volos ... British Forces in Greece'.[2] Remarkably, two other future Grand Bards were elected in the same year, George Pawley White (*Gunwyn*) and Denis Trevanion (*Trevanyon*), who were Richard Jenkin's immediate predecessors in that office.

The letter confirming his unanimous election survives in the Jenkin Archives. In it (after explaining that bardic robes were 'unobtainable owing to the Clothing Restrictions') Edwin Chirgwin (*Map Melyn*), Gorsedd Secretary and Herald Bard, stated: 'Your Bardic Name will be:– A<small>RWEDHOR</small> (Signaller)'. Today's bards will perhaps be surprised that it was once apparently in order for the Secretary to inform initiates of their bardic name, since it has long been the practice for the name to be largely the prospective bard's own choice. In any event, Richard Jenkin wasted no time in rejecting the injunction. Chirgwin's letter to Greece is dated 15 July, and the minutes of the Council meeting on 9 August record the name firmly as *Map Dyvroeth*, Son of Exile.[3]

Richard Jenkin's choice of bardic name clearly indicates that he had a strong feeling of disinheritance, on behalf of his Cornish father as well as himself,[4] and the fact that his six paternal uncles emigrated to the USA must also have made an impression on him.[5] Born in Derbyshire and educated in Lancashire, he later wrote of his early years, 'I never felt rooted anywhere'.[6] Part of his extraordinary drive to serve the cause of Celtic Cornwall no doubt sprang from this early feeling of alienation, and his empathy for other exiles was profound, as will be seen. Cornwall would always be home for him, and by his own account he had started to teach himself Cornish at the age of thirteen (i.e. in 1938/9) 'because it was my language'.[7] During his time at Oxford University in 1943-44 he had been a member of the Oxford Cornish Society and formed the Young Cornwall Movement with like-minded fellow students.[8] While serving in the army he practised Cornish in his spare time,[9] and in 1945, during his time with the Forces Broadcasting Service in Egypt, he joined the Cairo Cornish Association.[10] His longing to 'come home' to 'the place / Where generations bred my bone and brain' is expressed in his poem 'Cornwall recalled / Volos, Greece'.[11] As to the Cornish Gorsedd, he was corresponding with R.M. Nance (Grand Bard 1934-59) about its history and ethos (as well as other Cornish matters), from at least the early part of 1947. In April that year Nance wrote:

As for your queries – Gorseth Kernow does what it knows how to do to encourage the "Young Cornwall" groups ... without interfering with their management in any way, but it rather depends on these to find out the best way to help... Mars us dheugh whans a dhyscajor, da vya genef gweles neppyth a'gas Kernewek trawythyow, ha'y ewna ragough-why kens es y dhanvon arta dheugh. [*If you wish to have a teacher, I should be happy to see something of your Cornish on occasion, and to correct it for you before sending it back.*][12]

In May, Nance indicated how pleased he was at the high standard of Richard Jenkin's Cornish, adding, 'I feel sure that if you would send in your 500 words we should agree that you ought to be one of our Cornish bards by examination. We have among these several whose knowledge is probably much less than yours'. In another letter he stated that candidates were not expected to write their '500 words' without recourse to reference books. ('All reasonable allowances are made.')[13] Having received the desired submission – 'a series of anecdotes about John Stone as told me by my father'[14] – Nance replied that it is 'up to the average standard of those that we have in the past accepted. I am sure that we shall have in you a very useful and sincere worker for Cornwall'.[15] Richard Jenkin himself acknowledged that at that time it was a comparatively straightforward matter to gain entry into the Gorsedd by examination in Cornish. It was for this reason that when the Gorsedd introduced the much more rigorous tripartite examinations in 1962, he took the advanced grade examination (and the oral) 'as an example', passing with distinction.[16]

Unsurprisingly, the prospective new bard could not be at Windmill Hill, Launceston for the Gorsedd ceremony on 30 August 1947 and so was initiated by proxy 'without having ever seen a Gorsedd',[17] his bardic certificate being sent to him in Greece. (He sent fifteen shillings [75p] as his subscription, but only five shillings were due, because as the Treasurer later explained, 'Bards by examination do not pay the initiation fee of 10/-'. All such marks of difference between bards have long since disappeared.)[18] In a letter in Cornish to R.M. Nance (whom he addresses as 'Ow Mordon ker ha bryntyn' [*My dear, excellent Mordon*]) in September, he acknowledged receipt of his certificate and asked the Grand Bard about the Awen symbol of three descending rays used by the Gorsedd (a subject to which he would return), about the organisation's forma-

Gorseth Kernow

Grand Bard:
R. MORTON NANCE (MORDON),
"Chylason,"
Carbis Bay.

Deputy Grand Bard:
HENRY TREFUSIS (MAP MOR),
Trefusis, Falmouth.

Treasurer:
EDGAR REES (CARER LOSOW)
30, Morrab Road,
Penzance.

Secretary:
EDWIN CHIRGWIN (MAP MELYN),
St. Cleer, Liskeard.

15/7/47.

Dear Mr. Jenkin,

I have much pleasure in informing you that you have been unanimously elected a Bard of Cornwall by Examination in the Language. Initiation will take place at the Gorsedd to be held at Launceston at 3 P.M. on Saturday August 30th, but inability to be present will in no way invalidate your election.

The programme for the day is :—

Annual Meeting — Launceston College — Noon.
Lunch for Bards — 1
Gorsedd — 3
Tea for Bards — 5
Concert in Guildhall — 7.

There is an Initiation Fee of 10/- payable at your convenience to the Treasurer (above), and thereafter an Annual Subscription of 5/-. Robes are unobtainable owing to the Clothing Restrictions.

Your Bardic Name will be :—

<u>ARWEDHOR</u> (Signaller)

and I should appreciate your favourable reply.

Yours very faithfully,

Edwin Chirgwin
Secretary + Herald.

Letter, dated 15 July 1947, from Edwin Chirgwin, informing Richard Jenkin of his election to Gorsedh Kernow

tion and history and related issues. He made it clear that he wished to get down to serious work for the Celtic cause.[19] His father, who had been ordained as an Anglican priest in 1932, accepted the living of St Gennys in 1947 and was thus enabled to return to Cornwall – 'yndelma y-tewetho agan dyvroeth', wrote Richard (*so may our exile end*).[20] Shortly before the end of the year he was released from the Royal Signals,[21] and he returned to the UK in 1948.

Circumstances, however, did not allow him to settle permanently in Cornwall till 1959 (the year of Nance's death), by which time he was married with a young family, though he attended his first Gorsedd ceremony in 1948, at Carwynnen, Camborne.[22] He stood for membership of the Gorsedd Council as early as 1952, when he polled just twenty votes, coming twenty-eighth out of thirty-two candidates.[23] He continued to apply his mind to Gorsedd issues nevertheless, including the recurring question of differentiation between so-called 'language bards' and the rest.[24] In a letter to him in 1953, largely concerned with the Cornish language and the Gorsedd, Nance wrote: 'If your article [a short piece in Cornish enclosed with the letter] suggests that bards by examination really are considered as coming in at a back door by the Gorsedd Council, of course it is wrong, but if you think that not enough honour is paid them, that is a point to be considered.'[25] Richard Jenkin was unable to attend the 1953 Gorsedd because of a work posting to Wales, leading Nance to write to his protégé: 'I hope that it will be only a short time before you can come back to Cornwall, where there is so much waiting for you to do.'[26] In 1957 his wife Ann Trevenen Jenkin (*Bryallen*) was initiated as a bard by examination in the Cornish language, as was another future Grand Bard, Hugh Miners (*Den Toll*), with whom Richard Jenkin would have many dealings in the coming years.

Gorsedd Councillor
Richard Jenkin was co-opted to membership of the Council of Gorsedh Kernow in 1958 and again, unanimously, at the Council meeting on 15 October 1960.[27] He was to serve as a Council member for the rest of his life. At the next meeting about three months later the Grand Bard, E.G. Retallack Hooper (*Talek*), proposed that Richard be appointed Gorsedd Secretary to replace Edwin Chirgwin (who had died in November 1960), a proposal which was carried unanimously.[28] Suggestions were made at this meeting about ways of easing the considerable

burden of duties which fell to the Secretary. One of these suggestions was to separate the office from that of Herald Bard, which had previously been held jointly with it. (The Herald Bard calls to the Horner to sound to the four quarters of Cornwall at the Gorsedd ceremony.) With this in mind F.B. Cargeeg (*Tan Dyvarow*) was appointed Herald,[29] but in the event he served only two years in that office (1961-62), no doubt because of his election as Deputy Grand Bard in the latter year. Richard Jenkin had stood in for Edwin Chirgwin as Herald Bard at the 1960 ceremony, and in 1963 he took up the office officially (and temporarily, according to Council minutes), remaining as Herald until 1972, when he was himself installed as Deputy Grand Bard.[30] (He was evidently a reliable back-up in times of need, having deputised for Edmund Hambly (*Gwas Arthur*) as Swordbearer at the 1956 Gorsedd ceremony.)[31]

At the Closed Gorsedd (or AGM) on 3 June 1961, the Council for the three years to 1964 was elected and the new Secretary's position ratified.[32] As the Gorsedd minute books and other records make clear, the Secretary's duties are indeed extensive and varied. The public role played by him or her in the Gorsedd ceremony is a minor one compared to the administrative (and to some extent ambassadorial) tasks they are called upon to carry out, and Richard Jenkin had to perform them at the same time as doing a full-time job and helping to bring up a family. This led to his resigning from the post at the Council meeting on 21 October 1961, feeling that he was unable to devote enough time to carrying out his duties efficiently. He suggested that 'as well as a Secretary, a Master of Ceremonies should be appointed to be responsible for all details of ceremonial organisation, and to relieve the Secretary of some of his work which was too much for anyone in full time employment'. After discussion of ways in which the situation could be improved, he 'agreed to stand again and promised to be as efficient as he could manage to be, and was re-elected'. It was also decided to elect a Ceremonial Sub-committee, on which he would serve *ex officio*.[33] His duties evidently included those of host, since at the 1961 Gorsedd ceremony, the harp accompaniment to the Cornish songs was provided by Armel Geraud, a Breton girl who was staying with her sister at the Jenkin house in Leedstown.[34]

At a special Council meeting at Retallack Hooper's house in Camborne on 9 September 1961, there was discussion of the question of introducing three orders into the Cornish Gorsedd, i.e. druids and ovates in addition to bards, in the manner of the Welsh Gorsedd. This issue is brought up every so often within the college of bards, but there has never been enough support for introducing the additional orders. Richard Jenkin spoke against the idea at this meeting.[35] When it was discussed more widely at the Closed Gorsedd on 2 June 1962, feeling that there had been a suggestion of his acting improperly in the matter (which he did not accept), he again offered his resignation as Secretary but received a unanimous vote of confidence from the meeting.[36]

In the Council election of 1964 Richard Jenkin polled more votes than any other candidate, and in October he was re-elected unanimously as Secretary.[37] After a further year, however, he felt unable to continue, and his resignation was accepted 'with regret'. He agreed to carry on as Acting Secretary till the next Council meeting (5 February 1966), when Christopher Bice (*Gwythenek*) was elected to succeed him.[38] His secretarial duties during this interregnum included writing a letter on behalf of the Gorsedd Council to the Secretary of State for Education and Science, in protest against the proposal to move the Camborne School of Mines to Plymouth.[39] Also in 1965, he and Ann Jenkin saw through the publication of *Cornwall: the hidden land*, which includes a brief account of Gorsedh Kernow.[40]

Richard Jenkin's resignation as Secretary did not prevent his continuing to work for the Gorsedd as a conscientious member of Council. At the 1967 Closed Gorsedd, for example, he and Denis Trevanion opened a discussion on 'the place of the Gorsedd in the Community life of Cornwall'.[41] It is clear that his own contribution was a forceful appeal for a more positive approach on the Gorsedd's part to contemporary Cornish life. He said that 'some Cornish people regarded the Gorsedd as "play acting in blue nightshirts" or as a "house of lords for the Old Cornwall Societies". The work it did needed to be better known, and that included its competitions and work of the language board. The Gorsedd must lead, and must be more involved in the life of the community. It should be interested in the development of new industries and endeavour to mould Cornwall to make it suitable for modern life.'[42]

Later in 1967 he was one of those deputed to confer and report on the practicalities of a weekend conference with particular reference to the work of Gorsedh Kernow and the furtherance of Cornwall and its people.[43] After a good deal of preparatory work, this event, on the theme 'Towards a future Cornwall', was held in Newquay on 22/23 March 1969. The report on the conference ended with a statement by the Gorsedd, welcoming the University of Exeter's proposal to establish what would become the Institute of Cornish Studies.[44] Also in 1969 Richard Jenkin was one of the bards who recorded a number of Cornish-language readings for a long-playing record issued by the Cornish Language Board.[45]

Deputy Grand Bard (1972-1976)
At the Gorsedd Council meeting on 22 April 1972, Cecil Beer (*Map Kenwyn*) announced his intention to resign as Deputy Grand Bard at the end of May.[46] Two valid nominations were received for the vacant post, those of Richard Jenkin and Hugh Miners. The resulting postal ballot of Council led to the former's election by twelve votes to eight.[47] His duties began immediately after the results were announced in July, when he, Grand Bard Denis Trevanion and former Grand Bard George Pawley White were asked to prepare a report which would present the views of the Gorsedd on the names to be given to the new district authorities in Cornwall following local government reorganisation.[48] Richard Jenkin was installed as Deputy Grand Bard after the Gorsedd ceremony at Launceston Castle on 2 September, his sponsors being Cecil Beer, Hugh Miners and Christopher Bice.[49] Having served out what would have been the remainder of Beer's term as Deputy, he was re-elected unopposed for 1973-76, as was Denis Trevanion as Grand Bard.[50]

The Grand Bard and Deputy hold *ex officio* positions on the Gorsedd Council, the one as Chair, the other as a Councillor. The Deputy will take over the Grand Bard's duties in the latter's absence (often on other Gorsedd business) and take on some of the ceremonial, administrative, consultative and ambassadorial responsibilities of office as required. Deputy Grand Bards also have specific roles of their own. The Gorsedd minute book gives some idea of the numerous tasks performed by Richard Jenkin during this time – conscientious, steady and largely undramatic.[51] Quite enough drama, however, was to unfold in the more prominent years of office to come.

At the Gorsedd Council meeting on 3 July 1976, the result of the ballot to elect the next Grand Bard was announced: in another contest with Hugh

Richard Jenkin (right) newly-elected Grand Bard, with Hugh Miners, newly-elected Deputy Grand Bard, 1976 (copyright Peter Hughes)

Miners, Richard Jenkin had scraped home by thirteen votes to twelve. (The only other Deputy to have progressed to the office of Grand Bard had been Nance, though since 1976 this progression has become the norm.) In view of the fact that there had been no nominations for the office of Deputy Grand Bard, the Secretary, Peter Laws (*Crugyow*), proposed Miners as Deputy, and the Grand Bard elect seconded this proposal, which was agreed unanimously by Council.[52]

The new leader's connection with Mebyon Kernow was not lost on the press. 'MK leader Grand Bard' was the *West Briton* headline after his election, and their report after his installation described him as 'a leading figure in the county's nationalist movement'.[53] In an interview with the *Camborne-Redruth Packet* he disposed of the matter succinctly before moving on to real Gorsedd concerns:

> He said that the fact that he was chairman of a political party had no effect on his work for the Gorsedd. "Both are concerned with the future of Cornwall and both are working for Cornwall, but from completely different angles," he said ... [D]uring his term as Grand Bard he would like to see the Gorsedd put more emphasis on work with the youth of Cornwall.[54]

He wrote on another occasion that most bards, while loyal to Celtic Cornwall and its distinct culture, did not see the need for it to have its own political institutions, although those candidates for bardship who shared his own political beliefs were likely to qualify by their work in cultural fields. '[W]hen I speak as Grand Bard,' however, 'I am representing a body of people of all political opinions and none... whose work has shown that it is inspired by Cornwall and a desire to serve the Cornish people and to maintain their separate identity and culture.'[55]

Grand Bard, first term (1976-1979)

Richard Jenkin was duly installed as the sixth Grand Bard of Cornwall by Denis Trevanion on 4 September 1976 at the well-attended forty-eighth Gorsedd ceremony at Hayle ('on the windswept playing fields of Highlanes County Secondary School', as the *Cornish Guardian* put it). His first official duty was to install his Deputy. In his speech he expressed the hope that he would be able to live up to the standards of his predecessors and his wish that encouragement of the young people of Cornwall in their interest in her history and language would continue. Further development of the Gorsedd competitions would be an excellent means to this end.[56]

The duties of Grand Bard are of course even more demanding than those of Deputy Grand Bard or Secretary. He or she is the public face of the Gorsedd and is called upon to attend, and often speak or officiate at, numerous gatherings of all kinds, as well as being a member of various external committees, usually as a direct representative of the Gorsedd. There is not only a national but an international role, with respect to the Celtic countries and to the countries associated with the Cornish diaspora. Dealing with the media and with numerous organisations and individuals (both bards and non-bards) are among their many other duties. Richard Jenkin took all of these very seriously and carried them out responsibly, with a sense of the honour his office entailed and a conviction that Cornwall's individuality and culture were enhanced thereby. He was also generally in favour of a proactive approach in order to combat perceived threats to Cornwall's well-being, and he regularly called upon his fellow-bards to play their part in promoting the Gorsedd and thereby Cornwall itself: 'You are the point of contact between the public and the Gorsedd.'[57]

At the Closed Gorsedd on 3 June 1978 he stressed the importance of the six new signs on the Cornish border 'proclaiming for all to see the word KERNOW'. The signs had been achieved after a long, hard campaign by the Gorsedd, and the Grand Bard urged that as many as possible should contribute to their cost. He also indicated that production of new (Unified) Cornish dictionaries had been delayed, so that it was now proposed to issue supplements. (Three of these were to appear between 1981 and 1995, by which time other spelling systems for Cornish were being strongly championed by many bards.) He was positive about the future: 'The Gorsedd should be greatly encouraged by the high calibre of new bards, and in particular the number of young people who are qualifying through Cornish, and whose enthusiasm must be utilised to carry the Cornish cause to even greater expression in the life of our people.' Looking ahead to the planned Cornish Eisteddfod, he hoped that meanwhile an exhibition of the current year's Gorsedd competition entries would be mounted in libraries in the major Cornish towns 'so that people could learn more of the work of the Gorsedd and the standards being produced'. Furthermore, 'If we can plan wisely, the next 50 years should see as great a growth and achievement as our first 50 years.'[58]

Among his many other duties in 1978, the Grand Bard had to turn his attention to submitting evidence on Council's behalf to the Boundary Commission, objecting to their proposal that Cornwall and Plymouth should form one constituency in the future European Parliament and stressing that Cornwall should have its own representative.[59] (This appeal unfortunately failed, indeed the current European constituency of which Cornwall forms a part includes far more of South-West England than it did originally.)

Hugh Miners's *Gorseth Kernow: the first 50 years* was published in August 1978, and it was agreed in Council that the Grand Bard and others would deal with 'any financial matters arising'.[60] In the book its author thanked him for writing the foreword and (with others) for 'many corrections and helpful suggestions'.[61] Richard Jenkin himself took stock at this milestone in the Gorsedd's history, when it was 'appropriate to remind ourselves that the Gorsedd exists to embody the National Spirit of Cornwall in all its aspects'. He also discussed the foundations for a Cornish Eisteddfod which were being laid by Gorsedh Kernow and other organisations: 'it is our responsibility to bring it into being, as our predecessors brought into being the long-awaited Gorsedd 50 years ago'. In the same paper he returned to the theme of 'the Cornish in Exile', stressing the part that the Gorsedd must play 'to maintain and strengthen the links between all Cornish people and their homeland', encouraging those of the diaspora to enter the Gorsedd competitions, identify with Cornwall and return home when they can. The great importance which the 'Son of Exile' attached to this work is clear: 'We could make the reception of representative exiles part of the Ceremony… But as individuals we should work to reduce the need for involuntary exile and to provide opportunities for permanent return of our Cornish people without whom our nation cannot continue.'[62]

As early as October 1976 Council had been discussing the 'Golden Jubilee' Gorsedd ceremony of 1978. It was intended to stage it at Boscawen-Un, site of the inaugural Gorsedd of 1928, and it was agreed that the invitation to Charles, Prince of Wales and Duke of Cornwall, to be initiated as a Cornish bard should be reissued for the Jubilee Gorsedd. (The invitation was declined in due course.)⁶³ At the 1977 Closed Gorsedd the Grand Bard had emphasised that all bards should become involved in Jubilee Gorsedd events, and he urged that the occasion should be celebrated 'with ceremony and dignity'.⁶⁴ By the spring of 1978 it had been decided that there would be a separate Jubilee Day at Boscawen-Un on 21 September, as well as the Gorsedd ceremony itself at the Merry Maidens, St Buryan, on 2 September. The Ceremonial Sub-committee met on 15 April, and its recommendations were put to Council a week later.⁶⁵ The Archdruid of Wales, *Geraint* (Geraint Bowen), and former Archdruid *Gwyndaf* (Evan Gwyndaf Evans) would attend on 2 September.⁶⁶

The Jubilee Gorsedd of 1978 was a great success, notwithstanding the theft of the Swordbearer's regalia in August, which became a particular issue for Richard Jenkin as Chairman of the Ceremonial Sub-committee.⁶⁷ According to reports, the ceremony attracted over 160 bards, at that time the largest number ever assembled, and an audience of 2,000. In his opening words the Grand Bard stated that the Gorsedd 'had developed during the past 50 years according to the vision of its founders until it had become a very real presence in the cultural life of Cornwall. "We intend that it should grow and work in the same way"'. At the ceremony he presented a special Jubilee medal to Michael Cardew (*Myghal an Pry*), who had been initiated at the 1928 Gorsedd, and later in the day to A.K. Hamilton Jenkin (*Lef Stenoryon*), the only other surviving bard from that inaugural ceremony. For the first time bards by examination in the Cornish language constituted the majority of initiates, forty-six years after they had first been admitted at the 1932 Gorsedd. A display of bardic regalia and work submitted for Gorsedd competitions was held in Penzance on the same day. The evening concert included a new work 'Trio Gorseth'.⁶⁸

Reports indicate that a hundred bards attended the shortened 'golden jubilee commemoration Gorsedd' at the Boscawen-Un stone circle on 21 September 1978, fifty years to the day after the first modern Cornish Gorsedd had been held there. Richard Jenkin's speech recalled the original bards, especially the first two Grand Bards, Henry Jenner (*Gwas Myghal*) and R.M. Nance, 'great men and loyal servants of the Cornish nation'. He also read a communication from *Geraint* 'which stressed the message "be for ever Cornish"'.⁶⁹ In addition to these celebrations, a successful Gorsedh Kernow Jubilee Exhibition was held in Truro.⁷⁰

Richard welcoming his daughter Morwenna as a Cornish bard, Bodmin, 1979

In his Chairman's address at the Closed Gorsedd in June 1979, Richard Jenkin stressed that the overriding problem facing Cornwall was the lack of employment for young people, forcing them to leave their home. No doubt reflecting his own feelings and experience, he also said that 'despite this exodus, there were so many who had a very deep sense that Cornwall was their homeland even though they might live a long way away'. He made a plea for all Cornish people to 'do everything possible to maintain the National Spirit of Cornwall'. At the meeting a warm vote of thanks to him for his three years as Grand Bard was carried 'with acclamation',[71] and at the Council meeting on 21 July 1979, he and Hugh Miners were unanimously re-elected for a second three-year term.[72]

Almost as many bards attended the Gorsedd in 1979 as in the jubilee year. Striking a familiar note, one of the groups Richard Jenkin included in his welcome was 'all the "exiles" who had returned'. He initiated a record number of twenty-three new bards, including his elder daughter Morwenna (*Kestenen*) for proficiency in Cornish, 'a particularly proud moment'.[73]

Grand Bard, second term (1979-1982)

In the Grand Bard's letter of January 1980, Richard Jenkin again conveyed his high hopes and enthusiasm for the first Cornish Eisteddfod, still over three years away, calling on all bards to work for its success and to encourage other organisations to take part. It had been 'a dream since the Gorsedd was founded' and 'a way in which the Gorsedd and the Cornish people in general can come into a closer relation'. 'The Gorsedd's own competitions would form part of the Eisteddfod in 1983.' He also called upon bards to make sure that it grew as an institution and became an established part of Cornish life,[74] a theme to which he returned at the Closed Gorsedd in June that year, in the first annual address of his second term. As to the college of bards, for him it was 'a body of people under one law, whose aim was to help one another and not to work in isolation'. He strongly supported the Institute of Cornish Studies and deplored the attitude of those who sought to stamp out research into Cornish culture for economic reasons, suggesting (to applause) that all bards should ask candidates at the following year's County Council elections whether they supported the Institute.[75] (This may be the closest he came to bringing politics into a non-political organisation. Although very active in Cornish politics he strove, quite rightly, to keep the Gorsedd strictly non-political, clearly recognising the importance of its non-partisan integrity.)

The 1980 Gorsedd ceremony was held at Saltash on 6 September. In his address Richard Jenkin proclaimed, 'Across the Tamar we can see England ... in its proper place. May it stay there. To Saltash and its people I say "Be forever Cornish".'[76] (He was to issue a similar rallying cry at the Gorsedd at Torpoint in 1987, when he said of east Cornwall, 'We must watch over it now and forever.')[77] On 8 September 1980, following an appeal by the Welsh Archdruid elect at the Cornish Gorsedd, Richard Jenkin and Peter Laws, as Grand Bard and Gorsedd Secretary, were signatories to a letter to the Home Secretary in support of the Welsh Gorsedd's approach to the Government, urging them to honour the pledge to give the planned fourth television channel in Wales to the Welsh language. (The announcement that the Government would do so came a few days later, and S4C was duly launched in 1982.) On the other hand, Council also decided that the Grand Bard should convey its feelings verbally to the Archdruid of Wales about the 'political' speech of the Archdruid elect at the 1980 Gorsedh Kernow tea, in view of the policy of the Gorsedd, mentioned above, to keep clear of politics.[78]

In the Grand Bard's message early the following year, he designated 1981 'a year of preparation', indicating that bards must be ready to take advantage of opportunities for the advancement of Cornish culture offered by the changes to local broadcast media scheduled for 1982. Preparation needed to be made for the International Celtic Congress in Cornwall in 1982, and of course for the first Cornish Eisteddfod in 1983, in which the Gorsedd should play a leading role. 'In this year of preparation Cornish culture will be called upon to show its relevance to the present and future of Cornwall,' he wrote. 'The Gorsedd and its bards must take part in this. Admittance to the Gorsedd is not simply a recognition of work already done for Cornwall but a pledge to work together in unity to support the complete expression of the Celtic National Spirit of Cornwall.' In the final paragraph, written in Cornish, he welcomed the progress made in writing in the language and called for a new body of Cornish literature to be established.[79]

He returned to this subject at the Closed Gorsedd in June 1981, commending the new organisations that had been set up to teach Cornish to the very young. He stressed that the Gorsedd was principally concerned with the Cornishness of Cornwall and 'asked all Bards to promote amongst the public the need to uplift Cornwall and to make Cornish people proud of being Cornish'. He also discussed a potent symbol of such Cornishness, the Cornish flag, encouraging bards to fly it in celebration of the Duke of Cornwall's wedding,[80] and he was active at this time in encouraging Cornish councils to fly the flag on St Piran's Day (5 March).[81]

The open Gorsedd in September 1981, held at Nance, Illogan, saw another record attendance by bards of almost 200. The Grand Bard stressed that the purpose of the institution was 'to show our love of Cornwall, its language and its traditions... We meet in peace within this ancient round to show our loyalty to Cornwall and to honour the workers for Cornwall.' He also 'emphasised the devoted work being carried out to uphold and extend the use of the language.

This was one of the first objects of the Gorsedd.' There was, however, still much work to do 'especially in official circles and in the Press'. He again expressed hope that truly Cornish items would be part of the output of Radio Cornwall and urged bards to keep up the pressure to bring this about.[82]

It was on St Piran's Day 1982 that Truro City Council flew the Cornish flag for the first time, and this change of mind was due to the intervention of Richard Jenkin as Grand Bard, who explained that the flag was referred to much earlier than the founding of Mebyon Kernow and thus should not be considered 'political'.[83] He returned to the subject in his annual message to bards ('Preparing for a full year in 1982'). Having claimed for the Gorsedd that it 'represents every aspect of Cornish culture', he added that he was 'pleased to see the increasing number of Cornish flags in the circle around the Gorsedd, just as there is an increasing number... flying throughout the land. Mordon recognised it as the flag for all Cornishmen to fly, and so do I.'[84] Like Nance (and others) before him, he acknowledged the importance of symbolism to the Cornish cause,[85] and he initiated a discussion on the flag within Council at the meeting on 24 April 1982.[86] In his annual message for that year he expressed the hope that he had 'helped the Gorsedd to play its part in the life of Cornwall today'. This was evidently meant as a farewell of sorts, as was a more explicit statement which was destined not to be fulfilled: 'This is the last time I shall be writing in the Gorsedd newsletter as Grand Bard.'

He returned once more to the importance of the Cornish Eisteddfod at the Closed Gorsedd in June. It was 'intended to be a great celebration of all aspects of Cornwall for all Cornish people' and 'a unifying occasion' in which the Gorsedd could give a lead. He was again enthusiastic about the progress of the Cornish language, stating that 'examinations were going from strength to strength, and that the Language Board, an integral part of the Gorsedd, was thriving'. He gave a heartfelt tribute to Retallack Hooper, third Grand Bard, for his fifty years of untiring work for the Gorsedd, saying that he 'had even relinquished his livelihood for it'.[87] (Jori Ansell (*Caradok*) was later to make much the same point about sacrificing personal advancement for the Cornish cause with reference to Richard Jenkin himself.)[88]

On 10 July 1982, in the course of the last Council meeting before the Gorsedd ceremony at which he was to step down as Grand Bard, Richard Jenkin announced that he was giving, on behalf of his family, a new trophy for the Gorsedd competitions, the 'Cornish Crystal' for Cornish language prose.[89] He summed up at this point in his bardic career by saying, 'I have been at every Gorsedd but three in the last 35 years. I have not only loved Cornwall and its past but I have tried to work for its survival into the future as recognisably Cornish, a Celtic country. This is my Cornwall, a quartz crystal from the rock, fractured, imperfect, but shining from its many facets.'[90] A six-year term had become the normal period in office for a Grand Bard, indeed Gorsedd rules in force at that time stipulated that no more than two successive three-year terms could be served, and at the same July meeting Richard Jenkin announced that Hugh Miners had been elected to succeed him. 'It was agreed to record the greatest thanks of the Council to the retiring Grand Bard... for the six years hard work he had undertaken as the 6th Grand Bard of Cornwall.' Hugh Miners thanked him personally for the way he had carried out his duties and for his work towards the Cornish Eisteddfod, adding that he (Miners) 'felt sure they would all work closely and happily together'.[91]

At the Gorsedd ceremony at St Just on 4 September 1982, Richard Jenkin presented a framed certificate 'of love and respect' to Retallack Hooper, to mark his fifty years as a bard and his distinguished contribution to the Gorsedd. There was another proud moment for the outgoing Grand Bard when he initiated his younger daughter Loveday (*Myrgh an Tir*), the fourth member of the Jenkin family to be elected to bardship for proficiency in Cornish. He also installed Hugh Miners as his successor in the highest office of Gorsedh Kernow.[92]

A time of crisis
Though largely unsuspected at the time, the elevation of Hugh Miners to the Grand Bardship was to lead to a temporary schism within the Gorsedd, a period of great anguish and upheaval not only for the organisation itself but also for particular individuals within it. There is a great deal of documentation in which the details of the worsening crisis can be traced, but the outline of the story is easily told. Though Hugh Miners started with firm support within the Gorsedd Council, as his term of office went on, unease grew among its members as to his leadership style, to the point where, in the end, he stood alone against

the rest of the Councillors and withdrew his candidature from the 1985 election for Grand Bard. It was Richard Jenkin who had been put up as Council's alternative candidate – a steadying hand at an anxious time – and he was unanimously accepted as Grand Bard designate in July 1985.[93] Some of the statements made around this time (particularly during 1985-86) were extremely personal, and the arguments were sometimes very acrimonious. The strength of feeling aroused and the offence caused in some quarters during the crisis period can scarcely be overstated – the wounds cut very deep. Ironically, and tragically, those on both sides of the dispute felt that they were working for the greater good of the Gorsedd and out of Christian motives. Richard Jenkin was closely involved with events as they unfolded, being at the heart of affairs as the preceding (and succeeding) Grand Bard and a long-standing and experienced member of Council.

When Hugh Miners became Grand Bard, election to bardship had long been open to those who passed the third-grade Cornish Language Board examination at a sufficiently high level. From at least 1981 he had, as a 'bard by examination' himself, expressed the view that a more rigorous approach should be taken towards ensuring that such candidates were not initiated as bards automatically for this achievement alone, but that long-term commitment to the service of Cornwall should also be demonstrated, in accordance with the Gorsedd Constitution.[94] He was by no means the first to voice such concerns, indeed criteria for bardship had been discussed periodically since at least 1935.[95] It is of course a perfectly defensible point of view, one with which most bards would probably agree. It certainly had supporters within Council, though other Councillors had strong reservations, feeling that existing methods of scrutiny were sufficient.[96] After long discussion it was decided that a sub-committee should be set up to debate the issue of admission in general. Richard Jenkin served on this sub-committee, which held a lengthy meeting on 1 December 1982. The members agreed to recommend that a full citation should be submitted for every candidate and that its contents should be subject to close scrutiny before invitations to bardship were issued.[97] The matter continued to be discussed in Council and in Closed Gorsedd sessions, and in due course a much more rigorous screening process for prospective bards was introduced.[98]

Tensions within the Gorsedd Council had started to grow from a fairly early stage of Hugh Miners's tenure, however, and by 1985 the disaffection of the Council, having experienced his methods as unacceptably autocratic, was virtually complete, though he retained some support among the wider college of bards. In reply to a letter from a bard in July 1985, Richard Jenkin outlined Council's position: a decision had been taken that it was not in the best interests of the Gorsedd that Hugh Miners should serve a second term; as Grand Bard, he had been determined to run the Gorsedd not by consensus, but by fiat; another candidate had therefore been proposed, with Council's overwhelming support; having withdrawn from the election, Hugh Miners now seemed minded to cause as much discord and harm to the Gorsedd as he could. Richard Jenkin also put forward a robust defence of 'bards by examination' and the way in which they were nominated, naming well-known figures who had been elected for their language skills but who had also made their mark in other fields of Cornish studies. The tone of the letter is measured but the degree of feeling is apparent.

In Hugh Miners's own account of events from the time of his installation as Grand Bard,[99] and elsewhere, he singled out Richard Jenkin for particular criticism, often in strongly-worded and very personal terms. The situation as a whole clearly reflected far wider disagreements than just the question of membership criteria, but it was the proposed initiation of a bard for proficiency in Cornish which was the immediate threat to the 1985 Gorsedd ceremony. A special meeting of the Gorsedd Council was convened on 3 September as a result of Hugh Miners's refusal to receive Jürgen Zeidler at the Gorsedd or to sign his certificate of initiation to bardship, on the grounds that (according to Miners) evidence of his ongoing commitment to Cornwall was lacking. Like the other 'language' candidates, Dr Zeidler had passed the Cornish Language Board's third-grade examination at a sufficiently high level to be elected as a bard. (He had also previously won the Mordon-Caradar Rosebowl as first prize for Cornish verse in the 1984 Gorsedd competitions and was to win the same prestigious award in 1989, though he was not present to receive it in person on that occasion.)[100]

It was decided unanimously to send a delegation to Hugh Miners to convey the Council's wish that he conduct the Gorsedd exactly as prescribed, which would include his installing Richard Jenkin as his successor. Contingency plans were made in case he declined to do so.[101] In the event, having received assurances from Jürgen Zeidler as to his sincerity and intentions, at the eleventh hour Hugh Miners agreed to initiate him (as *Map an Dherowek*), and at the end of the ceremony, held on 7 September 1985 at Perran Round, he installed Richard Jenkin. His speech as outgoing Grand Bard was forthright (though no individuals were named) and there was no eulogy to his successor, which he felt would be hypocritical.[102]

It should be said that during Hugh Miners's term of office, Richard Jenkin had other preoccupations as well as the increasing tensions within the Gorsedd. The hard work put in by him and Ruth Moss (*Kewny*), Competitions Secretary, in making such a success of the first Cornish Eisteddfod (5-12 March 1983) was acknowledged at the Council meeting in April that year, when it was also decided that he could wear R.M. Nance's plastron at Gorsedd ceremonies – an appropriate arrangement, in view of Nance's influences on his bardic career.[103] And much later, a letter dated 20 July 1985 (the same date as his election in Council to a third term as Grand Bard) which addressed him as 'Richard Jenkins, High Druid' [sic] (one of a batch of material from more esoteric Celtic sources) must have been welcomed as positive light relief.[104]

Grand Bard, third term (1985-1988)

It was, then, a highly unsettled Gorsedd that Richard Jenkin had to preside over and help to bring back on course. As his address to the bards in Gorsedd Newsletter 21 (1985) put it: 'I have been chosen by your elected Council... to try to restore the confidence, harmony and co-operation that have been missed recently.' He called for bards' help and support, and stated that the Council 'has been anxious to maintain the dignity of the Gorsedd and has made no public statements... Let us now work together for the good of the Gorsedd and of Cornwall.'

One of the first actions of the new Grand Bard and Council was the convening of an extraordinary Council meeting on 12 October to review the aftermath of recent events, including aspects of the way in which the previous Grand Bard had acted in office. The issues raised were still very much alive. Hugh Miners had called for a Special Meeting to discuss the emendation of the Gorsedd rules and Constitution, with a certain amount of support from some other bards. A report was before Council, and this was intended to form the basis of a statement to be sent to all bards. Seven particular ways in which Hugh Miners 'had lost the confidence of the Council' were listed, and there was also an account of his withdrawal in June of his nomination for the Grand Bardship and the consequent unopposed election of Richard Jenkin. It was decided that a Special Meeting of all bards would be held on 14 December.[105] At the regular Council meeting on 26 October, Richard Jenkin read a communication to him from the absent Hugh Miners, who wished to protest strongly against the conduct of the meeting a fortnight earlier. At the same meeting it was made clear that the Grand Bard would serve on the Admissions, Ceremonial and newly constituted Revision of Rules Sub-committees.[106]

In a letter from Richard Jenkin to another bard during this period, he acknowledged that Hugh Miners 'sincerely believes that his ideas and plans would be for the good and benefit of the Gorsedd, and some of them were good, but these were often presented in a way that alienated those whose help he needed to carry them out'. This letter is mainly concerned with matters of Gorsedd constitution and organisation, in the light of the forthcoming special meeting for all bards on 14 December. At this meeting Richard Jenkin, as Chairman, stated that its purpose, as the Council saw it, was to give an impartial account of recent events and to explain the loss of confidence in Hugh Miners's leadership felt by Council members. The minutes record that following a debate, a recess was called so that an agreed statement could be considered by the Grand Bard, Peter Laws, Peter Pool (*Gwas Galva*), lawyer and bard, and Hugh Miners. Among other matters recorded in the statement, the parties to it accepted 'that all have acted in good faith and in accordance with their views as to the interests of the Gorsedd and of Cornwall' and considered that these interests required that the matters in dispute should not be investigated further. All personal attacks by bards on 'the honour and integrity' of other bards were to be deplored and should cease immediately, and confidence in Richard Jenkin as Grand Bard and in the other Gorsedd officers was affirmed. The Council was requested to send a copy of the resolution to all bards, and the desire was expressed that no further communications should be sent to bards 'regarding recent differences within the Gorsedd'. The statement was put to the meeting by Richard Jenkin, seconded by Hugh Miners and carried unanimously.[107] That, one might think, should have been the end of the matter.

At the Council meeting on 19 April 1986, however, the Grand Bard read out a letter which expressed Hugh Miners's contention that the Special Meeting in December had been incorrectly minuted.[108] By the following meeting (7 June) Peter Pool had discussed the situation with Richard Jenkin and Peter Laws and had sent a long reply which included another call for an end to 'this painful and protracted dispute'.[109] The Closed Gorsedd was held on the same day, and at this meeting Richard Jenkin commended to bards the creation of the Forth an Syns (Saints' Way) between Padstow and Fowey, of which he had attended the official opening on 25 October 1985, reported the success of the Gorsedd Proclamation Ceremony in Truro Cathedral chapter house in February 1986, stated that the Gorsedd had played its full part in the second Cornish Eisteddfod that year, noted that the 1987 Gorsedd would represent the 40th anniversary of the initiation of three future Grand Bards (George Pawley White, Denis Trevanion and himself), and extended the sympathy of the college of bards to Cornish miners and their families in the current crisis within the tin industry. The Gorsedd intended to lobby the European Economic Community on their behalf. He stated that the college of bards 'must express its deep sympathy for and understanding of the anger and frustration' felt by the tin workers. The industry had been a major formative influence in the whole of Cornwall. 'Every Cornish person must feel that a part of their heritage is being torn away,' and the bards must ensure that the gravity of the devastation likely to be caused is widely understood. Earlier in the year the Council had sent a letter on the subject to the Queen, the Duke of Cornwall, the Prime Minister and others in an attempt to protect the industry and thereby secure local employment, but to little effect.[110] Peter Laws made an oblique reference to the Gorsedd's own crisis when he paid tribute in his Secretary's report to the Grand Bard and all those 'who had unstintingly supported him in what had been a very difficult year'.[111]

In 1986 the well-attended Gorsedd ceremony was again held at the Merry Maidens. The bards 'were glad to be in St Buryan parish', said Richard Jenkin, 'because this and neighbouring Paul were places where the language was spoken fluently not too long ago'.[112] The Grand Bard made a point of expressing his pleasure in welcoming the strong Australian presence at the ceremony, and a record four bards from Australia were initiated. He was also present as Grand

Bard at the unveiling of a plaque on the Barbican at Plymouth to honour the 19th-century Cornish forebears of many South Australians.[113]

There was discussion at the Council meeting on 25 October 1986 of a pugnacious interview given by Hugh Miners, reported in the *Cornishman* of 25 September. Richard Jenkin had been contacted by the newspaper and had stated that the allegations made in the interview were baseless and that 'the matter was now closed'. If only it were. The Gorsedd minutes record Peter Laws's outlining local and national media reports of Hugh Miners's outspoken complaints during October and November 1986. This had led to considerable harassment of himself as Secretary and of the Grand Bard, among others. The Council would prepare a press statement of its own, and further harassment should be referred to Richard Jenkin.[114]

It is clear that during the crisis feelings ran extraordinarily high among those most closely affected and a great deal of anguish was caused to them, their families and to a lesser extent, members of the college of bards. There are still those who well remember with sadness the distress and upheaval of those years, but even at the time the crisis aroused only passing interest beyond the Gorsedd, and today many bards are unaware that it ever occurred, even though for a time the Gorsedd appeared to be in danger of splitting apart. It survived, nonetheless, and perhaps stronger than before. From that period of catharsis came, for example, a new Constitution and standing orders, the introduction of Gorsedd Conference Days and a further tightening up of criteria for bardship.

There were of course other matters to which the Grand Bard had to give his attention. As Chairman of the Ceremonial Sub-committee, he reported to the meeting on 27 November 1986 that the Cornish bards in Australia had expressed a wish to have a form of ceremony for use on appropriate occasions and he had formulated a draft accordingly. The sub-committee agreed to recommend Council's approval for this 'Ceremonial Order for Australian Use', and in due course Richard Jenkin conveyed Council's approval for an Australian Assembly of Bards, which however was not to be designated a Gorsedd.[115] The Australian bards were to elect a leader for his approval.[116] He later wrote to Ronald Daw (*Map Moonta*) in Australia, indicating that the Assembly had been approved by the Grand Bard and Council.[117]

In January 1987 it was agreed that new standing orders for Gorsedd elections should be adopted, including a new transferable vote system for the election of the Grand Bard.[118] At the same meeting, by way of contrast, the Council considered an application to station a recently-invented portable doughnut-making machine on the Gorsedd field. This was declined, since the Gorsedd had its own catering arrangements.[119]

The new Constitution (including standing orders for elections) was approved at the Closed Gorsedd on 6 June 1987. The changes to the rules included the stipulation that a Grand Bard should serve for three years and not be eligible for a second term till after an interval.[120] In his Chairman's Report at the meeting Richard Jenkin was generally positive, saying that 1986/87 had been a good year, with high attendance at the open Gorsedd and a successful inaugural all-day meeting in October. He hoped that this social and cultural event would become part of the Gorsedd year.[121] (Gorsedd Conference Day is indeed now well established. Richard Jenkin had led the working party which had organised this first conference and played a similar role in helping to draw up the programme for the second such event in October 1987.) Following the emphasis placed by several speakers on the need for bards to be 'bound in honour' to show loyalty to Cornwall as a Celtic nation, the Grand Bard said that the following Easter's Celtic Congress, held in Newquay, would help to portray Cornwall in that light.[122]

Richard Jenkin's final Chairman's Report at the Closed Gorsedd held on 4 June 1988, in which he thanked all bards for their loyal support during his nine years in office, was received with great appreciation by the assembled bards. He spoke of the tremendous revival of Cornish feeling in South Australia and New South Wales and said that the new ceremony for the Australian Assembly had been used for the first time. (This was on 5 March 1988 in Ballarat.)[123] At the meeting itself there was a long debate about the Cornish language, after which there were large majorities in favour of allowing any of the Cornish orthographies to be used in Gorsedd competition entries and for the continuation of Unified Cornish for official Gorsedd use:[124] as Jori Ansell put it, Richard Jenkin 'very shrewdly proposed – and, due to the great respect in which he was held, persuaded the Council to accept – that the Gorsedd should continue to use Unified Cornish'.[125] Though he was a firm supporter of UC, which he had been using for about fifty years, he did not wish to debar potential entrants to the competitions, of which he was perhaps the strongest supporter in the Gorsedd's history (see Appendix 3 below). Contention between the various forms of Cornish had been gaining momentum since the mid-1980s and at times the arguments between competing advocates became strident and personalised. This had the potential to cause another major split within the Gorsedd (as well as the wider Cornish movement), and the fact that this was largely avoided was due in no small measure to Richard Jenkin's advocacy of accommodating forms he did not support personally. Rather than alienate sections of the college of bards by switching its official position, the Gorsedd was kept above the fray by holding its nerve and maintaining its stance.[126] (When a change in Gorsedd practice was eventually made, in 2009, it was to the Standard Written Form of Cornish, which had been evolved after extensive academic input and consultation with advocates of the contending orthographies to become the officially sanctioned form for educational and formal use. The change was achieved relatively smoothly, and schism within the Gorsedd was avoided.)

At the conclusion of the Secretary's Report at the 1988 Closed Gorsedd, Peter Laws pointedly extended special thanks to Richard Jenkin and the Treasurer Helen Derrington (*Chun*) 'with whom he worked in complete harmony for the good of the Gorsedd'. Richard Jenkin himself had previously written that he hoped his successor would 'experience the same support and friendliness from bards as I have',[127] and it was announced at the Council meeting on 16 July 1988 that John Chesterfield (*Gwas Costentyn*) was to be the next Grand Bard. At this meeting Peter Laws paid another warm tribute to Richard 'for all the work that he had done over the past three years, two of which had been particularly difficult and very trying indeed and it was agreed to record the Council's great appreciation for his nine years as Grand Bard of Cornwall in the Minutes'.[128]

In a letter in July 1988, Richard Jenkin outlined his intention to 'retire into the background' after stepping down as Grand Bard, saying that if the post of President of the Federation of Old Cornwall Societies were offered to him he would decline. 'Strange as it may appear to some,' he wrote, 'I am of a retiring disposition... I don't want to be the official spokesman for any body. Furthermore, if I moved from one high office to another some might think that, like another Past Grand Bard, I was determined to reach the top of every organisation I was in.'[129] His intention was not altogether fulfilled – for one thing, in

1991 he was indeed elected President of the FOCS and accepted the position.¹³⁰

Arrangements for the Diamond Jubilee Gorsedd in 1988, at which Richard Jenkin would step down as Grand Bard for the last time, were in hand from 1986 onwards. The ceremony would be proclaimed in April 1988 during the Celtic Congress, and among other special features a commemorative plate would be made for the occasion. Three bards were involved in the commissioning and design of this plate, one of whom was the Grand Bard himself, whose advice led to the decorative border being given 'a more Celtic flavour'.¹³¹ He also drafted a message in Cornish for Australians of Cornish descent, hoping that many of them could travel to Cornwall in the jubilee year and including the familiar injunction 'Re bons y bynytha Kernewek' [*May they be for ever Cornish*].¹³² Before the ceremony, held at Poldhu on 3 September, Richard Jenkin, standing on the steps of the Marconi Memorial, spoke by satellite link to former Deputy Grand Bard Cecil Beer in Melbourne. 'The message was doubly fitting, as five Australians were initiated as bards during the ceremony in the afternoon.'¹³³ And it was at that ceremony that Richard Jenkin, sixth and eighth Grand Bard of Cornwall, installed Dr Chesterfield as his successor and quit the Grand Bard's chair for good.

Elder statesman (1988-2002)

Richard Jenkin's work for Gorsedh Kernow did not of course end after the 1988 ceremony, and a selection of his activities is mentioned here. As a past Grand Bard he was entitled to a seat on the Gorsedd Council, of which he remained an active member and a consistent attendee. He also continued to serve on various sub-committees, notably the Competitions and Ceremonial Sub-committees, and his house continued to be used on occasion as one of the venues for Gorsedd meetings.¹³⁴ His exemplary overall attendance record can be seen in the Council Attendance Book.¹³⁵ In 1992 he was one of three former Grand Bards to accompany Grand Bard Jori Ansell to Retallack Hooper's home to present him with a plaque to honour his service in that office (1959-64) and his sixty years of bardship.¹³⁶ Five years later it was his own turn to be honoured for long service, when on 6 September 1997, the day of the Gorsedd ceremony, he was presented with a certificate in appreciation of his fifty years' service as a bard.¹³⁷

The Holyer an Gof publishers' award was instituted, under the auspices of the Gorsedd, in memory of the Cornish publisher Len Truran (*Holyer an Gof*) soon after his death in 1997, and Richard Jenkin duly became a member of the award committee – a natural choice, in view of his own literary output.[138] On 24 October 1998, the Gorsedd Conference Day in Falmouth included a talk by him about the life and work of Retallack Hooper.[139] During a discussion about St Piran's Day and the Cornish flag at the Council meeting on 13 November 1999, Richard Jenkin suggested that Cornwall County Council (as it was then called) should be approached for support to make 5 March an officially recognised Saint's Day in Cornwall, a cause which is still advocated today.[140] The annual St Piran's Day parade in Truro had been instigated by him in 1983 (the day itself being the first day of the first Cornish Eisteddfod, of which he was Chairman) and he had long been a defender of the validity of the flag, as noted earlier.[141] The Gorsedd Conference Day in October 2000 was held in conjunction with the John Harris Society, and when it transpired that various speakers were unable to attend, Richard was one of those who took their places, reading from his own literary works.[142]

He felt well enough to attend the Gorsedd ceremony at Pensilva on 7 September 2002, where (for the second time) he was awarded the Jack Evans Cup for English verse by a Cornish poet, but he suffered a heart attack two days later. Unsurprisingly neither he nor Ann Jenkin was able to attend the Council meeting on 26 October 2002, and he died on 29 October, three weeks after his 77th birthday. Even at that meeting, however, there is evidence that he continued working for Cornwall through Gorsedh Kernow right to the end. He remained a member of the Competitions Sub-committee, and under the relevant section in the minutes of the meeting it is noted that '[a] letter had been received from Map Dyvroeth giving suggestions for the prose and poetry sections'. (He was certainly well qualified to advise in this area, as Appendix 3 will testify.) In the words of Grand Bard John Bolitho (*Jowan an Cleth*), 'He was a reference point of navigation from whom everyone in the Gorsedd took their bearings.'[143] The bilingual funeral service of this 'great Cornish patriot' was held at Crowan Parish Church on 9 November. Among the many members of the large congregation associated with Gorsedh Kernow was Hugh Miners.[144]

At the start of the next Council meeting (1 February 2003), there was a two-minute silence in memory of Richard Jenkin. John Bolitho paid tribute to him as 'an invaluable member of the Gorseth Council... whose counsel would be sorely missed', and Ann Jenkin responded with thanks for the thousands of tributes to Richard which she had received. As she reiterated in Gorsedd Newsletter 40 (February 2003), she was still receiving charitable donations to the Richard Garfield Jenkin Memorial Trust, which would therefore be kept open till the next open Gorsedd on 6 September 2003 'so that we can continue to remember a great Cornishman fittingly'. This serves as a reminder that Richard's association with the Cornish Gorsedd was shared by his family. Ann Jenkin and their daughters Morwenna and Loveday were bards, Ann and Loveday served on the Gorsedd Council, and Ann was the first woman to be Deputy Grand Bard and the first to be Grand Bard (1997-2000), indeed the first woman to head any of the three Brythonic-language Gorseddau. In the words of Jori Ansell, '[Richard] was... very proud and supportive of Ann during her six busy years as Deputy and then Grand Bard, always at hand to give a word of advice from his considerable experience', a statement confirmed by Ann herself in her own tribute. She also pointed out the breadth of knowledge he brought to his lifetime of service within the Gorsedd as an 'organisation safeguarding the culture, language, history, identity and nationhood of Cornwall'. One of the achievements of his many writings was to have enhanced the importance of the Gorsedd, and his 'inspiration and leadership will long be remembered and his influence on Cornish cultural perspective... not forgotten'. As she said, 'he led wisely and well'.[145]

Numerous other tributes were published, in the local and national press, at home and abroad, in Cornish, Breton and English, in print and on line. Douglas Williams (*Lef ha Pluven*) was glad that Richard had 'lived to see many dreams fulfilled'. Some of his character traits as recalled after his death will have stood him in good stead in view of his trials as Grand Bard: 'Never bitter, violent or aggressive in his views, he always believed in peaceful persuasion, but strongly emotive language.'[146] For someone 'never altogether happy in the public eye' Richard Jenkin was a remarkable leader, 'a chosen leader, rather than one who had sought to lead'. 'He has, over the years, been an inspiration to successive generations and will continue to inspire us all.'[147]

Appendix 1: Richard Jenkin and the spirit of Gorsedh Kernow
As the above account has indicated, Richard Jenkin gave much time and thought to the history and nature of the Gorsedd, bardship and associated concepts. 'Bards must be ready to help one another in their work for Cornwall. *Loyalty to Cornwall as a Celtic Nation* and to the Gorsedd is imperative,' he wrote, emphasising parts of the Gorsedd Constitution relating to bards' personal responsibility. He appreciated the difficulty of judging the worth of a potential bard's work in the light of the Gorsedd's ethos and knew that it was possible to do important Cornish research without having the least feeling for Cornwall's individuality.[148]

Like his mentor Robert Morton Nance before him, he was also deeply interested in Gorsedd symbolism, and, again like Nance, he wrote down his reflections on the subject while Grand Bard. In one of his essays, 'The symbolism of the Gorseth' (a title also used by Nance),[149] he discussed the deep significance of the Awen as well as the bardic circle, the Men Omborth (dais) and the individual elements of the ceremony itself. He wrote that his own practice respecting the 'cry of peace' was to 'usually direct the question to the left; to the right; and directly forwards, to follow the rays of the AWEN'. He referred to the allegiance to Gorsedh Kernow symbolically expressed by new bards at their initiation 'through its representative figure, the Grand Bard' by placing their hands between his. 'Note that the Grand Bard does NOT say 'my a'th tegemer' – I admit you, but 'ny a'th tegemer' – we admit you, that is, he is the spokesman for the Gorseth as a College.' The gesture was 'more highly symbolic than the handshake given by the Archdruid to Welsh initiates'. When the bards leave the Circle at the conclusion of the ceremony 'the procession is joined by Old Cornwall Societies and other Cornish Associations, symbolising the unity of the Gorseth with the people of Cornwall. This is often neglected nowadays and I wish it might be more commonly observed.' He concluded:

> The main symbolic themes are the threefold nature of creation; trinity in unity; the recurrent cycles of eternity; truth, justice, love; Peace, but not apathy; loyalty to Cornwall, its people, its culture, its language; the determination to survive and to maintain the identity of Cornwall by all means possible. These symbols, like Celtic art, are interwoven, shape-changing, and carrying overtones of other symbols so that there is a har-

mony and multi-layered meanings in the ceremonial of Gorseth Kernow.[150]

In these words the Grand Bard, the poet and the preacher come together, leaving no doubt that Richard Jenkin attached profound importance to the meaning of the Gorsedd ceremony – a phrase like 'the recurrent cycles of eternity' is not used lightly by such a writer.

Appendix 2: Richard Jenkin and Gorsedd Church Services
Richard Jenkin was once reported as having said that the Gorsedd was 'an entirely Christian organisation'.[151] Though he was speaking in the context of an article on the supposed druidical associations of the Midsummer Bonfire celebration, this statement is stretching a point, in that there is no religious restriction on admissibility to bardship, and parts of the ceremony are not specifically Christian. That Richard Jenkin himself was a committed Christian, however, there is no doubt, nor that he was a fine preacher: 'Cornwhylen a-leverys bos Map Dyvroeth an gwella pregowther-oll yn Kernewek' [*Cornwhylen* (Revd Richard Rutt) *said that Map Dyvroeth was the best preacher of all in Cornish*].[152]

The Gorsedd Cornish-language church service is held on the Sunday following the previous day's open Gorsedd ceremony, and Richard Jenkin was a regular attendee. He also played a part in the service from as early as 1951, when he read one of the lessons.[153] He again read the New Testament lesson at the service on 7 September 1952. One feature of that occasion strikes an incongruous note: 'The flag of St George, patron saint of England, flew over the parish church of St Cleer on Sunday afternoon.' Order was restored the following year, when the Cornish flag flew at St Ives parish church.[154] Richard Jenkin played a part in the service on many other occasions and preached the sermon every year during the nine years he was Grand Bard.

His sermon for the 1986 service at St Buryan Parish Church shows how he viewed the honour of membership of the college of bards and is another illustration of his interest in 'the spirit of Gorsedh Kernow'. The text for the sermon was from the parable of the vineyard: '… I will give unto this last, even as unto thee',[155] and part of his address (English version) reads:

> To bards among us I want to suggest that this great spiritual truth has a pale and weak reflection in our Gorsedd. We receive a call to enter the Gorsedd and work for Cornwall. It matters not at all whether the call is early or late... nor whether our knowledge is great or small. If the call comes and we... promise to work faithfully for Cornwall... then we are received among the bards... and we are... equal in the fellowship of the Gorsedd... The Grand Bard is not of a different order but, for a time, the first among equals. There is not one of us who is a perfect bard who could claim by merit alone to enter the circle. So our imperfect world reflects the perfect design of God like the vineyard in the parable reflects the kingdom of heaven.[156]

The parallel with the Christian doctrine of salvation is explicit.

He did not confine himself to the annual September service, however. Around Christmas 1977, for example, he gave an address at the service to commemorate the bicentenary of the death in December 1777 of Dolly Pentreath. This was arranged by the Cornish Language Board, which had been founded in 1967 by the joint resolution of Gorsedh Kernow and the Federation of Old Cornwall Societies. By virtue of their offices of Grand Bard and FOCS President respectively, Richard Jenkin and Hugh Miners were co-chairmen of the Board at that time. Drawing a lesson from the life of Dolly Pentreath, he spoke of the 'duty to hold fast to that which was good in our life, whether we were only one or many ... "Dolly made my destiny and the course of my life, for Cornish changed my life and brought me back to Cornwall...".[157]

Appendix 3: Richard Jenkin and the Gorsedd competitions – the elusive existence of Garfield Richardson

Richard Jenkin's literary achievements are explored elsewhere in this book, but a brief account of his contributions to the competitions of the Cornish Gorsedd (and Eisteddfod, under Gorsedd auspices) is not out of place here. He regularly called for more people to enter the competitions and certainly set an example in this field. His remarkable record has been noted by Jori Ansell, among others: 'Ef a-waynyas moy a bewasow yn kesstryfow an Orseth rak scryfa yn Kernewek (ha Sowsnek), del grysyr, es denvyth aral.' [*He probably won more prizes in the Gorsedd competitions (writing in both Cornish and English) than anyone else*].[158]

Over the years, Richard Jenkin submitted entries in the classes for Cornish verse, Cornish prose, and English verse 'on a Cornish subject' or 'by a Cornish poet'.[159] Among the Jenkin papers are preserved twenty-seven certificates awarded to him in these classes between 1957 and 2002, ranging from 'Commended' to First Place. The first time he won a class was in 1962 for Cornish prose, and he took first place and the Jack Evans Cup for English verse in 1974 and (as noted above) 2002. (Extraordinarily, in this, the year in which he died, he also won two other awards, for Cornish and English verse.) In 1992 he won the Mordon-Caradar Rose Bowl for Cornish verse and four other awards, and in 1995 he took first place and the Cornish Crystal (the award he had presented to the Gorsedd in 1982) for Cornish prose.

With one exception, he won these awards in years when he was not Grand Bard. It is the Grand Bard who presents the awards, and he or she is one of the signatories of the certificates. There would be a slightly farcical element to authenticating a certificate awarded to oneself with one's own signature, but the trick was pulled off in 1986, when he won a commendation for Cornish verse. It is far from the case, however, that (with this one exception) he refrained from entering the competitions when he was Grand Bard. He simply used a second pseudonym. Entries to the competitions had to be submitted under a pseudonym in order to preclude foreknowledge by the judges of the identity of entrants and thus avoid any question of bias. ('Lew Du' ['Black Lion'] and 'Cothwas Coynt' ['Funny Old Chap'] were two of those used by Richard Jenkin.) The true identity of entrants is revealed only after awards have been decided. During the years of his Grand Bardship, therefore, his 'true' identity for competition purposes became Garfield Richardson. This is perhaps better described as word play than a pseudonym, since he was indeed Garfield, son of Richard. The use of this parallel identity obviously appealed to him since he continued to use it in years when he was no longer Grand Bard, sometimes winning awards under his real name and his alias in the same year.

As Garfield Richardson, between 1979 and 1995 he won at least a further twenty-eight certificates, fourteen of them signed by himself as Grand Bard. Two of these were in 1992, so that in that one year he won seven awards. He took first place and the William Morris Cup for English verse on a Cornish subject at the first Cornish Eisteddfod in 1983 (as well as three other awards in the same year). In fact, his alter ego took first place in one class or another in each of the first five Eisteddfodau, as well as other awards. Naturally, Garfield Richardson could not be present in person to receive his accolades. (His home address, in London or Manchester, was coincidentally the same as that of Richard Jenkin's sister.) Richard had some fun with his friend Garfield, who took on a life of his own. In the late 1980s Richard read and discussed Garfield's poems in at least one poetry reading, received a letter from him ('Dear Mr Jenkin…') and contacted at least one publisher on his behalf.[160] 'Mr Jenkin' was a serious man, but he did not lack a sense of humour.

Appendix 4: Richard Jenkin as ambassador to Wales and Brittany
Cornish bards are encouraged to forge and maintain links with other Celtic peoples, notably by attending the Gorseddau of Wales and Brittany, often as designated representatives of Gorsedh Kernow. Members of any one Gorsedd are honorary members of the other two and send delegates to their ceremonies, and it is a pleasurable duty for a Grand Bard in particular to feature on these occasions. Richard Jenkin took his wider Celtic activities very seriously. During his time as a bard, he represented Gorsedh Kernow at numerous Welsh and Breton Gorsedd ceremonies, starting with the Breton Gorsedd of 1955, which he attended with Denis Trevanion, and ending with the Welsh National Eisteddfod at Llanelli in 2000.[161]

At the Closed Gorsedd on 5 June 1982 he spoke of the wonderful welcome which he and the other Cornish delegates had received at the Breton Gorsedd that year. He also revealed a plan to hold the first combined Welsh, Breton and Cornish Gorsedd in Brittany in the summer of 1983, using the three Brythonic languages. (This would be in addition to the three individual Gorseddau, which would be held in the normal way.)[162] Regrettably, this event did not take place at that time, but – like other Gorsedd visions – the plan was eventually realised, in 1999, when both Richard and Ann Jenkin attended, the latter as Grand Bard.[163]

Notes
1. The full designation is Gorsedh Berdh Kernow (The Gorsedd of the Bards of Cornwall). The most accessible publication on the organisation is Rod Lyon (2008) *Gorseth Kernow / The Cornish Gorsedd: what it is and what it does*, [n.p.]: Gorseth Kernow. When, in 2009, the Gorsedd replaced the orthography of Unified Cornish with that of the Standard Written Form of Cornish for 'official' use, this entailed a change in

spelling from 'Gorseth' to 'Gorsedh'. Within this chapter, the latter spelling is used in the phrase 'Gorsedh Kernow' and the adopted Welsh word 'Gorsedd' (plural 'Gorseddau') in an English context, though the amendments to the Constitution adopted in 2013 include the use of 'Gorsedh' in the English as well as the Cornish version of the document. The spelling of the word in quotations is of course in the form of the original.
2. Cornwall Record Office, X1104/1/1, Cornish Gorsedd Minute Book, p. [249].
3. CRO, X1104/1/1, p. [251].
4. 'Jenkin, Richard Garfield', file in the 'Bards' Biographies' series, Cornish Gorsedd Archives.
5. Richard Jenkin, 'My Cornwall', ms., [1982], Jenkin Archives.
6. Richard Jenkin, Letter to Victoria L. Morgan, 16 March 1993, Jenkin Archives.
7. Richard Jenkin, Paper, [1978], Jenkin Archives.
8. 'Notes on Richard G. Jenkin', ms.; R.M. Nance, Letter to Richard Jenkin, 22 April 1947; Jenkin Archives.
9. Richard Jenkin, Letter to Victoria L. Morgan, 16 March 1993, Jenkin Archives.
10. Undated cutting [*West Briton*, 1977?], Jenkin Archives.
11. Published in *Cornish Magazine*, vol. 5, no. 1, May 1962, p. 28. A copy in the Jenkin Archives is dated 1946.
12. R.M. Nance, Letter to Richard Jenkin, 22 April 1947, Jenkin Archives.
13. R.M. Nance, Letters to Richard Jenkin, 19 May 1947 and 15 June 1945 [misdated], Jenkin Archives.
14. Richard Jenkin, 'My Cornwall', ms., [1982], Jenkin Archives.
15. R.M. Nance, Letter to Richard Jenkin, 25 May 1957 [i.e. 1947], Jenkin Archives.
16. Richard Jenkin, Letter to Victoria L. Morgan, 16 March 1993; Richard Jenkin Chronology; Examination certificate; Jenkin Archives.
17. Richard Jenkin, Letter to Victoria L. Morgan, 16 March 1993, Jenkin Archives.
18. E.A. Rees (*Carer Losow*), Letter to Richard Jenkin, 4 January 1951, Jenkin Archives.
19. Richard Jenkin, Letter to R.M. Nance, September [1947], Jenkin Archives.
20. Richard Jenkin, Letter to R.M. Nance, 29 October [1947], Jenkin Archives.
21. Sea landing permit (release to the UK) dated 26 December 1947, Jenkin Archives.
22. 'Notes on Richard G. Jenkin', ms., Jenkin Archives.
23. CRO, X1104/1/1, p. [374].
24. The term 'language bard' is not used officially, there being no longer any distinction made between the types of achievement leading to qualification for bardship. Discontinuation of all indicators of differentiation between bards was approved at the Gorsedd Council Special Meeting on 4 January 1986 (CRO, X1104/1/5, Cornish Gorsedd Minute Book, pp. 114-115).
25. R.M. Nance, Letter to Richard Jenkin, 20 June 1953, Jenkin Archives.
26. R.M. Nance, Letter to Richard Jenkin, 25 June 1953, Jenkin Archives.
27. CRO, X1104/1/1, pp. [372], [344].
28. CRO, X1104/1/1, p. [345]; *Cornishman*, 2 February 1961.
29. CRO, X1104/1/1, p. [347].
30. *Western Morning News*, 5 September 1960; CRO, X1104/1/3, Cornish Gorsedd Minute Book, pp. 3, 25; CRO, X1104/1/4, Cornish Gorsedd Minute Book, p. 40.
31. *Western Morning News*, 3 September 1956.
32. CRO, X1104/1/1, p. [351].
33. CRO, X1104/1/1, pp. [357]-[359].
34. *Cornishman*, 7 September 1961.
35. CRO, X1104/1/1, p. [361]. See also CRO, X1104/1/4, pp. 228-229; Peter W. Thomas (2007) 'Robert Morton Nance and Gorseth Kernow' in Peter W. Thomas and Derek R. Williams (eds) *Setting Cornwall on its feet: Robert Morton Nance, 1873-1959*, London: Francis Boutle, p. 209.

36 CRO, X1104/1/1, pp. [367]-[368].
37 CRO, X1104/1/3, p. 24; 'Circular to all Bards August 1964' (copy in chronological Gorsedd files, Cornish Gorsedd Archives).
38 CRO, X1104/1/3, pp. 42-43, 45.
39 'Jenkin, Richard Garfield', file in the 'Bards' Biographies' series, Cornish Gorsedd Archives (letter dated 10 November 1965). The letter was printed in *Cornish Magazine*, vol. 8, no. 8, December 1965, p. 171.
40 Richard and Ann Jenkin (1965) *Cornwall: the hidden land*, Bracknell: West Country Publications (2nd ed. (2005), Leedstown: Noonvares Press). The Gorsedd is described on pp. 4-5 of the original edition and on pp. 11 and 13 of the revised edition.
41 CRO, X1104/1/3, pp. 68, 75.
42 *West Briton*, 8 June 1967.
43 CRO, X1104/1/3, pp. 88 ff.
44 CRO, X1104/1/3, pp. 146, 149-150.
45 Kesva an Tavas Kernewek / The Cornish Language Board ([1969]) *Cornish Language* (IBC/LP/3624). The year of issue is found in the chronological Gorsedd files, Cornish Gorsedd Archives.
46 CRO, X1104/1/4, p. 25.
47 CRO, X1104/1/4, pp. 28, 35.
48 CRO, X1104/1/4, p. 37.
49 CRO, X1104/1/4, p. 35; *Cornish and Devon Post*, 9 September 1972.
50 CRO, X1104/1/4, p. 58.
51 CRO, X1104/1/4, pp. 35-127, 140-144.
52 CRO, X1104/1/4, p. 124; *Western Morning News*, 5 July 1976; *West Briton*, 8 July 1976.
53 *West Briton*, 8 July 1976 and 9 September 1976.
54 *Camborne-Redruth Packet*, 8 September 1976.
55 Richard Jenkin, Paper (undated), Jenkin Archives.
56 *Cornish Guardian*, 9 September 1976.
57 Gorsedd Newsletter, no. 24, 1987.
58 CRO, X1104/1/4, p. 191; unidentified newspaper cutting, 8 June 1978, chronological Gorsedd files, Cornish Gorsedd Archives.
59 CRO, X1104/1/4, p. 179.
60 CRO, X1104/1/4, pp. 165, 220.
61 Hugh Miners (1978) *Gorseth Kernow: the first 50 years*, Penzance: Gorseth Kernow, pp. 3, 6.
62 Richard Jenkin, Paper, [1978], Jenkin Archives.
63 CRO, X1104/1/4, pp. 128, 136, 166.
64 CRO, X1104/1/4, p. 151; *West Briton*, 9 June 1977.
65 CRO, X1104/1/4, p. 169; *Cornishman*, 7 September 1978.
66 CRO, X1104/1/4, p. 175.
67 CRO, X1104/1/4, pp. 181-182, 186.
68 Unidentified newspaper cutting, 31 August 1978, chronological Gorsedd files, Cornish Gorsedd Archives; *Sunday Independent*, 3 September 1978; *Western Morning News*, 4 September 1978; *Cornishman*, 7 September 1978.
69 *Western Morning News*, 23 September 1978; *Cornishman*, 28 September 1978.
70 CRO, X1104/1/4, pp. 188, 191.
71 CRO, X1104/1/4, pp. 218, 222-223.
72 CRO, X1104/1/4, p. 205.
73 *West Briton*, 6 September 1979.
74 Grand Bard's letter (January 1980), Jenkin Archives; *Western Morning News*, 4 February 1980. See also Peter

W. Thomas, op. cit., pp. 183-184.
75 CRO, X1104/1/4, p. 244; photocopy of unidentified newspaper cutting, [12(?) June 1980], supplied by Derek R. Williams.
76 Gorsedd Newsletter, no. 15, 1981; *Western Morning News*, 8 September 1980; *West Briton*, 11 September 1980.
77 *West Briton*, 10 September 1987.
78 CRO, X1104/1/4, pp. 233-234; Gorsedd Newsletter, no. 15, 1981; *West Briton*, 11 September 1980.
79 Gorsedd Newsletter, no. 15, 1981; *Western Morning News*, 4 April 1981.
80 CRO, X1104/1/4, pp. 270-271; *West Briton*, 11 June 1981.
81 *West Briton*, 25 February 1982.
82 Gorsedd Newsletter, no. 16, 1982; *West Briton*, 10 September 1981.
83 *West Briton*, 4 March 1982. For Richard Jenkin's summary of historical references to the Cornish flag, see his letter to the *West Briton*, 5 December 1985.
84 Gorsedd Newsletter, no. 16, 1982; *Western Morning News*, 29 March 1982.
85 See Peter W. Thomas, op. cit., pp. 208-209.
86 CRO, X1104/1/4, p. 278.
87 CRO, X1104/1/4, p. 301; *West Briton*, 10 June 1982.
88 Jori Ansell (2003) 'Old Cornwall remembers: Richard Jenkin' in *Old Cornwall*, vol. 12, no. 12, Spring 2003, pp. 61-62.
89 CRO, X1104/1/4, p. 284; *Western Morning News*, 3 September 1982; *Cornishman*, 9 September 1982.
90 Richard Jenkin, 'My Cornwall', ms., [1982], Jenkin Archives.
91 CRO, X1104/1/4, pp. 283, 287; *Western Morning News*, 12 July 1982.
92 *Cornishman*, 9 September 1982.
93 CRO, X1104/1/5, pp. 71-76.
94 CRO, X1104/1/4, pp. 250, 277.
95 CRO, X1104/1/1, p. [116].
96 CRO, X1104/1/4, pp. 250, 277.
97 CRO, X1104/1/4, pp. 284-285, 288, 292, 294, 297.
98 CRO, X1104/1/4, pp. 333, 335; CRO, X1104/1/5, pp. 18, 54.
99 Hugh Miners, Paper (with ancillary documents), dated 9 March 1987, Cornish Gorsedd Archives.
100 *Western Morning News*, 3 September 1984; *West Briton*, 7 September 1989.
101 CRO, X1104/1/5, p. 85-86.
102 Hugh Miners, Letter to Peter Laws, 30 August 1985, Cornish Gorsedd Archives; *Western Morning News*, 9 September 1985; *West Briton*, 12 September 1985.
103 CRO, X1104/1/4, pp. 310-311.
104 Lynne Cassell, Letter to Richard Jenkin, 20 July 1985, Jenkin Archives.
105 CRO, X1104/1/5, pp. 87-92.
106 CRO, X1104/1/5, pp. 95, 101-102. The Revision of Rules Sub-committee presented their proposals for a revised set of rules, drafted by solicitor Peter Pool, to the Council meeting on 25 October 1986. After some amendments, the final version was approved at the 1987 Closed Gorsedd (CRO, X1104/1/5, pp. 165-166, 220, 250).
107 CRO, X1104/1/5, pp. 107-110, 113.
108 CRO, X1104/1/5, pp. 116, 137-138.
109 CRO, X1104/1/5, pp. 145-147.
110 CRO, X1104/1/5, pp. 114, 191-192; *Western Morning News*, 9(?) June 1986.
111 CRO, X1104/1/5, p. 197.
112 *Cornishman*, 11 September 1986.
113 *Western Morning News*, 6 September 1986; *West Briton*, 11 September 1986.

114 CRO, X1104/1/5, pp. 175-177, 181-182.
115 CRO, X1104/1/5, pp. 171, 182-183, 211, 231, 310; *West Briton*, 12 February 1987; CRO, X1104/1/8, Cornish Gorsedd Minute Book, meeting of 7 November 1998.
116 *Western Morning News*, 1 February 1987.
117 Richard Jenkin, Letter to Ronald Daw, 7 March 1987, chronological Gorsedd files, Cornish Gorsedd Archives.
118 CRO, X1104/1/5, p. 180.
119 CRO, X1104/1/5, p. 187.
120 CRO, X1104/1/5, p. 250; *West Briton*, 11 June 1987.
121 CRO, X1104/1/5, pp. 248-249.
122 CRO, X1104/1/5, pp. 161, 230; *West Briton*, 11 June 1987.
123 CRO, X1104/1/5, p. 283; *West Briton*, 9 June 1988; The first Assembly in Australia of the Bards of the Gorsedd of Cornwall, March 5th, 1988, Ballarat, Victoria (booklet, copy in chronological Gorsedd files, Cornish Gorsedd Archives).
124 CRO, X1104/1/5, p. 312.
125 Jori Ansell, funeral tribute to Richard Jenkin, Crowan Parish Church, 9 November 2002.
126 CRO, X1104/1/7, Cornish Gorsedd Minute Book, p. [63]; CRO, X1104/1/8, meeting of Competitions Sub-committee, 24 November 1998; CRO, X1104/1/9, Cornish Gorsedd AGM Minute Book, meeting of 2 June 2001.
127 Gorsedd Newsletter, no. 25, 1988.
128 CRO, X1104/1/5, pp. 284, 316; *West Briton*, 21 July 1988.
129 Richard Jenkin, Letter to Helen Derrington, 1 July 1988.
130 CRO, X1104/1/6, p. 47.
131 CRO, X1104/1/5, pp. 164-165, 268; [*Camborne-Redruth?*] *Packet*, w/e 10 September 1988.
132 Richard Jenkin, 'Dhe bobel Kernow yn Australya', ms., [1988], Jenkin Archives.
133 CRO, X1104/1/5, pp. 358-359; *West Briton*, 8 September 1988 and 8 June 1989.
134 See e.g. CRO, X1104/1/5-X1104/1/9 passim.
135 CRO, X1104/3/1.
136 CRO, X1104/1/6, p. 126.
137 Chronological Gorsedd files, Cornish Gorsedd Archives.
138 Ann Jenkin, 'Richard Garfield Jenkin, Map Dyvroeth – Son of Exile, 9/10/1925-29/10/2002', posthumous tribute.
139 Gorsedd Newsletter, no. 36, 1999; *West Briton*, 29 October 1998.
140 CRO, X1104/1/8, meeting of 13 November 1999.
141 *Western Morning News*, 11 March 2003.
142 CRO, X1104/1/8, meeting of 28 October 2000.
143 *Western Morning News*, 31 October 2002.
144 *Camborne-Redruth Packet*, 6 November 2002; *Western Morning News*, 12 November 2002.
145 Jori Ansell (2003); Ann Jenkin, 'Richard Garfield Jenkin, Map Dyvroeth – Son of Exile, 9/10/1925-29/10/2002'.
146 *Cornishman*, 7 November 2002.
147 Jori Ansell (2003); *Western Morning News*, 12 November 2002.
148 Richard Jenkin, Paper (undated), Jenkin Archives.
149 Peter W. Thomas, op. cit., p. 208.
150 Richard Jenkin, 'The symbolism of the Gorseth', ms. and typescript, Jenkin Archives. For details of the ceremony, see Rod Lyon, op. cit.; Solempnytys Gorsedh Berdh Kernow / Ceremonies of the Gorsedd of the Bards of Cornwall (booklet to accompany the open Gorsedd ceremony).

151 *Western Morning News*, 22 June 1999.
152 Jori Ansell (2003).
153 *Cornish Guardian*, 6 September 1951.
154 *Cornish Times*, 12 September 1952; *West Briton*, 5 December 1985.
155 Matthew 20, 14b, King James Version.
156 Cornish text and English translation accompany a letter, Revd Frank Warnes (*Den Gwarnek*) to Richard Jenkin, 26 August 1986, Jenkin Archives.
157 *Cornishman*, 5 January 1978.
158 Jori Ansell (2003), with translation from the English version of his funeral oration; Ann Jenkin, 'Richard Garfield Jenkin, Map Dyvroeth – Son of Exile, 9/10/1925-29/10/2002'.
159 On at least one occasion he also acted as a competition judge, in a non-literary section. See *West Briton*, 5 September 1985.
160 Richard Jenkin, ms. notes for a poetry reading, [1989?]; Garfield Richardson, Letter to Richard Jenkin, 17 April 1989; Richard Jenkin, Letter to *Cornish Scene*, 19 April 1989; Jenkin Archives.
161 CRO, X1104/1/1, p. [319]; chronological Gorsedd files, Cornish Gorsedd Archives.
162 CRO, X1104/1/4, pp. 287, 301; *West Briton*, 10 June 1982.
163 CRO, X1104/1/4, p. 313; Rod Lyon, op. cit., p. [37]; chronological Gorsedd files, Cornish Gorsedd Archives.

Acknowledgements

Various individuals and organisations have contributed to the research for this chapter. For their unfailing help and forbearance I should like particularly to thank Ann Trevenen Jenkin, Derek Williams and Esther Johns, as well as David Thomas and the rest of the staff at the Cornwall Record Office.

Celtic Cornwall lives on

Richard G. Jenkin

In time past Cornwall was an independent Celtic country. After the Romans lost their grip on Britain we Cornish had our own kings, our own laws, our own church, our own language – Celtic laws, Celtic church, Celtic language.

Then came the English. After four centuries of freedom Cornwall was conquered. Our kings and nobles were killed or dispossessed. Our church was subjected to Canterbury, our laws replaced, our language no more the language of the rulers.

Doubtless our nobles had bards to sing their praises and recite their pedigrees. But when the nobles are no more the bards disappear. A century after the English conquered Cornwall they themselves in their turn were conquered by the Normans. The Normans took our land for their profit. Stories of our kings were of no interest to Bassets, St Aubins, Blanchminsters, Granvilles and later the Carews and Elliots. But the people, the serfs, remembered Arthur and Mark, Casvelyn, Massen, Cadiek, Rialobran, Costentyn Kernow, Doniert and others. There were no learned men to keep the records and now we can see our kings only through dark mists of folklore – as Professor Charles Thomas says, it is likely that the last memories of Rialobran formed the giant Holiburn on Hannibal's Carn not far from his memorial, the Maen Scryfa, and that Cadiek of Rescadiek became the "General Jig" of Camborne folklore.

In Wales and Brittany often the gentry were descended from the old kings and were proud of their lineage but in Cornwall all the gentry were strangers and the memories of Cornish freedom were dangerous to them. Yet still our nobles have their memorials, Meyn Scryfa or Inscribed Stones – Rialobran, Cuneval, Tegernomal, Doniert, Ricat, Cunedauc, near to 40 of them. They are also remembered in our placenames – Tremodret; Lesteedur; Rescadjeeg; Cartuther; Cargenwen.

Always the strangers tried to stamp out Cornish things. Our saints were honoured by the people but the bishops tried to bring in foreign saints – Martin in place of Meriadoc; Nicholas in place of Finbar; Felicitas at Phillack and possibly others where the Cornish saint is now forgotten. However, the people and their priests loved their church and their saints and, indeed, helped to save our language through their miracle plays. It is a pity that more have not survived. Tantalising references exist to other plays besides the ones we still possess.

The stranger nobles and lords of the manors were English in all their ways. It was not the great land-owners who made the revolts of 1497 and 1549 but the people, the lesser gentry, farmers, labourers and their parish priests. The pressure from above turned our history and legends into drolls and folktales and turned our language into a tongue of labourers, miners and fishermen. We must honour the few gentry who were loyal Cornishmen:– Humphrey Arundell; Winslade; Nicholas Roscarrock; Scawen; Boson; Keigwin; James Jenkin of Alverton; Tonkin; Hals; perhaps Borlase and Davies Gilbert. Nevertheless, the majority wished only to be English.

They have nearly succeeded in Anglicizing Cornwall. The Post Office, when asked for a stamp for Cornwall, like all the other Celtic parts of Great Britain, can say 'We will not give a stamp or all the other counties of England will want one'! Nowadays the local government of Cornwall is organized completely as in an English county. Its Council has no more power than English County Councils and the English believe Cornwall is now only a part of England.

Yet the people, some people, still fight on. Some 80 years ago people began to re-learn Cornish. It was no profit to them. They learned it because it was their own language. And today people learn it for the same reason. The spirit of Cornwall began to re-awaken with the founding of the Cornu-Celtic Society, followed by the Federation of Old Cornwall Societies, then the Gorsedd, the Celtic Congress, Cornish Wrestling Association, Tyr ha Tavas and others. All spoke of the Cornish Nation and Mebyon Kernow was founded to claim the rights of the Cornish Nation.

But Cornwall is not yet fully awake. It is still possible for the English to smother Cornwall and turn its sleep into the sleep of death. We, in the whole hosts of the Cornish Movement, are the spurs to awaken Cornwall to new life. If we succeed the Cornwall of the future will truly be a Celtic country; if we fail Cornwall will be only an English county. The end will not be seen by us, perhaps, but it will be made by our actions now. If God wills we shall re-awaken the Cornish people and they will ensure that Cornwall will be a Celtic Country and will not be only an English county.

[Translated from an address in Cornish entitled 'Kernow, Gwlas Keltek py Conteth Sawsnek?' and published under his bardic name *Map Dyvroeth* in *New Cornwall*, vol. 17 no. 3, Summer 1972]

'Years of dreaming and scheming...': Esedhvos Kernow

Derek R. Williams

Introduction
On Saturday 2 February 1980, Ruth Moss (*Kewny*), the Cornish Gorsedh's competitions secretary, outlined to a meeting of its council the progress being made towards holding the first Cornish Eisteddfod in March 1983. Richard Jenkin, who was four years into his first term of office as Grand Bard, stressed that an eisteddfod had been a dream since the founding of the Gorsedh and called on all bards to work for its success so that it became 'an established part of Cornish life'.[1] He was still chairing the eisteddfod committee at the end of the decade when he wrote to fellow bards to remind them of the impending third festival of its kind. 'We want the Esethvos to show what the Cornish can do in every aspect of culture,' he enthused, 'especially our own native culture but also our contribution to, and expertise in, European culture generally.' First and foremost, he wanted it to be 'the Esethvos of all Cornwall and all Cornish people'.[2] Before examining his pivotal role in the establishment of the Eisteddfod of Cornwall in 1983 and its continued success over two decades, it is necessary to view that role in the light of previous attempts by a number of committed individuals – usually working from within the Cornish Gorsedh – to provide Cornwall with a celebration or festival of indigenous Cornish culture.

Towards a Cornish National Eisteddfod

Writing in *Gorseth Kernow: the first 50 years*, Hugh Miners (*Den Toll*) described the principle of an eisteddfod as being 'inherent in the foundation of Gorseth Kernow', the two concepts being 'intertwined'. He concluded:

> To many, the eventual holding of a Cornish Eisteddfod would seem an attractive and important contribution to the cultural life of Cornwall, but it would have to be on the basis of complete mutual trust and cooperation between all of the bodies and organisations concerned. There are so many bards who are also members of these organisations, and so much good-will already exists between them and the Gorsedd, that such cooperation should not be too difficult to come by in order to produce an event which, far from "poaching" should enhance the work and status of them all.[3]

It was concerns over any such perceived 'poaching' that dominated early calls for Cornwall to have its own eisteddfod. The founding members of the Old Cornwall societies in the immediate post-World War I era and those same Cornish activists working towards the establishment of a Cornish Gorsedh in 1928 are together considered to have been amongst the first to propose, too, a Cornish cultural event. Among them was Reginald F. Reynolds, who is generally considered to have been initiated as a Welsh bard (*Gwas Piran*) in 1899.[4] In August 1917 he wrote to D. Rhys Phillips, a Welsh bard and secretary of the Celtic Congress, of 'advocating a Cornish Eisteddfod in the summer following the conclusion of peace', having first put forward the idea 'on the occasion of a Royal coming of age'.[5] The content of the rest of the letter indicates that his suggestion was made pre-war. Reynolds was almost certainly referring here to the 18th birthday of the future Edward VIII on 23 June 1912 and part of his contribution to the lengthy correspondence on the subject of a Cornish eisteddfod in the local newspapers in 1923 substantiates this suggestion, for he wrote then of '[h]aving published an outline of a Cornish Festival in 1912'.[6]

The initiator of this debate, which was reported in the pages of both the *Western Morning News and Mercury* and *The Cornubian*, was 'Den, a' Gernow' who noted the growth in stature of the annual bandsmen's festival at Bugle from small beginnings in 1912. Describing how a London Cornishman had given voice to an idea that had occupied his mind for many years – namely, 'Why cannot we have a Cornish Eisteddfod?' – he suggested that the Bugle meeting could be made a nucleus for an annual gathering with singing competitions, band contests, folk dancing, wrestling, hurling, and perhaps rock drilling. All this would constitute 'a spontaneous gala week for the Cornish race'.[7] 'Den, a' Gernow"s emphasis on the need for cooperation and coordination on the part of existing societies was not enough to placate 'Not a bandsman' who, while supportive of the idea of a Cornish Eisteddfod, appealed to those who were entertaining 'any idea of hybridizing this great event' to leave "Bugle-day" out of the equation.[8] Writing from the Tregenna Castle Hotel, St Ives – his Cornish base throughout the decade – Reginald Reynolds saw the debate as proof that many favoured an event supportive of the Royal National Eisteddfod of Wales, the appeal of which had 'the religious fervour of patriotism'. He saw competitors in any Cornish Festival doing so 'for the honour of Cornwall' and suggested that the first step should be the immediate formation of a small committee, with which those interested, himself included, could keep in touch.[9]

Cornwall's musicians were canvassed for their views; others working in the burgeoning Cornish Movement also joined the fray. Of the former, Dr C. Rivers of Redruth, who was involved with the Cornwall Symphony Orchestra, the Camborne and Redruth Choral Society, and the West Cornwall Musical Society – all of which were, it seems, struggling financially – thought that some such movement as an eisteddfod would be both an important factor in 'cultivating music' and 'a big advertisement [for local music societies]'.[10] Lady Mary Trefusis, one of the honorary secretaries of the Cornwall Music Competition (Asedhvos Canoryon Kernow, to give it the Cornish-language title then in use) and a leading figure in Cornish folk dancing, took the opposite view and emphasized the difference in the aims of the eisteddfod movement from those of the music competitions which had been held in Cornwall and elsewhere for years. Whereas the Welsh Eisteddfod was 'kept going by the large money prizes given' and was 'partly a sort of amusement festival', the music competition movement was purely educational, with money prizes being either non-existent or very small indeed. 'The Eisteddfod belongs to Wales,' she concluded, its companion, the music competition, having gone some way towards fulfilling Sir Arthur Quiller-Couch's idea some ten years previously of a large Cornish festival of song, music and dance.¹¹ Another opponent of the idea was Major A.W. Gill of Truro, the other honorary secretary of the Cornwall Music Competitions and president of Truro City Band. Echoing Lady Trefusis's rather disparaging remarks, he thought that the Eisteddfod principle did not raise musical taste or standards, being 'a popular form of amusement'.¹² Responding to the letters of 'Den, a' Gernow' and Reginald Reynolds, Robert Morton Nance, future Grand Bard of Gorsedh Kernow, thought that the cooperation of all the existing societies in Cornwall in making one big Cornish Festival or "esedhvos" outwardly resembling the Royal National Eisteddfod of Wales was achievable. He believed, though, as did Reginald Reynolds, that the life and soul of the latter was the gorsedd and in order for the Cornish "esedhvos" to have a Celtic standing, it was necessary to have something in Cornwall that might at least be recognised in Wales and Brittany as 'the best that Cornwall can do towards forming such a [bardic] court'.¹³ Some three weeks later, though, as Peter Thomas points out, Nance changed tack slightly, playing down the relative status of the Gorsedd and elevating the eisteddfod to the position of 'first object'.¹⁴

Henry Jenner, Cornwall's future first Grand Bard, addressed the concerns of those who saw the advocates of a Cornish Eisteddfod as 'poachers'. There was no need, in his opinion, for an Eisteddfod to enter into rivalry with the Cornwall Music Competition or with the folk-dancing festivals. Excellent though their work was, these two institutions had no more to do with 'the Celtic aspect of Cornwall' than had Dr Rivers' symphony concerts. Any musical content in the Asedhvos would have to be along different lines, such as competitions in the discovery of folk songs. A beginning, though, should be made with the Gorsedh.¹⁵ Jenner continued to press for an acceptance of the principle of a Cornish Eisteddfod when the matter was subsequently discussed by the committee of the Cornwall Music Competition, but in the face of continued opposition from Lady Mary Trefusis and others, reluctantly agreed that it was premature to pass any resolution.¹⁶ *The Cornubian* thought that there were enough enthusiasts in Cornwall to make a Cornish Eisteddfod a certainty for 1924 if they combined with the various branches of the Old Cornwall societies. 'What better medium could be used to enlarge our sympathies for all things Cornish than a combined county Eisteddfod?' asked the writer in conclusion.¹⁷

During the middle and closing years of the 1920s and throughout the 1930s, various members of both the Federation of Old Cornwall Societies and the Cornish Gorsedh, notably Jenner and Nance, continued to raise the subject. Early in 1928, the latter wrote – as he had done three years previously in the first issue of *Old Cornwall* – of the long-standing object of establishing in Cornwall 'something akin to the Welsh National Eisteddfod', while at the first Gorsedh at Boscawen Un on 21 September that same year, Charles Henderson (*Map Hendra*) described the day's events as 'but a step towards the greater festival of an eisteddfod'.[18] The following year, Grand Bard Henry Jenner foresaw 'someday a Cornish Eisteddfod Association which, with the Gorsedh in its centre, might include the Cornwall Music Competitions, the Folk-dancing Festival, the Band Competitions, the Wrestling Tournaments and last, but by no means least, the various activities of the Old Cornwall Societies – everything, in fact, that makes Cornwall Cornwall.'[19] At the annual meeting of the Gorsedh on 9 September 1932, the possibility of its activities being expanded to encourage 'the arts of music, poetry etc.' was discussed, with Walter Barnes (*Pen Ylow*), founder-conductor of the Penzance Orchestral Society, proposing 'early steps to combine with the Cornwall Music Festival, to create an eisteddfod'.[20] Canon Henry Jennings (*Saws Degemerys*) thought it was better for the movement to be slow and permanent than to try and rush matters and moved that the proposal be referred to the Gorsedh council. While conferring bardship on outstanding performers in the Cornwall Music Festival was investigated and referred to the Festival's committee, the specific proposal of a Cornish Eisteddfod seems to have disappeared off the radar.[21]

Just before his installation as Grand Bard in 1934,[22] Nance spoke again of his hope for the realisation of his 'first object' and many others would echo his sentiments at pre- and immediately post-war gorsedhow. As Hugh Miners pointed out, those sentiments were heartfelt, but often cautious in tone, centring on allaying the fears of those members of the Cornwall Music Festival who felt that first the Federation of Old Cornwall Societies and then the Gorsedh were 'poaching' on their preserves.[23] It would be the 1970s before real progress was made and 1983 before the dream of those early Cornish activists was realized.

Enter Richard Jenkin

On 3 August 1957, ten years after he had received Richard Jenkin into the

Gorsedh, Robert Morton Nance wrote to him as follows:

> I hope this will reach you in time. We should all wish that Cornwall should be represented at the [Welsh] Eisteddfod and no-one could do this better than yourself. Please consider any words of greeting that you may use as official...[24]

With *Mordon*'s blessing Richard duly attended the event at Llangefni, Anglesey, combining it with a holiday in north Wales. To my knowledge, this was his first official visit to Wales' premier cultural festival and he went on to attend on at least five subsequent occasions. Crucially, perhaps, three of those five visits – in 1976, 1980 and 1981 – fell within the period when he was either Deputy Grand Bard or Grand Bard of Gorsedh Kernow and when serious consideration was again being given to something similar in Cornwall. As editors of *New Cornwall*, Ann and Richard Jenkin always stressed the need for Cornwall and her culture to be seen in relation to her sister Celtic countries, and Richard cannot fail to have been impressed by the scope of the Welsh National Eisteddfod and stimulated by his attendance in the late 1970s and early 1980s.

Richard's work for the Gorsedh is explored elsewhere in this book, but a few significant events underline his growing importance in its hierarchy. Early in June 1967, for instance, he was elected to the Gorsedh Council at its annual general meeting where, significantly, it was suggested that the increasing co-operation between the Gorsedh and the Cornwall Music Festival might eventually lead to a Cornish Eisteddfod.[25] Furthermore, at the Closed Gorsedh which followed, one of the opening speakers – on the subject of 'The Gorsedd in the community life of Cornwall' – was Richard Jenkin who said that the Gorsedh should develop its services to Cornwall by playing a leading role in the life of the community.[26] Re-elected as Grand Bard that same day was G. Pawley White (*Gunwyn*), who during his two three-year terms in office was instrumental in putting the Gorsedh centre-stage in Cornwall. Although it was not realised until some years later, his ambition was for Cornwall to have an eisteddfod as successful as that in Wales – although on a smaller scale – with the competitions successfully inaugurated by the Gorsedh as an integral part of it.[27] For *Gunwyn*, as for so many others, 'the principle of an Eisteddfod was inherent in the foun-

Richard addressing the Welsh National Eisteddfod, Flint, 1969 (?)

dation of Gorseth Kernow' the two concepts being 'intertwined'.²⁸

On 4 September 1976, a couple of months after attending the Welsh National Eisteddfod in Cardigan as the official Cornish delegate, Richard was installed as Grand Bard of Gorsedh Kernow at Hayle, having served as Deputy Grand Bard since 1972. Thereafter, the idea of an Eisteddfod for Cornwall gathered some momentum, the *Western Morning News* announcing on 18 October 1977 that the possibility of an event giving scope to 'Celtic influence and the Cornish language' was being considered by the Gorsedh and that a meeting was to be arranged with the Cornwall Music Festival.²⁹ Also held during that year was an open meeting where a sub-committee was formed to look into the possibility of an Eisteddfod of Cornwall taking place every five years, although this was later reduced to three.[30] The decade closed with a public meeting where there was great support for the staging of an Eisteddfod in March 1983 involving as many Cornish associations as possible, including brass bands, music and drama groups, Women's Institutes and the Floral Art Society.[31] In the middle of November 1979 the local press reported that Truro looked set to be the venue for the first-ever Cornish Eisteddfod which would bring together the Cornwall Music Festival, the Cornish Gorsedh competitions and Cornwall's drama festival. Addressing the public meeting at which the decision was made to go ahead with the festival and to appoint a steering committee, Richard Jenkin, as Grand Bard, said: 'I want every aspect of Cornish culture to be drawn into the eisteddfod so that Cornwall can show its achievements to the world.'[32] Speaking early the following year, he underlined the lengthy genesis of the project:

> This has been a dream since the Gorsedd was founded and it is for us to bring it into being and to make sure that it grows and becomes an established part of Cornish life. It is the way in which the Gorsedd and the Cornish people in general can come into a close relationship.

Much remained to be done and he called on all bards to work for its success and to encourage other organisations to take part.[33]

Needless to say, he worked tirelessly himself for the project. Further visits to the Welsh National Eisteddfod at Lliw Valley, west Glamorgan in 1980 and Machynlleth in 1981 will have reinforced the potential of such an event. In the aftermath to what was promoted as 'Cornwall's First National Eisteddfod', Richard's work included either writing or helping to write an official constitution for it. In a draft of this document, the Cornish Eisteddfod is described as 'a periodic... celebration of Cornish culture... produced by the co-operation of bodies which contribute to the cultural life of Cornwall'. There was no need for contributing bodies to be wholly cultural as long as they were promoting some aspect of Cornish culture. The Eisteddfod was to be controlled by its Council (Consel an Esethvos), the final authority in Eisteddfod matters, and organised for the Council by an Executive Committee (Consel Gwruthyl), which would manage its affairs. The Council would meet at least once a year – ideally two or three times – and more frequently as the Eisteddfod itself approached.[34] The fifteen-point constitution was eventually agreed by the Committee and recommended for adoption, but not before it had been checked by solicitor Peter Pool (*Gwas Galva*). In a letter to Richard Jenkin dated 19 January 1985, Pool suggested various amendments or additions to the draft constitution. He commented, for instance, on the fact that it did not deal in any way with the relationship between the Eisteddfod and the Gorsedh, which he was not alone in viewing as 'a close and special one' and one which needed to be spelt out in the constitution. 'I am sure,' he continued, 'that you, as a former Grand Bard [Richard's first two terms in office had ended in 1982], will be the first to realize that the future relationship of these two bodies will be of immense importance, and it is worth a good deal of effort to get it right now…' Between 1973 and 1983 Richard was chairman of Mebyon Kernow and was still serving as the party's deputy chairman at the time of Peter Pool's letter. Eight months later he would begin a third term as Grand Bard. It is therefore of more than passing interest that one of the amendments suggested by *Gwas Galva* and eventually adopted was the addition to Rule 1, which concerned the cooperation of contributing cultural organisations, of the sentence 'The Eisteddfod shall be non-political.' Pool judged that although the addition of this clause would not preclude organisations such as Mebyon Kernow taking part, it would facilitate any future recognition of the Eisteddfod as a charity.[35]

Cornwall's First National Eisteddfod: Esedhvos Kernow 1983

Richard was chairman of the committee which coordinated five successful eisteddfodau between 1983 and 1995 and was deputy chairman for the sixth festival of Cornish culture in 1998. He clearly headed very organised and dedicated teams which included in the early days Ruth Moss as secretary and Richard Radcliffe as publicity officer. Radcliffe was instrumental in ensuring maximum publicity for the event and throughout 1982 and the first two months of 1983 the local press whetted the public's appetite with headlines such as 'Cornish eisteddfod aims high', 'Luxon heads Eisteddfod programme', and 'Cornwall's first Eisteddfod – no longer a dream'.[36] In September 1982 Richard Jenkin and fellow judges – artist Ben Maile and graphic designer Peter Sugden – chose the

Poster for Esedhvos Kernow, 1983

design of Cornish bard Dennis Ivall (*An Den*) as the logo for the Eisteddfod and this was first used when the full programme, with international baritone Ben Luxon (*Caner Canow*) topping the guest list, was released that same month. On St Piran's Day (Saturday 5 March), 1983, '[years] of dreaming and scheming reached a colourful climax', as the *West Briton* put it, with the proclamation of the Gorsedh by Grand Bard Hugh Miners at the High Cross in Truro launching a week of Cornish cultural events. Describing the event at the time as 'an historic occasion, the fulfilment of a dream nurtured by generations of Cornish Bards for 60 years',[37] *Den Toll* underlined how successful, both financially and artistically, the first eisteddfod had been that year in a letter designed to garner support for future festivals. Although it was 'too much to say that "Esethvos Kernow, 1983"... captured the same rapturous enthusiasm accorded in Wales to the Royal National Eisteddfod', it was the hope and trust of the organisers that that enthusiasm would, in time, come.[38] Hubert Julian (*Ylewyth Methodyst*), who was treasurer for much of the 1980s, wrote of the first eisteddfod as having of necessity to be planned 'on an experimental and modest scale'. Its overall success, though, encouraged the committee to press ahead with plans for a second and more ambitious festival in 1986.[39]

At the 3rd Perranporth Conference, which was held on 20 and 21 April 1985, Richard contributed to the debate on Cornish cultural life, specifically whether there was such a thing as Cornish culture and, if so, what its make-up was, or whether there could be said to be only a culture of a more general kind in Cornwall. As chairman of the Esedhvos committee, he spoke of its hopes and plans for the second eisteddfod the following March.[40] Whereas the inaugural event had been sponsored by Gardinia Windows (South-West) of Hayle and supported with a grant from Cornwall County Council and an interest-free loan from Carrick District Council, the 1986 event drew in funding from a wide range of bodies, including the Celtic Congress, Cowethas an Yeth Kernewek, the Cornish Assembly, and the Cornish Associations of Cardiff, London, West Kent, and Worthing, as well as from a dozen or so individuals, including Richard and the late David Penhaligon (*Penhelygen*).[41] Cornish dancing at the High Cross by Ros Keltek was to have inaugurated the second eisteddfod, but poor weather meant that this did not happen and, as the snow got heavier after the bardic procession, the proceedings moved into the Chapter House. Richard

Letter card for Esedhvos Kernow, 1983

had been elected to a third term as Grand Bard the previous September and, in welcoming the Eisteddfod to Truro, described it as 'a home for the people of Cornwall to display the best of Cornish life and to take part all together in a festival of the people who make music, dance, drama, literature and crafts'.[42]

Esedhvos Kernow 1989
One of Richard Jenkin's last duties as Grand Bard was attending the Welsh National Eisteddfod at Newport in July 1988. Although John Chesterfield (*Gwas Costentyn*) began his term of office that September, Richard was still chairman of Esedhvos Kernow and, as such, wrote to fellow bards on 1 February 1989 to encourage them to support the forthcoming festival not only by making donations, but also by attending the various cultural activities being offered and helping to steward the events and exhibitions. 'We want the Esethvos to show what the Cornish can do in every aspect of culture,' he continued, 'especially our own native culture but also our contribution to, and expertise in, European culture generally. We also want it to be the Esethvos of all Cornwall and all Cornish people, so many different places will have events

and we hope that future Esethvosow will spread even wider.'[43] He wished for cooperation rather than competition, so every attempt was to be made to keep separate days for separate events. The overriding aim was to have a festival of the arts 'produced by Cornish people for Cornish people... all home produced'.[44]

Since 2006 the focus of Esedhvos Kernow has changed radically from being a three-yearly festival lasting over a week in March and running in tandem with the Cornwall Music Festival to a smaller, two or three day annual event adjacent to the Gorsedh. One integral feature of the Eisteddfod which has for obvious reasons not migrated to early September is the St Piran's Day procession, which Richard organised as part of Cornwall's first eisteddfod. Writing as Eisteddfod chairman early in 1989, he invited various Cornish organisations to assemble in St George's Road, Truro, for the march to the High Cross. Members of each organisation able to attend were asked to bring their St Piran's flag and their banner, if they had one. 'They may also like to carry a placard with the name of your [sic] organisation on it – (but no slogan),' he continued. The procession was for all Cornish associations and was non-sectarian and non-political. On previous occasions some participants had worn distinctive or traditional Cornish dress, and this had helped enhance 'the festive spirit of the occasion'.[45] Led by piper Merv Davey (*Telynor an Weryn*), about 100 people duly paraded through Truro's streets on Sunday 5 March.

Although its theme of cooperation throughout the cultural life of Cornwall meant that the third Eisteddfod was home grown, by its very scope and quality it also had an international dimension. For instance, baritone Benjamin Luxon again featured as the guest of the Cornish Music Guild's composers' workshop and concert at the Chapter House, Truro, on the opening day. Although Truro was the focal point, between 4 and 18 March events, talks and exhibitions were also held in Perranporth, Devoran, Lostwithiel, Pool, and St Austell. A major feature was an exhibition at the Royal Institution of Cornwall of work produced by a wide range of artistic and cultural organisations such as the Cornwall Guild of Weavers, the Federation of Old Cornwall Societies, Cornwall Family History Society, and Cornwall Association of Local Historians.[46]

A 'high tide' for Esedhvos Kernow?

Brian Coombes (*Cummow*) has described Esedhvos Kernow as having a 'high tide' in the mid-1990s when he was Grand Bard, with Richard's support being 'fundamental'.⁴⁷ The document entitled 'A Constitution for the Cornish Eisteddfod and its organisation', which was agreed and recommended for adoption by the Annual General Meeting c.1982-83, stipulated that its controlling body, the Eisteddfod Council, should meet 'at least once a year and at other times as necessary'.⁴⁸ In his original draft Richard had been more specific, adding 'ideally 2-3 times and more frequently as the Eisteddfod approaches'.⁴⁹

As chairman of the Council for the eisteddfodau held in 1992 and 1995, he was clearly keen that no momentum was lost in between events, and on 29 June 1990 its Executive Committee met to consider proposals for Cornwall's Fourth Eisteddfod. Proposed dates for the event were on the agenda of a Council meeting that September and just over a month later the organisation held its AGM. Among the items considered at St Mary Clement Methodist Church on 2 November were the formalisation of a policy for the organisation of a Fourth Eisteddfod and a discussion of further plans. In February 1991 Richard sent out notices about the annual St Piran's Day procession to organisations involved in planning the event, including the Cornwall Arts Forum, the Federation of Old Cornwall Societies, the Royal Institution of Cornwall, and the Celtic Congress.⁵⁰ Of course, the following year, the event which was jointly organised by Richard and Peggy Morris and reported by the *West Briton* under the headline 'Marching quietly on the pride of St Piran', marked the start of the Fourth Eisteddfod. Meanwhile, the previous March a letter to Richard from Eisteddfod secretary, Ruth Moss, reminded him of the next meeting – presumably of the committee (Consel Gwruthyl). 'With less than a year to go before Cornwall's Fourth Esethvos,' she wrote, 'it is necessary for events to be planned and halls booked... I know you haven't an organisation as such but I reckon you're representing the Gorsedd!'⁵¹ Documents from the period indicate how thorough the planning and preparations for the Eisteddfod were. Council meetings were often held immediately after Committee meetings and many of the agenda items were discussed by both bodies. The Council meeting held on 17 February 1992, for instance, which was probably the last before the Eisteddfod, had twenty-six items on its agenda, including the St Piran Day procession, the Friends of Glasney College, a Catherine Rachel John lecture, Truro and Falmouth Old Cornwall Societies meetings, and a Cornish Language Film Day.⁵²

As well as serving Esedhvos Kernow as either chairman or deputy chairman between 1983 and 1998, Richard found time to enter its competitions – both as Richard Jenkin (Leedstown) and Garfield Richardson (Llandysul, Wales)! In the 4th Eisteddfod of 1992 he was awarded the Edith Warmington cup in the English verse category and was highly commended for his Cornish-language verse entry. Three years later, he won the Esedhvos cup for his Cornish-language verse. Recognition of his long-standing service came in 2001 when, on his retirement as a founder member from the Council, he was made an honorary life member of Esedhvos Kernow on the occasion of the 7th Eisteddfod at a service in Truro Cathedral.

The mid 1990s could lay claim to being a 'high tide' for Cornwall in a number of ways. With the 500th anniversary of the 1497 Cornish uprising on the horizon, a small committee was established in 1994 to act as a coordinating body for the many events planned to commemorate the event. At the core of Keskerdh Kernow ('Cornwall Marches On') or Keskerdh Kernow 500 as it eventually came to be known, was a great march to London in the footsteps of the rebels of 1497, but the commemoration also included 'cultural, educational and promotional events celebrating the best in Cornwall both within Cornwall and beyond'.[53] There is more than a strong echo here of Richard Jenkin's letter to fellow bards in February 1989. Richard briefly joined the Keskerdh Kernow marchers as they crossed Polson Bridge into England on the morning of Saturday 31 May 1997 and took photographs of them.

Conclusion

Richard Jenkin's death in October 2002 meant that he did not see the 8th Eistedddfod in 2004 – the last in the form in which it had taken place since 1983. The new millennium saw those organisations which had hitherto been at the forefront of the Cornish movement – Gorsedh Kernow, Esedhvos Kernow, the Celtic Congress and (later) Keskerdh Kernow – gradually work more closely together, with the continuing support of such bodies as the Cornwall Federation of Women's Institutes and the Federation of Old Cornwall Societies. In 2005 discussions took place to change the focus of the Eisteddfod from a three-yearly, week-long event parallel with or adjacent to the Cornwall Music Festival in Truro in March, to a smaller two- or three-day event in tandem with the Gorsedh each year. This was seen as bringing it back to its original purpose of extending cultural activities around the Gorsedh, and with the exception of the 11th event in 2008 when Esedhvos Kernow combined with Dehwelans, this has been the pattern ever since.[54] A further change was agreed at the Annual General Meeting of Esedhvos Kernow on 28 April 2009 when the organisation became a sub-committee under Keskerdh Kernow, which had charitable status.[55] It was hoped that a widening of the cultural and linguistic platform in Cornwall would result from linking Esedhvos Kernow more closely with the Gorsedh and the more junior Keskerdh Kernow. Whether or not this will be the case remains to be seen, but Richard Jenkin's pivotal place in the establishment and promotion of Esedhvos Kernow in a Cornwall which continues to march on can never be in doubt.

Notes

1. *Western Morning News*, 4 February 1980
2. Letter dated 1 February 1989 in Esedhvos Kernow files at Cornwall Record Office, Truro
3. Den Toll (Hugh Miners), *Gorseth Kernow: the first 50 years*, Gorsedh Kernow, 1978, p. 52
4. There is some doubt about this. See Cornish Bards of the St Ives Area, Gorsedh Kernow, 2010, p. 42
5. National Library of Wales, D. Rhys Phillips 2, item 4171, letter from Penzance, 23 August 1917
6. 'Can there be a Cornish festival?' Undated *Western Morning News* cutting in envelope addressed to R.M. Nance, Esq and marked '"Cornish Eisteddfod" Correspondence 1923. Previous to formation of Cornish Gorsedd', Esedhvos Kernow files at Cornwall Record Office, Truro
7. Undated [but pre-September, 1923] *Western Morning News* cutting in '"Cornish Eisteddfod" Correspondence 1923...' envelope
8. 'Bugle-Day', letter to the *Western Morning News* from Newquay, 3 September [1923] in ibid.
9. 'Can there be a Cornish festival?'
10. 'Should county have an eisteddfod?', *Western Morning News*, 7 September 1923, in ibid.
11. Ibid.
12. Ibid.
13. Letter dated 5 September [1923], in ibid. See also Peter W. Thomas, 'Robert Morton Nance and Gorseth Kernow' in Peter W. Thomas & Derek R. Williams (eds), *Setting Cornwall on its Feet: Robert Morton Nance, 1873-1959*, Francis Boutle, 2007, pp. 183-184.
14. Peter W. Thomas, p. 184
15. *Western Morning News*, 27 September 1923, in '"Cornish Eisteddfod" Correspondence 1923...'
16. 'Music in Cornwall. Cautious regard of Eisteddfod plan', undated *Western Morning News* cutting in '"Cornish Eisteddfod" Correspondence 1923...'
17. 'A Cornish Eisteddfod', *The Cornubian*, 20 September 1923
18. Den Toll (Hugh Miners), p. 52
19. 'Bards, Druids and the Gorsedd', MS in Box 3 of the Robert Morton Nance Collection, Courtney Library, Truro. Extracts are reproduced in Derek R. Williams (ed), *Henry and Katharine Jenner: A Celebration of Cornwall's Culture, Language and Identity*, Francis Boutle, 2004, p. 196

20 Ibid; *A Summary of the Minutes of the Cornish Gorsedd* (August 1928-September 1939), Gorseth Kernow, n.d., p. 9
21 *A Summary of the Minutes...*, p. 9
22 Peter W. Thomas, p. 184
23 Den Toll (Hugh Miners), p. 51
24 Letter in Jenkin family archive
25 *New Cornwall*, vol. 15, no. 2, Summer 1967
26 Ibid.
27 *West Briton*, 16 July 1970, p. 15
28 Den Toll (Hugh Miners), p. 52. Gunwyn's words may have formed part of a lecture entitled 'Towards a Cornish National Eisteddfod' which was delivered at Old County Hall, Truro, on 7 June 1971
29 'Gorsedd Bards consider new festival', *Western Morning News*, 18 October 1977
30 Ann Trevenen Jenkin, 'Important Outline Information on Esethvos Kernow/Eisteddfod of Cornwall', November 2008
31 bid.
32 *West Briton*, 15 November 1979
33 'Cornish Plan Eisteddfod', *Western Morning News*, 4 February 1980
34 'Draft. A Constitution for the Cornish Eisteddfod and its organisation', n.d., in folder marked 'Esethvos Kernow – draft constitution and some history and press cuttings', Cornwall Record Office, Truro.
35 Letter in 'Esethvos Kernow – draft constitution...'
36 *West Briton*, 6 March and 16 September 1982, and 24 February 1983
37 'Eisteddfod Dream Becomes Reality', *West Briton*, 10 March 1983
38 Undated letter in Esedhvos Kernow files at Cornwall Record Office
39 Hubert Julian, 'Cornwall's Eisteddfod 'stakes its claim'', *Cornish Scene*, vol. 1, no. 5, February/March 1986
40 Paul F. Smales, 'The Third Perranporth Conference, 1985', in material relating to the Eisteddfod of Cornwall in Jenkin family archive
41 Programmes and press cuttings (tan folder), with outline of Esedhvos Kernow dates, in Esedhvos Kernow files at Cornwall Record Office, Truro
42 'Weather forces festival inside', unidentified newspaper cutting in blue scrapbook of miscellaneous photographs, leaflets etc., in Esedhvos Kernow files, Cornwall Record Office, Truro
43 Letter in Esedhvos Kernow files, Cornwall Record Office, Truro
44 '14-day festival of the arts', *West Briton*, 2 March 1989
45 Undated circular [circa February 1989] in material relating to the Eisteddfod of Cornwall in the Jenkin family archive
46 'Packed arts programme for Esethvos', *Western Morning News*, 1 March 1989; Esedhvos Kernow Programme
47 Letter to the author, 19 November 2011
48 Esedhvos Kernow files at Cornwall Record Office, Truro
49 Letter in folder marked 'Esethvos Kernow – draft constitution...', Esedhvos Kernow files, Cornwall Record Office, Truro
50 Esedhvos Kernow files, Cornwall Record Office, Truro
51 Letter dated 20 March 1991, Esedhvos Kernow files, Cornwall Record Office, Truro
52 Esedhvos Kernow files, Cornwall Record Office, Truro
53 Simon Parker (ed), *Cornwall Marches On: Keskerdh Kernow 500*, Keskerdh Kernow, 1998, p. 2
54 Ann Trevenen Jenkin, November 2008
55 Ann Trevenen Jenkin, 'Esethvos Kernow – a Positive Step Forward', press release dated 6 May 2009, Esedhvos Kernow files, Cornwall Record Office, Truro.

Sermon: Saint James/Pregoth: Synt Jamys

Richard G. Jenkin

In the name of God, the Father, and the Son, and the Holy Spirit, Amen. Our text is verse ten of the fourth chapter of the Epistle of James: Humble yourselves in the sight of the Lord and he will lift you up.

Today we are assembled in the church of St James. Who was James? In the New Testament three Jameses are mentioned: among the disciples, James son of Zededee, brother of John the beloved disciple, and James son of Alphaeus. There is also James, called 'the brother of the Lord', who wrote the Epistle which contains our text and became leader of the church in Jerusalem after the Crucifixion. Peter, foundation-rock of the church, deferred to him.

There is not much known about any James, no more than is known of our Cornish saints. Who was our St James here? He was James son of Zebedee, sometimes called James the Great to distinguish between him and James son of Alphaeus, called James the Less. This does not show their spiritual rank but, probably, their physique. James the Less is so described in St Mark's Gospel Ch. 15, v. 40. They were nicknames. In the same way, doubtless, were made our Cornish family-names Ennear (the long), Leah (less), Behenna (littler).

Let us see what we do know of James. He, his brother John and his father Zebedee were fishermen and partners with Simon, nicknamed Peter by Christ, and Andrew his brother. The four young fishermen were among the first disciples called by Jesus to follow him. They were not very poor. They had their own boats and John was known by the Chief Priest and was able to enter the Chief

Priest's palace when Jesus was arrested, leaving Peter at the door.

James and John, sons of Zebedee, were fiery followers of Christ. One day Jesus set out towards Jerusalem with his disciples. They wanted to stop in a Samaritan village. Samaritans and Jews were unfriendly to one another, like Protestants and Catholics in Ulster. Entry was refused. "Let us call down fire from heaven like Elijah and burn them up," cried James and John. But Jesus said, "You do not know of what manner of spirit you are. The Son of Man came not to destroy men's lives but to save them." And he gave them the nickname 'Sons of Thunder'.

With Peter, James and John were the three disciples who were with Jesus the most frequently, who stood on Mount Tabor where Christ was transfigured and watched with him in Gethsemane. Their mother was so proud of their closeness to Jesus that she urged them to ask Jesus for the seats on his right and left hand when he entered his kingdom, but Jesus said, "To sit on my right hand and on my left is not mine to give." Did they remember his words when Jesus was dying with a thief at his right hand and a thief at his left? And the ten, when they heard the request of the sons of Zebedee, began to be angry with them, but Jesus said to them, "Whosoever of you will be the chiefest, shall be servant of all." The mother of James and John and also the mother of James the Less were the women with Mary Magdalene at the tomb of Jesus.

After Christ's resurrection, when Peter and John were teaching in the temple and being arrested by the Chief Priest's men, we hear nothing about James and the last word we read in the Bible about him is that Herod the king killed him with the sword.

So, though James had been a disciple close to Jesus, like Peter, Andrew and John, he was one of the first to be martyred and could not carry the message of Christ to other generations as did Peter and John. One might think that his promise was unfulfilled – that his martyrdom was a waste of his training. But God does not see as man sees. Man would expect all twelve Apostles to become missionaries and great teachers and evangelists, but one was a traitor and of the eleven faithful, only Peter, John and Matthew were active in the work of the church after the Ascension, it seems. God chose the others for other purposes.

James, the first Apostle to be martyred, was greatly honoured by following generations and, according to tradition, his body was carried to Spain to

Santiago de Compostela – St James of the field of the Stars. Santiago de Compostela is in Galicia, a region where British Celts went about the same time as they went to Brittany, though they did not keep their language so long. Santiago became a place of pilgrimage for all Europe. So important was it that the badge of St James – a cockle-shell – was the badge of all pilgrims. Santiago was very popular in Cornwall. Ships sailed direct to Galicia. All kinds of people went: landlords like Otho Bodrugan and Ralph Beaupre who went in 1324; priests like the rector of St Erme who went in 1330 to Compostela and Rome; and others like the forty pilgrims carried to Santiago by William Rose in his ship the 'Seinte Marie' of Truro in 1396 – a mediaeval package-tour. Pilgrims from Wales, also, crossed the sea to Cornwall and travelled along the north coast of Cornwall, where there were several chapels of St James, including Jacobstow, marking, perhaps, their path. They would have the opportunity to see the Cornish places of pilgrimage of Perranzabuloe, St Michael's Mount, and Holy Trinity, St Day, before they left the south coast of Cornwall to sail to Santiago.

Perhaps the Cornish were attracted to Sant Iago because his name was similar to the old Celtic name Iacut, Iago, and coming from it the Cornish family-name James. Iacob became Iacobus and Iacomus in Latin; Iacopo and Iachimo in Italian; Iago and Jayme in Spanish; Jaume in Provencal; Jacques and James in old French; and James in English.

Pilgrimage from Cornwall stopped after the Reformation of the Church but we may be sure of this – Richard Carew of Antony House, who knew Spanish well enough to translate Spanish books, would sit in this church and know that this James was the same saint as Sant Iago of Compostela.

What was a pilgrimage? It was not wholly a pleasant voyage to a sunny land, a mediaeval 'holiday of a lifetime' on the Costa del Sol. Partly, perhaps, but it was also a period of spiritual awakening, of deeper thoughts about life and death and the purpose of life, of spiritual communion with one who walked and talked with Jesus himself. The changes in Christian life of thousands upon thousands caused by Santiago de Compostela were, probably, greater in every way than the changes caused by James son of Zebedee in his short life. Though his life was humble, in and beyond his death he was lifted up by God to be a beacon to Christians in the West, far from Palestine. The purposes of God are hidden from us but we can be sure of it – choices of men, good or evil, will be used by God to carry out his own purpose and will. A life may end, as it seems, in failure and still make changes in following centuries. In that way, the life of Anne Frank may seem short and wasted, but how many people have been moved by it in more than forty years after her death?

What lesson for ourselves can we draw from what is known of James? Surely, it is this: we ought to do the work which is set before us, as best we can, not fearing failure nor hoping for success. Neither one nor the other is in our hands. God will use our endeavours in his Great Plan as he used the Apostles in ways we know not. We humble ourselves in the sight of the Lord and he will lift us up and put us in his great pattern. Our work may flower in our lifetime or in ages we shall not see or remain for ever unknown to mankind like the work of so many Apostles, but if we do it as best we can, however humble, God will lift it up. The stone which the builders rejected shall become the headstone of the corner.

Humble yourselves in the sight of the Lord and he will lift you up. May God bless us and the work we do in his name. Amen.

Y'n Hanow Dew, an Tas, Ha'n Map, ha'n Spyrys Sans, Amen. Agan testen yu gwers dek a'n peswera chaptra Epystol Jamys: Omhuvelheugh yn gwel an Arluth hag ef a wra agas drehevel-why.

Hedhyu ny yu cuntellys yn eglos Synt Jamys. Pyu o Jamys? Y'n Scryptor Noweth try Jamys yu meneges: yn mysk an Dhyskyblyon, Jamys map Zebede, broder Jowan an dyskybel caradow, ha Jamys map Alfeus. Yth esa ynweth Jamys, hynwys 'broder an Arluth' nep a scryfas an Epystol hag ynno agan testen ha dos ha bos hembrynkyas an eglos yn Jerusalem wosa'n Crowsyans. Peder, carrek-fundyans an eglos, a blegyas dhodho-ef.

Nyns us mur gothvedhys a Jamys-vyth, namoy del yu gothvedhys a'gan syns a Gernow. Pyu yu agan Synt Jamys omma? Ef yu Jamys map Zebede, trawythyow hynwys Jamys an Mur rak dyberth yntredho ha Jamys map Alfeus, hynwys Jamys an Byghan. Hemma ny dhysqueth aga roweth spyrysek mes, hep mar, braster aga horfow. Jamys an Byghan yu descryfys yndelma yn Awayl herwyth Mark, chaptra 15, gwers 40. Leshynwyn o. Yn keth forth, hep dhowt, o gwres agan hynwyn-tylu Kernewek: Ennear (an hyr), Leah (lyha), Behenna (byghanna).

Gwren-ny gweles pyth a wodhon a Jamys. Ef, y vroder Jowan ha'y das Zebede o pyscadoryon ha kevrannoryon gans Symon, leshynwys Peder gans Cryst, hag Andrew y vroder. An peswar pyscador yowynk o yn mysk an kensa dyskyblyon gelwys gans Jesus dh'y sewya. Nyns ens-y pur voghojek. Yth esa dhedha aga hucow aga-honen ha Jowan o aswonys gans an Arghoferyas hag ef a allas entra lys Arghoferyas ha Jesus ow-pos dalghennys, ow-casa Peder dhe'n darras.

Jamys ha Jowan, mebyon Zebede, o holyoryon danek a Gryst. Un jeth Jesus eth un hens wor tu ha Jerusalem gans y dhyskyblyon. Y a vynnas gortos yn pendre Samarytanow. Samarytow ha Yedhewon o mur anwhek an yl dh'y gyla, kepar ha Protestans ha Catholegyon yn Ulster. Dones aberveth o neghys. "Gwren-ny gelwel tan a nef kepar ha Elyja ha'ga howllesky," a gryas Jamys ha Jowan. Mes Jesus a leverys, "Ny wreugh-why aswon a by par spyrys ough-why. Ny dheth Map Den dhe dhystrewy enevow tus mes dh'aga sylwel." Hag ef a ros dhedha leshanow 'Mebyon Taran'.

Gans Peder, Jamys ha Jowan o an try dyskybel esa gans Jesus an moyha menough hag a sevys war'n Meneth Tabor mayth esa trelyes fysmant a Gryst adheragtha hag a wolyas ganso yn Gethsemane. Aga mam o mar wothys a'ga ogaster dhe Jesus mayth ynnyas-hy aga govyn orto rak an esedhow dh'y barth dyghow ha dh'y barth cleth hag ef owth-entra yn y wlascor, mes Jesus a leverys, "Esedha an barth dyghow dhym hag an barth cleth, henna ny'm bus-vy dhe ry." A wrussons-y perthy cof a'y eryow ha Jesus ow-merwel gans lader dhe barth dyghow ha lader dhe barth cleth dhodho? Ha'n dek, pan glew sons govyn mebyon Zebede, y tallathsons bos serrys orta, mes Jesus a leverys dhedha, "Ahanough nep a vynno bos moyha, a vyth gonesek dhe buponen." Mam Jamys ha Jowan, hag ynweth mam Jamys an Byghan, o an benenes gans Marya Magdala dhe'n beth Jesus.

Wosa Dasserghyans Cryst ha Peder ha Jowan ow-tysky y'n templa hag ow-pos dalghennys gans tus arghoferyas, ny ny glew travyth yn kever Jamys, ha'n ger dewetha a wren-ny redya y'n Bybel yn y gever yu Herod an myghtern dh'y ladha gans cledha.

Ytho, kyn fya Jamys dyskybel ogas dhe Jesus, kepar ha Peder, Andrew ha Jowan, ef o onen an kensa dhe vos mertherys ha ny allas-ef don negys Cryst dhe dhenythyansow erel kepar del wruk Peder ha Jowan. Y hyller tyby bos y ambos hep keweras – bos y vertherynsy scul a'y dhyscans, mes ny wel Dew kepar del wel mapden. Mapden a dhesefsa pupoll an deudhek Abostol dhe dhos ha bos cannasow an eglos ha dyscadoryon vur hag awayloryon, mes onen o traytour hag a'n unnek lel saw Peder, Jowan ha Mathew o bysy yn ober an eglos wosa'n yskynnans Cryst, del hevel. Dew a dhewysys an re-erel rak ken towlow.

Jamys, an kensa Abostol dhe vos mertherys, o muronorys gans denythyansow a sewyas ha, herwyth hengof, y gorf o degys dhe Spayn dhe Santiago de Compostela – Synt Jamys a'n Gwel Ster. Yma Santiago de Compostela yn Galythya, randyr mayth eth Keltyon a Vreton Vur adro dhe'n keth termyn y eth dhe Vreten Vyghan, kyn na wythsons-y aga yeth termyn mar hyr. Santiago a dheth ha bos tyller perghyrynsys rak Europ-oll. Mar ughel o y vry mayth o arweth Synt Jamys – crogen-cocla – an arweth pup perghyryn-oll. Santiago o mur gerys gans an bobel yn Kernow. Gorholyon a wolyas kewar dhe Alythya. Pup eghen a bobel a wruk mos: tyrogyon kepar ha Otho Bodrugan ha Ralf Beaupre nep eth y'n vledhen myl tryhans peswar war'n ugans; oferysy kepar ha'n rector Synt Erm nep eth y'n vledhen myl tryhans dek war'n ugans dhe Gompostela ha Rom; ha re-erel kepar ha'n deu ugans perghyryn degys dhe Santiago gans William Rose yn y worhel 'Seinte Marie' a Druru y'n vledhen myl tryhans whetek ha peswar ugans – vyach-bagas an Osow Cres. Perghyrynas dyworth Kembry ynweth a dremenas an mor dhe Gernow ha lafurya a-hes an arvor cleth a Gernow, mayth esa nebes chapellow Synt Jamys, ynweth Jacobstow, ow-merkya, martesen, aga hens. Y fya dhedha an dro dhe weles an tylleryow perghyrynsys Kernewek a Dreth Peran, Meneth Myghal Sans, ha'n Drynsys Sans, Synt Day, kens y dhe asa an arvor dyghow a Gernow rak golya dhe Santiago.

Martesen an Gernowyon o tennys dhe Sant Iago awos bos y hanow kehaval dhe'n hanow Keltek coth, Iacut/Iago hag ow-tos dyworto hanow-tylu Kernewek Jago ha Bretonek, Jagu. Iago yu nes dhe'n hanow Ebbrow gwyr, Iacob, ages Jamys. Iago eth ha bos Iacobus ha Iacomus yn Latynek; Iacopo ha Iachimo yn Ytalek; Iago ha Jayme yn Spaynek; Jaume yn Provencal; Jacques ha James yn Frynkek coth; ha James yn Sawsnek.

Perghyrynsys dyworth Kernow a hedhys wosa Dasformyans an Eglos mes ny a yl bos sur a hemma – Richard Carew a Jy Antony, nep a wothva Spaynek da lowr dhe drelya lyfrow Spaynek, a esedha y'n eglos-ma hag aswonvos bos an Jamys-ma an keth sans avel Synt Iago a Gompostela.

Pyth o perghyrynsys? Nyns o-hy yn-tyen saw vyach whek dhe dyr howlek, gol a vewnans war Costa del Sol yn Osow Cres. Yn ran, martesen, mes hy o ynweth termyn a dhyfuna spyrysek, a brederow downa yn kever bewnans ha mernans ha'n towl bewnans, a gomunyans spyrysek gans onen nep a gerdhys ha leverel gans Jesus y-honen. An trelyansow yn bewnans Crystyon a vylyow war vylyow gwres gans Santiago de Compostela o, hep mar, brassa yn pup forth ages trelyansow gwres gans Jamys map

Zebede yn y vewnans ber. Kynth o huvel y vewnans, yn ha dres y vernans ef o drehevys gans Dew dhe vos golowva dhe Grystonyon y'n West, pell dyworth Palestyn. Towlow Dew yu cudhys dyworthyn-ny mes ny a yl bos sur anodho – dewysyansow tus, da po drok, a vyth usyes gans Dew rak avonsya y dowl ha'y volunjeth y-honen. Bewnans a dhewetho, del hevel, yn dyfygyans ha whath gul trelyansow yn cansbledhynnow a sew. Y'n forth-na, bewnans Anne Frank o ber ha scullyes, del hevel, mes pygemmys tus re bu muvyes ganso yn moy ages deu ugans bledhen wosa hy mernans.

Py dyscas ragon-ny agan-honen a yllyn-ny tenna adhyworth an pyth us gothvedhys a Jamys? Yn sur, ef yu hemma: y coth dhyn-ny dhe wul an ober us gorrys adheragon, gwella gyllyn-ny, nag owth-owna dyfygyans nag ow-quaytya sowynyans. Yma nanyl na'y gyla y'gan deudhorn-ny. Dew a wra usya agan stryvyansow yn y Dowl Mur kepar del usyas-ef an Abestely yn fordhow na wodhon-ny. Ny a wra omhuvelhe yn gwel an Arluth hag ef a wra agan drehevel ha'gan gorra yn y Dowl Mur. Agan ober a vlejyow y'gan bewnans py yn osow na welyn-ny py gortos pupprys hep gothvos mapden kepar hag ober mar lyes Abostel, mes mara'n gwren-ny gwella gyllyn, kyn fe mar huvel, Dew a wra y dhrehevel. An men a ve tewlys dhe-ves gans an wythoryon chy, henna a vyth gwres pen-men an gornel.

Omhuvelheugh yn gwel an Arluth hag ef a wra agas drehevel-why. Dew re'gan sono ha'n ober a wren-ny yn y hanow. Amen.

Gwesperow yn Eglos Synt Jamys, Antony, De Sul, 6es Mys Gwyngala 1987; Pregoth gans Map Dyvroeth, Barth Mur/Evensong in St James Church, Antony, Sunday, 6th September 1987; Sermon by Richard G. Jenkin, Grand Bard.

[Typescript in 'MSS English and Cornish, Verse and Prose', the Jenkin family archive.]

A voice heard all over the parish: Richard Jenkin, Helston and Old Cornwall

Ann Trevenen Jenkin

As can be seen from other biographical references in this book, Richard Jenkin was passionate about all aspects of Cornwall, past or present. This section deals with his involvement with Helston Old Cornwall Society and Helston Museum, as well as his wider Cornish links within the Helston and Lizard area. It also covers the Federation of Old Cornwall Societies, where he took an active part and became its president.

Before his return to Cornwall with his family at Christmas 1959, much work had been done in Helston to secure knowledge of the past. Helston Museum had been set up in 1949 by W. F. Dalton (*Tryger ryp an Logh* – Dweller by the Lake). In 1950, A. S. Oates (*Car Tyr Meneghek* – Friend of Meneage) had written a seminal book *Around Helston in the Old Days*. These two bards, together with Helston Old Cornwall Society, established in 1924, were essential in helping to save the knowledge of the history and customs of Helston, and in the early preservation of artefacts in Helston Museum, later called Helston Folk Museum.

The 1960s

When Richard Jenkin returned to Cornwall, he and his wife joined Helston Old Cornwall Society in 1960, and for many years he was also an active member of the Museum management committee. As a new teacher at Helston Grammar School, he was involved with pupils and activities there.

In 1961, he was also honorary secretary of Gorsedh Kernow, whilst at school he became president of the Helston Young Cornwall Society, which had as one of its members, Priscilla Oates, later very active in and a chairman of the London Cornish Association. The Young Cornwall Society was important in reminding young people what Cornwall was all about. Its leaders were Richard Jenkin, Dick Gendall (*Gelvynak* – Curlew), and a Miss Taylor, and meetings were held in the biology laboratory over lunchtime. Other members at that time were Neil Bourdeaux from Praze-an-Beeble and Janet Spargo (*Hellys Genys* – Helston Born). Activities included the study of place-names and their meanings, and an introduction to the Cornish language. There was also at least one summer outing from the school to Brown Willy and Rowtor, which Priscilla could remember. Eventually, like many societies, it ran its course and faded away, but it was important for some years.[1]

It was in 1961, too, that Richard Jenkin took part for the first time in the Crying the Neck ceremony arranged by Helston Old Cornwall Society, speaking in Cornish at Winnianton Farm, Gunwalloe. He was remembered by many as a tall and striking figure with a powerful voice, and he continued to take part every year until just before his death.

In 1962, with many other Grammar and Gwealhellis Secondary Modern School staff who were important adult actors in the ceremony, he was asked to take over the part of the dragon in the Hal an Tow, the oldest part of the celebrations held on Furry Day, usually on 8 May. A new costume, by theatrical costume designer Claire White, was made for him by Marjory Ballance, with advice from Bernard Williams, an opera singer. All three were from the St Ives art colony. According to newspaper reports, a 'skirmish with knights had been arranged' and '[T]his year… [the Dragon] a young and active creature… sparred purposefully with the knights in the street'.[2]

Family memories of this dragon were of a sandy-brown hessian which made up the actual costume, and a large head which rested partly on top of the head of the performer, making him about seven foot high – quite an imposing figure. Gold, silver and green scales were sown on all over the body. These were actually foil tops from large old-fashioned milk bottles, but they caught and reflected the light, which made the dragon stand out even more. One newspaper contained the following account:

> One of the most colourful spectacles of Helston Flora – the Hal an Tow – once again lived up to expectations – many aspects of life and legends are captured in this spectacle, and in the many verses of the tune we find such things [sic] as Robin Hood and his Merry Men and the capture of Spanish seamen by Elizabethan sailors. Each of these stories is enhanced by the colourful costumes, and this year there was that beautiful dragon…[3]

That May, the death was announced of J. A. Shimmin, Deputy Head, Manxman and bard *Map an Enesow* (Son of the Isles). He had been a founder member of Helston Grammar School's Young Cornwall Society, a supporter of both Helston Old Cornwall Society and the Hal an Tow, and an inspiration to many.

In June 1962, Richard Jenkin took part in Cornish in his first Old Cornwall Midsummer Bonfire ceremony in west Cornwall when he lit the bonfire at Wheal Burrow, Porthleven, and his wife Ann was Lady of the Flowers.

Richard continued to play the dragon in the Hal an Tow for four years, and Morwenna, the eldest Jenkin daughter, described the excitement of going with her father to watch the ceremony. 'At 8.30am on the 7th May 1966,' she wrote in her account, which won a commendation from the Gorsedh in 1966, 'I went with Daddy to see the Hal-an-Tow at Helston.' She describes all the characters and who played them, '… [b]ut best of all was the Dragon. Daddy was it last year.' She describes the ceremony, the song, and the route of the procession, and concludes:

> We went back to Penrose Secondary Modern School for refreshments. We had tea, orange juice and sandwiches. I enjoyed everything very much.[4]

That year, Richard changed his role to that of Town Crier in the Hal an Tow. The dragon costume had been very heavy, and skipping about all over the town was extremely hard work! He remained Town Crier for the next four years,

Richard as the dragon in Helston's Hal an Tow, Furry Day, May 1965 (Wallace A.S. Fuggle, courtesy of Helston Museum)

until the pressures of an ever-growing family and other demands on his time, made it difficult. He handed over to Howard Curnow (*Kernow* – a family name) in 1969, just after he had joined the staff of Helston Grammar School, and Howard has been in that role ever since, a familiar, well-known and striking figure on Furry Day.

During the 1960s, Richard Jenkin was on both the Federation of Old Cornwall Societies Publications Committee and its Editorial Board, and went on to sit on its Executive Committee between 1970 and 1991. In 1966, accompanied by his wife and daughter Morwenna, he also took part alongside other local Helston figures in the unveiling of the plaque to Michael Joseph at St Keverne. Richard and Ann had been founder members of Mebyon Kernow, which organised the event, from its formation in 1952.

The 1970s
In 1970, and for many years thereafter, he continued to take part in the annual ceremonies of the Midsummer Bonfire and Crying the Neck. This is his introduction to the Midsummer Bonfire ceremony:

Why are we here and what are we doing? Firstly, we are here because the Federation of Old Cornwall Societies exists, as its motto says, to "gather up the fragments that remain" – not merely to preserve them and record them, but to use them and pass on the living tradition to succeeding generations "that nothing be lost".

What we are doing requires a longer explanation. If you have one of those diaries that gives lots of general information you may see that tonight is Midsummer Eve and that June 21st, the longest day, is officially the first day of summer. That would appear to give us a summer about a week long. It may seem like that sometimes but it is really nonsense. Our Celtic forefathers were more practical. Their summer began around the 1st – 8th May, which is why at Padstow May Day they sing "adieu the merry spring for summer is a-cumen today", and here in Helston the Hal an Tow (8th May) has "For summer is a-come-o and winter is a-gone-o".

So in the Celtic calendar, summer ran from the beginning of May to the end of July; autumn or Harvest ran from the beginning of August to the end of October; winter was November, December and January, with mid-winter day around 21st December, balancing Midsummer Day. Spring was February, March and April. The year actually began with the eve of the first day of winter –Nos Calan Gwaf – now Hallowe'en.

Our ancestors based their year on the sun's progress, recognising in the sun the source of life, light and warmth and the destroyer of evil; and indeed the sun is all of these, though not as a god, but as a creature of God. They worshipped and helped their sun god by the sympathetic magic of bonfires, especially at his weakest at the mid Winter Solstice and, with rejoicing, at his strongest in Midsummer. The beginnings of the seasons were also marked with bonfires, especially the beginning of winter or Samhain fires of November, and the beginning of summer with Beltane fires in May.

The fires were symbolic purification too. Herbs and weeds were cast on them, people leapt through the flames and cattle were driven through the ashes to remove evil influences from them.

Now you may think it superstitious and unchristian to keep up memories of pagan rites, but our fathers in the faith, who made this land of Cornwall Christian long before Augustine came to the English, were wiser. They used the good to symbolise the best. So they put up stone crosses instead of menhirs; they consecrated holy wells as baptisteries and they tied the feasts of the people to the Festivals of the church.

Samhain, the beginning of the year and of winter, became All Saints' Eve – Hallowe'en – and perhaps its fires are unconsciously preserved in those of November 5th. Here, in Helston, Beltane, the beginning of summer, became May 8th, the feast of the appearance of St Michael; February 1st, the beginning of spring, became the eve of the Purification of the Blessed Virgin Mary, or Candlemas; August 1st, the beginning of autumn, became Lammas Day, and of course, the fires of the winter solstice became the Yule fires of Christmas, while the Midsummer celebration took place, as now, on the Eve of St John – Nos Golowan – St John, the cousin of Christ, the herald of the covenant between God and Man – a perpetual reminder of God's love and God's sacrifice – the saint who proclaimed with no uncertain voice the Coming of the Light of the World.

That is why we are here. We are standing in the Great Company of our forefathers, who, through the years, in their own way, as best they knew, sought the light. It is a company we should be proud to join.[5]

And so, at midsummer, traditional weeds and flowers are thrown on to the bonfire, with the verse spoken by the Lady of the Flowers, usually in Cornish and English:

> Otta kelmys yn-kemyskys
> Blejyow, may fons-y cowl leskys,
> > Ha'n da, ha'n drok.
> Re dartho an da myl egyn,
> Glan re bo dyswres pup dregyn,
> > Yn tan, yn mok!

> *[In one bunch together bound*
> *Flowers for burning here are found,*
> > *Both good and ill.*
> *Thousandfold let good seed spring,*
> *Wicked weeds fast withering,*
> > *Let this fire kill!]*

At the Crying the Neck ceremony in late summer, 1970, A.J. Butcher – at that time agricultural correspondent of the *Western Morning News* – described what he saw:

> Mr R. Jenkin, an MK enthusiast, Cried the Neck in Cornish. "Yma Genef. Yma Genef. Yma Genef", to which the crowd replied: "Pen Yar, Pen Yar, Pen Yar", his thunderous roar receiving the approbation of the crowd, with great shouts of "Houra, Houra, Houra". This ceremony was followed as usual by the beautiful hymn, "This is the field..."
>
> The entire ceremony left me with a feeling that this was not a mere recital of some forgotten phrases, but an excursion into the past and a look back at an age where farming was a life of unremitting toil, relieved only by occasional celebrations such as Crying the Neck.[6]

By 1976, the Helston ceremonies were supported by many other Old Cornwall societies and individuals, and that year, Edward Cunnack, (*Conoc* – a family name), who had become president on the death of Edward Dalton, welcomed the Suffragan Bishop of St Germans, the Right Reverend Richard Rutt.[7] Also present was the next Grand Bard of the Cornish Gorsedh, Richard Jenkin, and two former Grand Bards, Pawley White (*Gunwyn*) and Retallack Hooper (*Talek*). Michael Penlerick, tenant of Trebarvah Farm, cut the last bit of standing corn with his scythe and Cried the Neck. The questions and answers were repeated in Cornish by Mr Jenkin. In one of the driest summers on record, the bishop said a prayer which included a prayer for rain, and Helston's new Old Cornwall banner was on show for the first time. 'Beautifully woven in silk, employing two colours', its production owed much to the initiative of vice president Doris Treloar of Praa Sands.[8]

The 1980s

Martin Matthews describes as follows his memories of Richard:

> I first met Richard in the early 1980s. I became curator of Helston Folk Museum in 1980, and to further my knowledge of Cornwall, I became a member of the Old Cornwall Society. Eventually, I became President – a position I have held for a number of years.

Midsummer Bonfire and Crying the Neck were a part of Helston Old Cornwall Society's syllabus and it was during these celebrations that I met Richard. It was at these ceremonies that Richard excelled; because he always explained the reason for holding the ceremonies in a way that those gathered to celebrate could easily understand. His response to the prayers in the Cornish language were read with true feeling and always appreciated by those present who did not know the language.

Richard was gifted with a very loud voice and when "crying the neck" he really meant it to be heard "all over the parish".

If I was ever confronted with a place-name in Cornish or an interpretation of anything in the Cornish language, I would just lift the telephone and Richard was always willing to supply me with an answer. He never counted it a burden. Richard also had a long association with the museum and often popped in to see how things were.

I was confirmed as a bard of Gorsedh Kernow in 1988, taking the bardic name of "Carer Hellys" – Lover of Helston. This was when the ceremony was held at Poldhu. Richard was Grand Bard at the time and he greeted me as a friend and was thrilled for me.[9]

I will remember him as a friend who was always willing to help with anything to do with his beloved Cornwall.

The ceremonies continued through the years, but conditions and attitudes to harvesting were changing. June Lander wrote in the *Western Morning News* on 3 September 1982 of her interview with Alan Todd, later bard *Gwas Sythny* – Servant of Sithney, but at that time president of Helston Old Cornwall Society:

> We have to use a bit of poetic licence', said Alan. 'This is because the harvest wasn't actually finished, and the huge red combine harvester was waiting in the wings to do the job.

June Lander described the ceremony in detail, including the Cornish language input which '... the Grand Bard, Mr Richard Jenkin, uttered with great gusto'.

That same year, there is a photograph of Richard at the An Gof commemoration at St Keverne, with his young son, Conan, holding the Cornish flag.

1985 saw the formation of the Friends of Helston Museum, a group which

Richard 'Crying the Neck', Crowan, with standard bearer Sidney Medlyn, and – on Richard's right – Martin Matthews

Richard supported when he could, and in 1988, he was down on The Lizard for the Diamond Jubilee Gorsedh at Poldhu. He initiated Martin Matthews as a bard that year, and for the first time in Gorsedh history, he broadcast a radio message to Cecil Beer (*Map Kenwyn* – Son of Kenwyn), formerly Deputy Grand Bard, but then living in Australia:

> … Richard Jenkin symbolically recreated Marconi's first transatlantic message by telephoning Cecil Beer in Adelaide from the site of the Marconi monument. The *Cornish Guardian* pointed out that 'the message was doubly fitting as five Australians were initiated as Bards during the ceremony which followed in the afternoon'.[10]

This link was set up through the assistance of Goonhilly Satellite Station and showed the development of Gorsedh communications moving more quickly into the media world with which we are now so accustomed. Major Beer continued to formalise the Gorsedh Assembly in Australia to help keep up close bardic contacts with Britain. Indeed, with Richard Jenkin and the Council's agreement, a special plastron including both Cornish and Australian symbols was made in Cornwall, paid for by Cecil Beer and kept in Australia for ceremonies over there. It remains the property of Gorsedh Kernow.

When he wasn't taking part in both Gorsedh and Old Cornwall ceremonies at that time, Richard Jenkin was giving lectures when asked, both in Cornwall and outside. In 1989, for example, he spoke to Penzance Old Cornwall Society on 'The Exodus of the Celts from Cornwall'.

And so, the Old Cornwall cycle of lectures, talks, festive occasions and ceremonies continued every year, with Richard always taking an active part. In addition, there was the usual annual ceremony at St Keverne on 27 June to commemorate Michael Joseph 'An Gof' and Thomas Flamank.

The 1990s
In 1991, as incoming president of the Federation of Old Cornwall Societies, he spoke at the twenty-fifth anniversary 'of the history of the event and the decision to place the memorial plaque in 1966 as an everlasting tribute to the martyrs of Cornwall'.[11] There is an excellent photograph of him that year, as the new president, presenting Yvonne Gilbert of Liskeard Old Cornwall Society with the Kernow Goth trophy.[12]

In 1992, he spoke at the Crying the Neck at Tregaminion Farm, St Keverne. David Stewart's transcript of the speech, which was broadcast by Rod Lyon on Radio Cornwall on 6 September, reads as follows:

> Long ago, when man first became a grower of corn, the life of the people depended entirely on the success of each harvest, and the growth from the dry seed to the ripe corn showed them some divine life at work, and they believed that this divine life, personified in the corn maiden, lived in the growing corn.
>
> When harvest time came and the corn was being cut down, this divinity had to be appeased and propitiated and in some parts of the world

there were sacrifices – 'grab a passing stranger'.[13] Well, I don't think you are at risk tonight!

It was believed in Britain that the divine life in the corn retreated before the reapers into the last standing handful and it was important that it should not escape and be lost so that the fertility of the land would decrease, but that it should be kept on the farm to bring new life to the corn next year.

So when there was left only a handful of corn, as thick as a hen's neck, the farmer would cut it with ceremony and it was taken back to the farmhouse and made into a corn dolly, which remained there until the next harvest.

After the coming of Christianity, the ceremony was kept up but it was used as a means of announcing to the neighbourhood that the harvest on the farm was over. Each farm hurried to be the first to 'Cry the Neck' and the farmer would shout as loud as he could to let the whole parish know; once, twice, and thrice with his workers joining in the cheers, to carry the message far and wide. The neck was then taken back to the farmhouse and hung up there. And once the corn was gathered in and safely stacked, the farmer and his workers could then relax with the Dy' Goel Deys – the Feast of the Ricks – a harvest supper, when all would gather for a hearty meal and an evening of singing and dancing.

The autumn of 1992 saw the introduction of the annual Cartwright lecture at Helston Old Cornwall Society, with Anthony Cartwright, a lecturer in geography at Exeter University, giving the inaugural lecture on 'The Building Stones of Helston and District' to commemorate his late parents, Richard and Olive Cartwright, staunch members of the society. Dick was the pilgrimage secretary for a number of years until his death in 1983.[14]

In 1993, Richard helped to organise the Trevenen reunion on Furry Day for his wife's family, who attended from all over the world, including Hawaii, South Africa, Canada, Cornwall and England. That same year, Helston Old Cornwall Society organised the Summer Festival for members from all over Cornwall. David Stewart, the then secretary, reported in *Old Cornwall*:

> The people of Cornwall will well remember June 1993 for the torrential rain that fell during the early part of the month and the dreadful flooding that resulted...

Helston decided, however, to go ahead with the arrangements. David Stewart continued:

> As it was, only one item... was affected; the beautiful gardens of Lismore... had suffered terrible damage in the floods and had to be withdrawn from the programme...
>
> Nearly 600 people packed the Hall of Helston School to witness Federation President (and member of Helston OCS) Richard Jenkin perform the Opening Ceremony, with assistance from the Mayor of Helston, Mrs Brenda Banfield and the President of the Helston Society, Martin Matthews.[15]

The rest of the very varied programme went ahead, with visits and entertainment, including videos of the Helston Town Trail, Furry Day and the 1992 Gorsedh. Borough charters from Cornwall Record Office were on display in the Guildhall, guarded vigilantly by the Town Beadle and Mace Bearers in their splendid uniforms, and Helston Folk Museum was open. There were all sorts of other interesting activities to keep the visitors entertained, including displays of Cornish wrestling in the sunken garden and Cornish dancing in front of the Grylls monument and at the school. At the end of a very successful festival, the Roy Bissett Accordion Band struck up with Cornish songs and other favourite melodies while the visitors enjoyed a Cornish tea:

> And so a tremendously happy and friendly day drew to a close. The Helston Society thoroughly enjoyed the opportunity to share its historic town with so many appreciative visitors.[16]

Richard chaired the spring meeting of the Federation as president in March 1993, when sixty-five members from thirty societies were present in Truro. In August, he was on home ground with Helston Old Cornwall Society Crying the Neck at Binnerton, a Domesday Manor near Leedstown and the oldest building in Crowan parish. Over four hundred were welcomed by Martin Matthews, president, including visitors from Scotland and Brittany.[17] Richard gave his annual explanation of the ceremony before reading some of the prayers and Crying the Neck, both in Cornish. There are some splendid photographs of him

Crowan Parish Council, November 1994; Richard, back row, fourth from left (copyright Cornwall and Isles of Scilly Press)

holding aloft the last sheaf of corn as his voice echoed across the valley to Horsedowns, Trenwheal, Huthnance and beyond. Local farmer, Henry Giles, Cried the Neck in English, with Praze Male Voice Choir helping with the singing. On a fine clear evening, it was a memorable occasion. A service followed in Leedstown Methodist Church, where excellent refreshments were served.[18]

At the third annual Cartwright lecture that autumn, Richard G. Grylls, a relation of Ann's, gave a very full and well-researched lecture on the Grylls and Trevenen connections with Helston. Again, Richard – and to some extent Ann – had helped Richard Grylls, who lives in Tring, Hertfordshire, with much local Helston and Grylls research.

In 1994, Helston Old Cornwall Society had to move from Penrose Road to Helston Lower School because the numbers were too big for the room being used. Richard conducted the Cornish-language element of both the

Midsummer Bonfire at Beacon Crag, Porthleven, and of Crying the Neck at Churchtown Farm, The Lizard.

He helped, too, with the research and the writing of parts of *Leedstown in our Lifetime*, a book edited by his wife, and contributed a section on 'Some Cornish Place-names around Leedstown'. There was also an article by him outlining his biographical contribution and devotion to Cornwall. He concluded with a typically poetic Richard Jenkin sentence:

> This is my Cornwall, a quartz crystal from the rock, fractured, imperfect, but shining from its many facets.[19]

In that year, too, his second daughter, Dr Loveday Jenkin, was elected to Kerrier District Council as a Mebyon Kernow councillor, and this again gave him a great deal of pride and pleasure. It meant that she could work for the community which Richard had supported in so many ways for many years. (He was on Crowan Parish Council for thirty-one years, and a member of Leedstown Village Hall committee for nearly as long). Loveday served on Kerrier District Council for fourteen years, and at the time of its unfortunate dissolution, she was one of the six Executive members.

In 1994, Richard was present, alongside Martin Matthews, president, David Stewart, secretary, and other dignitaries, when Helston Old Cornwall Society celebrated its 70th birthday with a special cake. The Trelawney Singers entertained with a splendid programme of Cornish songs, Christmas carols, and light-hearted recitations.[20] Members were reminded of the formation of the society on 11 December 1924, when a meeting was held at Duke's Studio, Meneage Street. Adult membership cost 2/- and junior 1/-. Rule 15 of the society stated:

> As an amicable fellowship of lovers of Old Cornwall, all members are expected to converse without introduction at its meetings, and the society and its members shall lose no opportunity of saving and handling [sic] on whatsoever of Old Cornwall remains.[21]

While the style of speech may have changed in seventy years, the ethos of friendliness and sociability remains in Helston Old Cornwall Society up to the present day.

After helping with advice on the erection of Terry Coventry's An Gof statue at St Keverne in 1996 and supporting the An Gof march to London in 1997, Richard Jenkin gradually withdrew from more active events as his health deteriorated, but he strongly supported his wife Ann Trevenen Jenkin when she became the first female Grand Bard of Gorsedh Kernow that year. They were both founder members of the original Holyer an Gof committee, which was set up in 1996 as a publisher's award in memory of Leonard Truran, a close friend of theirs whose bardic name was *Holyer an Gof*.

In 1997, Ann attended the mayor's lunch with Richard on Furry Day as Grand Bard, just as her husband had previously done during his term of office. On that first occasion, the rector, Rev. David Miller, remembered his charm and charisma, and his deep knowledge of Cornwall, as he sat next to him at the meal.[22]

Final years

Over the next few years, Richard accompanied Ann at the start of the An Gof march to London and for various short distances along the route. He was present with her at the dedication of the Millennium Cross by Helston Old Cornwall Society on Sithney Common Hill in 1999, and as late as 2000 he led the Crying the Neck ceremony at Crowan, his home parish. In June 2002, he attended the Midsummer Bonfire, and three months later, just six weeks before his death, the Gorsedh at Pensilva.

Richard Jenkin died on 29 October. His funeral at Crowan on 9 November was a truly Cornish and Celtic occasion, with St Piran's flag flying from the church tower, and with harp music performed by his granddaughter Riwana from Brittany, some of his poems read by Bert Biscoe, and a eulogy given by Jori Ansell, past Grand Bard. His coffin was accompanied to the grave by Cornish bagpipes played by Will Coleman, and the size and make-up of the congregation reflected his wide Cornish interests. Among others, many members of the local Old Cornwall societies and the Federation of Old Cornwall Societies were present to say 'Godspeed'. The Cornish granite cross on his grave commemorates a great Cornishman as well as his strong religious beliefs.

After 2002, money from his memorial fund was used to purchase a St Piran's flag for Crowan church, and it still flies proudly from the tall tower ten years later on parish and Cornish occasions such as St Piran's Day. A seat was also provided for the churchyard, the inscription reading 'Ef a garas Kernow' (He loved Cornwall). There was also the setting up of the Trevenen Jenkin Memorial Fund with Helston Old Cornwall Society, to continue the work first started with the by-then-discontinued Cartwright lectures. Each October, Richard's name is remembered, together with that of his wife, at the annual Trevenen Jenkin lecture, the opening talk for the year.

A great Cornish patriot

In Spring 2003, the Federation of Old Cornwall Societies journal published a memorial tribute to Richard Jenkin by Jori Ansell, Past Grand Bard and member of Hayle Old Cornwall Society, who had delivered the eulogy at his funeral in 2002. His conclusion will have resonated with so many Old Cornwall readers:

> I myself was always struck by his kindly and understanding nature, even to those of us who at the time had little knowledge of Cornish matters. To many of us he was a good and caring friend, with an open and generous spirit. His gentle humour could be relied on to defuse many a difficult situation.
>
> His family will remember him as a loving and dedicated husband, father and grandfather. We, his friends and colleagues, will remember him first and foremost as a great Cornish patriot. His interest in Cornwall and Cornish was a passion, not an academic study. He has, over the years, been an inspiration to successive generations and will continue to inspire us all.[23]

Notes

1. Information from Priscilla Oates, now chair of Mullion Old Cornwall Society, and recently elected vice president of the Federation of Old Cornwall Societies.
2. Newspaper cutting, n.d. [May 1962] and *Evening Herald*, 8 May 1962.
3. Newspaper cutting, n.d. [May 1962]
4. Jenkin family archive.
5. Ibid.
6. *Western Morning News*, 2 September 1970.
7. He later learnt Cornish and became a bard.
8. *The Packet*, 3 September 1976.

9 Per Martin Matthews, *Carer Hellys* – Freeman of Helston.
10 Garry Tregidga and Treve Crago, *Map Kenwyn: The Life and Times of Cecil Beer*, Gorseth Kernow, 2000.
11 Stephen Ivall, *The Packet*, 18 July 1991.
12 Joan Rendell, *Old Cornwall*, vol. 11, no. 3, Autumn 1992, p. 154.
13 David Stewart's young son, Ben, found this phrase irresistible and it became a family saying!
14 *West Briton*, 30 January 1992.
15 *Old Cornwall*, vol. 11, no.6, Spring 1994, pp. 272-273.
16 Ibid.
17 'Leedstown Community News', *Western Morning News*, 4 September 1993.
18 Personal memories, Ann Trevenen Jenkin.
19 Ann Trevenen Jenkin (comp. and ed.), *Leedstown in our Lifetime*, Leedstown Women's Institute, 1994.
20 *The Packet*, 15 December 1994.
21 Ibid.
22 Personal memories, David Miller.
23 'Old Cornwall Remembers: Richard Jenkin', *Old Cornwall*, vol. 12, no. 12, Spring 2003, p. 64.

Acknowledgements

Melody Ryder; Helston Folk Museum – Helston Old Cornwall records; Martin Matthews, president, and Janet Spargo, committee member and former secretary, Helston Old Cornwall Society; David Stewart, former secretary Helston Old Cornwall Society, and secretary, The Friends of Helston Folk Museum; many other individuals and friends.

'Michael Joseph was a man…'

Richard G. Jenkin

Michael Joseph was a man
Who fought as well as anyone can.
He fought for us with all his might
And we'll remember him tonight.

His mighty arms were strong as oak
And heavy was his hammer stroke
His heart was great, and courage too,
And to friends he was always true.

The King of England taxed us sore
When on the Scots he waged a war
Our people groaned beneath his heel
And vowed to pay the king with steel.

There came to Michael Joseph's door
A band of men, both rich and poor,

[Unfinished poem in a spiral-bound A5 notebook in 'MSS English and Cornish, Verse and Prose', the Jenkin family archive]

'Breathing the fire of Cornish patriotism': *New Cornwall*

Derek R. Williams

If any one thing could be said to have encapsulated and bridged the political and cultural aspirations for Cornwall of Richard Jenkin, then it was *New Cornwall* which, with its very first issue in October 1952, set the tone for over twenty years of putting Cornish interests first. Despite its claim to being 'independent of all parties and societies'[1] and the frequent disclaimer of successive editors that it was not the mouthpiece of Mebyon Kernow, there is no denying that it was always 'strongly Nationalist in flavour'.[2] Indeed, it was surely no coincidence that the fledgling political movement had seen the light of day nineteen months earlier. It was surely no coincidence, either, that the first issues of Denys Val Baker's *Cornish Review* ceased publication in the summer of 1952. What is more, three of the four future editors of *New Cornwall* had contributed to this pioneering literary magazine, notably Richard Jenkin with 'The Case for Self-Government for Cornwall' and Richard Gendall with 'Cornish Nationalism', which was published in its last issue. Apart from *Old Cornwall*, the long-running journal of the Federation of Old Cornwall Societies, there would be no other publication with a uniquely Cornish outlook until May 1958, when Penpol Press' *Cornish Magazine* began its eleven-year run.

Richard Jenkin was not noticeably associated with *New Cornwall* from the very outset, its first editor being a certain 'R. Morris' – a nom de plume used by Richard Gendall. He was helped in the undertaking by Helena Charles, who led Mebyon Kernow for the first four years of the organization's existence. In

August 1953 Miss Charles became both editor and distributor, announcing that the magazine's founder Mr R.B. Morris was 'obliged to leave Cornwall for family reasons'.[3] *New Cornwall* continued to be edited and distributed by Miss Charles either monthly or bi-monthly until March 1956, although the misnumbering of the publication that was clearly a problem for most of its editors meant that the issue with which she relinquished her role as editor was actually dated February. 'The magazine for those who have the interests of Cornwall at heart', which remained its mission statement until 1964, reappeared in December 1956/January 1957 when Richard and Ann Jenkin assumed the editorship, convinced that *New Cornwall* had a part to play in the future of Cornwall.[4] Thereafter, either together or singly, they were responsible until the Summer/Autumn 1973 issue for what was a shining beacon of commitment.

Although Richard did not assume the mantle of editorship or joint-editorship of *New Cornwall* until early in 1957, his involvement as a contributor began four years earlier when the magazine's second issue contained a letter from him praising its appearance for filling a great need and wishing it 'all prosperity'.[5] He went on to say that he was one of the delegates from Cornwall who had attended the Easter Inter-Celtic Conference arranged by the Welsh League of Youth in Borth and appealed for *New Cornwall* readers to help him mount a photographic exhibition of all aspects of Cornish life at the next conference by sending him contributions. Richard attended this event for two subsequent years and as 'R.G.I' [sic] wrote a report of the 1954 conference for *New Cornwall*. It seems clear that the promotion of Celtic culture which would be a marked feature of the magazine throughout its existence was engineered largely by Richard, for that August it published a report of the Celtic Congress in Dublin which he attended during July, and a year later 'National Life in Cornwall', the Celtic Congress lecture which he delivered in Brest.[6] *New Cornwall* No. 6, March 1953, saw the first appearance of the 'Here and There' column, a pot pourri of pro-Cornish, pro-Celtic items which under the pen-name 'Pasco(e) Trevy(g)han' and with the disclaimer that the views expressed were not necessarily those of the editors, he would compile for virtually every issue from November 1955 onwards. Richard's other contributions prior to his editorship included a tongue-in-cheek, though heartfelt poem entitled 'Almost any Cornish town'[7] and a piece entitled 'Cornwall must live', which featured an account of his role in the founding of the Young Cornwall Movement at Oxford in 1944.[8]

'The future of New Cornwall is up to you'

The general development and changing fortunes of *New Cornwall* between 1957 and 1973 in the hands of Richard and Ann Jenkin can be gleaned from the magazine's editorials – especially those in the December/January or Christmas/New Year issues – and from local press reports. Especially in the early days, these editorials were invariably joint efforts, but over the years the increasing demands of family and other commitments meant that these progress reports or comments on topical issues became Richard's alone. In the very first issue of *New Cornwall* back in October 1952, the then editor 'R. Morris' made it clear that a major failing of the established local press was that it did not reflect the views of the public. From the outset, then, *New Cornwall* was designed as a forum for those Cornish people who had the interests of Cornwall at heart, and its editor appealed for readers to submit sound critical suggestions as to how Cornwall's many ills could be remedied. '[L]et us tackle our problems constructively and build a New Cornwall,' he concluded.

With the publication of the first number of volume 5 from a flat in Fore Street, Totnes towards the end of 1956, the editors made it clear in their opening piece titled 'An Appeal' that they intended to keep *New Cornwall* as an open forum for those who were interested in Cornwall, its past, present and future, and that they hoped to publish articles by people of very varying opinions. 'We therefore appeal to you,' they continued; 'if you do not agree with an article, don't stop reading New Cornwall, but start writing to us. We shall welcome all your letters, especially if we may print them.'[9] The future of the magazine was in the hands of its readers who 'must' help in three ways – firstly, by acting as 'local reporter[s]' and informing the editors of anything likely to be of interest to Cornish people; secondly, by finding another subscriber in the coming year; and thirdly, by renewing their subscriptions promptly. Donations would be welcome to ease the editors' 'initial difficulties'. On a practical level, it was intended to publish a double 8-page issue every two months, so that the yearly subscription would remain the same at 6/-. Two months later, the editors could report that they had received many letters welcoming the reappearance of *New*

Cornwall; as we shall see, criticism centred on an article entitled 'Suez and Hungary'. 'Letters to the Editors' included one from former editor Richard Gendall who expressed his delight at receiving a copy again after such a long break and at finding that the standard was still so high. He continued: '[T]he paper strikes me as being well laid out and easy to read – the larger headlines add to the effect. I only wish "New Cornwall" were several times the size!'[10] Not everyone would be as complimentary about the paper's readability as the years went by, but for now the prognosis was good.

One misapprehension concerning *New Cornwall* with which the editors had to contend throughout its existence was that it was the mouthpiece of Mebyon Kernow. From the outset, its status was open to question, with the authors of *Mebyon Kernow and Cornish Nationalism* arguing that although the magazine was 'technically an independent monthly publication, it was edited and distributed by leading members of the new society' and from 1952 onwards promoted '[t]he nationalist challenge of MK'.[11] In April 1953, issue 7 contained a rejection that *New Cornwall* was the organ of Mebyon Kernow. The disclaimer appeared again the following January, by which time the editorship had passed to Helena Charles, who was then, of course, chairman of Mebyon Kernow. Six months into their editorship, Richard and Ann Jenkin devoted their editorial in the June-July 1957 number to the issue. As a statement of intent or 'mission statement', it cannot be bettered:

> A West-country paper recently referred to 'New Cornwall' as 'the organ of "Mebyon Kernow"! This is a mistake. 'New Cornwall' aims to serve all who are truly interested in Cornwall. Naturally, activities of Mebyon Kernow are mentioned and some articles are written by members of that organisation, for it is one of the active and encouraging factors present in the Cornish scene to-day. However, the majority of our readers are not, so far as we know, members of M.K. and 'New Cornwall' is open to articles of varying points of view. We believe that news of present activities and events in Cornwall and free discussion of them lay the best foundations for planning future developments. Plans for these must take account of present conditions and be firmly based on the continuing tradition of Cornish life. Cornwall must neither be turned into a backwater, nor must it be stripped of all individuality and forced into a mould of uniformity.[12]

NEW CORNWALL

THE MAGAZINE FOR THOSE WHO HAVE THE INTERESTS OF CORNWALL AT HEART
Yearly 6/- *Edited by* Richard & Ann Jenkin, Flat 1, 29 Fore Street, Totnes, Devon
post free
PRINTED BY THE TRE POL PEN DUPLICATING SERVICE, 2 NEW STREET, PADSTOW

Volume 6. No. 5. August - September 1958.

Cover for New Cornwall, *August-September 1958*

Clarification was once again called for in the mid-1960s when the *Western Morning News* described the magazine as 'the journal of Mebyon Kernow, the Sons of Cornwall movement'.[13] In their response, titled 'Our Purpose', the editors stressed that their purpose was to produce a magazine for all members of the public who were seriously interested in Cornish affairs, whether they belonged to any society or none. 'NEW CORNWALL is an open forum,' they continued, 'and our contributors can, and do, express conflicting views. The majority of readers are not members of Mebyon Kernow. NEW CORNWALL is independent and self-supporting and does not receive any subsidy from any society or group.'[14] A few months earlier the *Cornish and Devon Post* had hedged its bets on the issue by saying that 'although it [*New Cornwall*] is not quite the official organ of a "Home Rule" political movement, there is no doubt as to where its heart lies'!'[15] The last word on the subject should go to Richard Jenkin who, in an interview conducted by the Cornish Audio Visual Archive on 14 February 2000, suggested in the measured language that was so characteristic of him the new approach to nationalism that he and Ann introduced when they took over as editors:

> We changed it from being a MK (more or less) internal magazine, to making it, or trying to make it, the magazine for the whole Cornish movement. And somewhere in it I wrote, 'New Cornwall is accused of being the Mebyon Kernow magazine. It's not the Mebyon Kernow magazine any more than it is the RIC magazine or the Cornwall archaeological magazine or any other society I belong to.' We wanted to cover the whole aspect of Cornish culture and development.[16]

A special enlarged issue marked the beginning of the Jenkins' second year as editors. In an editorial entitled 'A Year's Hard Labour!' they appealed once more to their readers to help *New Cornwall* be more representative by acting as reporters and submitting items of Cornish interest from their own area. Athough press-day had often found the editors 'frantically typing out and arranging' material,[17] they had enjoyed producing it and felt that it was rendering some service to Cornwall. The number of subscribers had increased by a fifth during 1957, although more were wanted north of Launceston and east of Padstow. The issue was praised for its use of photographs, to which the editors responded by pointing out that the process by which these were reproduced was expensive and raised the production cost considerably. Despite this, they hoped to print more photographs in the near future.[18] The spring of 1958 saw the publication of the first issue of the Falmouth-based *Cornish Magazine*. 'We are pleased to welcome once more a Cornish Magazine pleasantly illustrated and printed with an attractive cover,' wrote *New Cornwall*'s editors magnanimously. Its articles were varied and should, they thought, have a wide appeal, although this was perhaps a weakness. 'A Cornish Magazine must be Cornish in outlook and tone,' they continued, 'but many of the articles seem of rather too general interest, and are such as might appear in any County or National Magazine.'[19] By today's standards, the *Cornish Magazine* of the late 1950s and 1960s looks home-made, but it was a commercial venture. *New Cornwall*, on the other hand, was literally home-made, typed and roneoed[20] by the editors, with help from such committed individuals as Stephen Fuller. Despite any apparent shortcomings as regards production, it was praised for what matters – its content – with one newspaper pinpointing 'the growing width of its outlook' as *New Cornwall*'s 'outstanding quality' and concluding that it was 'becoming an exceedingly readable (if provocative) paper'.[21]

In January 1959 the editors' New Year message 'A Second Milestone' recycled some of the thoughts that they had expressed in previous editorials. Some issues during 1958 had been bigger than the normal eight pages and they hoped to continue this trend and introduce some illustrations. An encouraging trend was that the circulation had increased by a third, indicating that the magazine was supplying a need. This judgement was backed up by one local newspaper which thought that *New Cornwall* was 'growing up'. An air of more definite interest meant that it could no longer be classed as 'just another of those freak productions'. Furthermore, it considered that the magazine's aim of giving a picture of the Cornwall of the day was 'within measurable distance of being realized'.[22] For another local newspaper, *New Cornwall* was 'definitely a periodical to be taken seriously'.[23]

'Home Again'
The start of the 1960s heralded a very welcome change of circumstances for Richard and Ann Jenkin – a return to Cornwall. In their first two editorials they

expressed their hopes that from their Leedstown home they could work more effectively for Cornish interests in *New Cornwall*. There had been a further 17% increase in subscriptions during 1959, but more were needed if planned future improvements were to materialise. Inspired by the panorama from their new home – as far as Carn Brea, Tregonning Hill and Godolphin Hill, and even the tip of St Michael's Mount – Richard gave voice to two abiding themes in his writing: the periphery versus the centre and individuality versus uniformity. To someone who had just returned from living in different parts of England, including London, 'the faintly ashamed air of some Cornishmen who apologize for not being near "the centre of things" because one is so far from London' seemed quite ill-founded. 'Thank goodness one does not live near the centre of things,' he continued, 'even if there are problems of unemployment, unwise building development and other local difficulties to contend with. At least in rural areas the individual still is important and in few places more so than this side of the Tamar…'[24]

Over the next three years *New Cornwall* continued to thrive despite the pressures on its editors of holding down jobs, raising a young family and their increasing involvement with a wide range of Cornish organisations, including the Cornish Gorsedh – of which Richard became secretary in 1961 – and the Celtic Congress. Looking back at the beginning of 1962 over five years in charge, they noted that the work entailed in editing and dispatching the magazine had more than doubled and expressed their thanks to all who had helped and to those who had written articles.[25] Subscribers continued to increase – by 25% in 1960 and 15% in 1961 – but more were needed. So, too, were more roving reporters, more articles and more letters for publication so that *New Cornwall* might be 'truly representative of all shades of Cornish opinion'.[26] In addition, to all readers and more especially newspapers they wished to make it clear that the views expressed by contributors were not necessarily those of the editors.[27] The continued support of the local press was clearly seen as important and was by and large sympathetic, with the editors being praised for their 'courage and enterprise'[28] and for being 'go-ahead people' who were 'anxious to do everything possible to stimulate lively activity in the county'.[29] *New Cornwall* was variously described as a 'stout-hearted little magazine',[30] 'a fiercely patriotic publication' which had 'fought many a battle and backed many a Celtic cause'[31] and a 'patriotically Cornish publication'.[32] Not all reviews were complimentary, though, and as we shall see, these tended to focus on what some newspapers and some individuals alike saw as the publication's extreme pro-Cornish, pro-Celtic stance.

Dasserghyn

The first issue of volume 12 in January 1964 saw a wholesale redesign of *New Cornwall*. In an editorial entitled 'A New Departure' Richard and Ann Jenkin described it as 'a venture of hope'. In addition to a reduction in size from foolscap to quarto, there was for the first time a standardized cover by Cornish artist Mary Mills (*Morgelyn*) whose interweaving of a phoenix, the Cornish coat of arms and the Cornish word *Dasserghyn* was explained by Richard six years later. 'DASSERGHYN – Let us rise again – has been on our cover now for many years. It was intended to mark our belief in the renaissance of the Cornish nation in all its manifestations, and was linked with the symbol of the phoenix re-born from the flames.'[33] *New Cornwall* was itself an outcome of the renaissance of Cornish feeling, especially during the 1950s and 1960s, seeking as it did 'to serve the Cornish people in their fight to retain their identity and to develop their national life according to their own desires'.[34] The magazine's new guise and format were widely praised by the local press, with the *Cornish and Devon Post* describing it as '[n]ow resplendent in stiff covers (bearing of course the county colours of yellow and black)' and 'much easier to handle'.[35] More generally, *New Cornwall* would henceforth make greater use of Celtic symbolism and illustrations. Another change was the introduction of sequential pagination throughout each volume. One reader who particularly appreciated *New Cornwall* and its revamp was the English-born, Cornish-raised, Welsh-speaking Plaid Cymru radical John Legonna,[36] who that Easter wrote to the editors in his characteristically flowery style of Cornwall never being the same after the magazine's birth twelve years previously. 'Beneath an editorial banner,' he continued, 'an editorial perceptiveness that has marked a milestone on Cornwall's road: surely bringing our People's gratitude, however diffident, upon yourselves, a gerens whek [dear friends], courageous Editors: so deserving of congratulations...' Of the myriad he could proffer, one concerned the new format which, 'emblematic of the so-long-unheard-of real Cornwall, [was] much a step

Cover design for New Cornwall *by Mary Mills (Morgelyn), used from January 1964*

in the right direction: with its depicting of the fires of obliteration through which NEW CORNWALL rises. Arises, calling confident that our land, our Cornwall, our small but dear People too shall arise'.[37] Although Richard's short piece entitled 'New and Lively Publications' was intended to introduce three very different new magazines, it was surely meant, too, as a personal observation on *New Cornwall*:

> From time to time new periodicals appear and it is often the smaller ones which are the most interesting. Usually duplicated, they owe their very existence to an enthusiastic conviction that something important needs to be said and to a determination to overcome obstacles in the way.[38]

In the case of *New Cornwall*, over the next nine years of its existence until its demise in mid-1973 these obstacles – in the form of both personal and professional commitments – would increase. Apologizing for the delay in the appearance of the August 1964 issue, Richard cited 'successive illnesses and convalescences in the family of the editors' at the time when the material should have been in preparation.[39] With three young children, he and co-editor Ann were increasingly involved during these years in the flourishing Cornish scene. Their booklet *Cornwall: the Hidden Land* was published in 1965. Richard was elected to the Gorsedh Council in 1967 and as Deputy Grand Bard five years later. Mebyon Kernow responsibilities were increasing and he regularly attended the International Celtic Congress in either early spring or summer each year. Although *New Cornwall* editorials were sometimes signed 'The Editors' and sometimes by Richard alone, I think it is fair to say that henceforth there were routinely more articles signed either 'R.G.J' or 'R.G. Jenkin'. These editorials, too, tended to focus more on the issues of the day than, as was hitherto the case, being a mixture of these plus the mechanics of publishing the magazine.

The appearance of the first number of volume 15 in May 1967 marked a further change to *New Cornwall*. With the number of subscribers increasing sixfold during the ten years that the current editors had been in charge and the average size of each issue doubling, it was taking several weeks to compile and several weeks to duplicate 'in the limited "spare time" of the editors'. With

Page from Richard Jenkin's notebook showing rough outline of contents of New Cornwall, *vol 15, no 3, October-December 1967*

postal charges increasing, it was felt that it would be more economic in terms of both time and money to publish 'approximately quarterly' instead of six times a year.[40] Once again, the editors finished on a plea to their subscribers to pay promptly and to their readers to submit suggestions of topics for discussion and ways of serving Cornwall more effectively. Only constructive criticism, articles, letters and recommendations to potential subscribers could ensure the magazine's future success and continued existence.

With the new decade, the pressures increased. Having been elected deputy chairman of Mebyon Kernow the previous year, Richard was chosen in 1969 as the party's first prospective parliamentary candidate in the following year's General Election. The following year, Ann returned to work and this, together with the fact that there were now four children in the family, meant that she could no longer write for *New Cornwall*. Hitherto, she had contributed about a third of the articles, mainly cultural, literary and educational, as well as book reviews and some historical items. Clearly, something had to give and at the beginning of 1970 – with the fourth number of volume 16 – it was announced that in future the magazine would appear as and when material was available and ready. It was virtually a year before the first issue of what would prove to be the last volume saw the light of day. Richard Jenkin's editorial – 'Dasserghyn!' – was clearly intended to convey an upbeat message, with the publication's emblematic motto now seen as applicable to *New Cornwall* itself. After 'some months of travail', it was rising to new life again, although just as the Cornish situation was changing as new groups, new societies and new periodicals appeared, so too would *New Cornwall* itself. As it was entirely produced by voluntary labour, it was impossible to have fixed publication dates, although the editors hoped to be able to produce three or four issues a year.[41] In the event, issues two and three of the final volume were published in the autumn of 1971 and summer of 1972 respectively. A year later what would be the final number of *New Cornwall* was published – the first issue for which Richard assumed sole editorship in writing. A certain irony underlies his very downbeat editorial, one feels, for although the message of 'The harvest is plenteous but the labourers few' was worded in such a way as to refer to the Cornish situation generally, it clearly reflected the perilous situation in which *New Cornwall* found itself. The issue had been planned to appear during the previous winter and some of the material for it had been ready then, but lack of help and 'pressure of work of many kinds' had held it up. 'I would like to know,' he concluded, 'whether subscribers would prefer this size of issue appearing irregularly or smaller issues appearing more regularly. I would also be grateful for more contributions from those who have something to say about Cornwall.'[42]

Although there would be no further issues of *New Cornwall*, Richard Jenkin continued to receive letters about it and some readers continued to renew their subscriptions. The public silence surrounding the magazine's future appears to have lasted a further three years until June 1976 when a farewell letter was sent to all subscribers.

'Spreading the gospel of awareness…': themes and content
If *New Cornwall* was sometimes mocked by the local press and occasionally taken to task by a few of its readers for its pro-Cornish and perceived anti-English stance, there were no such qualms about the breadth of its subject matter. Indeed, Cornwall would arguably have to wait until the 1990s and the appearance of *Cornish Worldwide* and the earlier issues of *Cornish World* for anything approaching such an informed and comprehensive overview of Cornwall, the Cornish diaspora and the other Celtic lands.

As was the case for their predecessors, the overriding theme for editors Richard and Ann Jenkin was Cornish identity and how it could be preserved and promoted. Feeding into this were Cornish history and how it was portrayed – or, as was and often still is the case, ignored – and Cornish education. An offshoot of their concern for Cornish identity and something that was clearly very dear to Richard was the struggle between individuality and freedom on the one hand and uniformity and totalitarianism on the other. Here there was often a fusion of Cornish, British and world politics. Overspill (the relocating of thousands of Londoners to Cornwall), the threat posed to Cornwall's physical integrity by the deliberations of the Boundary Commission, and the Common Market (British membership of what has become the European Union) were all burning issues in the 1960s and early 1970s. We have already seen how the editors of *New Cornwall* felt obliged – at least on paper – to distance their publication from Mebyon Kernow, but they were both founding members and supporters – and in Richard's case, a leader and parliamentary candidate – so the work of that organisation cum political party was widely covered. So, too, was news from the other Celtic territories – Wales, Scotland, Ireland, Mann and Brittany – and the organisations devoted to promoting them, primarily the Celtic Congress and, from the early 1960s onwards, the Celtic League. Richard's 'Here and There' column was first and foremost a vehicle for pan-Celtic news. On the wider stage, the work of the Federal Union of European Nationalities (FUEN), which Richard supported, was publicized and championed. Naturally, *New Cornwall* also drew attention to the work of a host of other Cornish organisations.

Although, as Pasco Trevyhan, Richard once described himself as 'an uneconomic person',[43] there was plenty of coverage of the industrial and economic issues of the day in Cornwall, with prominence being given to concerns about transport, tourism, and to a lesser extent, fishing, mining and nuclear power. Balancing this coverage of what we might broadly call 'political' subjects were penetrating and interesting features about the cultural life of Cornwall, with the arts generally, literature and books, broadcasting, archaeology and, of course, the Cornish language all being covered on a regular basis. While both editors wrote under their own names, their bardic names, and pen names, a number of prominent individuals – sometimes named, sometimes not – helped make *New Cornwall* the excellent forum that Richard and Ann Jenkin wanted it to be. Contributors during their sixteen-year editorship included Inglis Gundry, Charles Thomas, Ken MacKinnon, John Legonna, Richard Gendall, Harri Webb, Francis Cargeeg, E.G.R. Hooper, Peter Pool and – to the last but two and last but one issues respectively – a young P.J. Payton, whose articles 'Dasserghyn' and 'Language Revival' gave his own fledgling views on the Celtic rebirth of Cornwall. A full examination of all the numbers edited by the Jenkins is well outside the scope of this chapter. However, this writer does propose to look in detail at four themes or subjects covered in either specific articles or on an issue to issue basis, and at the four major series that *New Cornwall* featured over the years, together with the controversy these sometimes generated. These subjects are Cornish identity and nationalism, Cornish history, the Cornish language, and tourism.

'Cornwall is the only 'Region' for the Cornish'

There are a number of articles and papers which can be seen as cogent expressions of Richard Jenkin's views on Cornish identity, Cornish and Celtic Nationalism, and individualism versus centralism – all of which taken together are central to the ethos of *New Cornwall*. These include 'National Life in Cornwall' (1955), 'Nations and Nationalism Today' (1964) and 'Freedom' (1968), which is reprinted in this volume. However, it is with the third issue edited by the Jenkins – that for April-May 1957 – that the writer proposes to start. Commenting on an article by Professor Anton Hilckman of Mainz University entitled 'The Submerged Europe', the unassigned editorial points out that, despite being general rather than particular, much of what it had to say was true of Cornwall and the other Celtic countries. It continued:

> A national or regional patriotism is a strong deterrent to the communist creed of "sameness", and the view that individuality is dangerous.
>
> Cornish individuality has always been strong and it seems a pity that we sometimes appear in danger of losing our "Cornishness" because of modern conditions of work, and the large-scale emigration of many good citizens. While we would hate Cornishmen to lose their pioneering spirit which has taken them out of Cornwall and abroad it seems that saturation point can be reached. Cornish people are now needed IN THE County in order to preserve that very Cornishness of which our emigrants are so proud.[44]

Towards the end of that same year, the editors announced that, as Cornwall was one of the six Celtic nations, they hoped to continue to print articles about one or other of them in most issues of *New Cornwall*. 'The more we know of one another, the more we shall understand our history, our present situation, and our probable future.' They considered that we could learn much from our Celtic cousins, their problems being often similar to ours, and their methods of tackling them capable of being adapted to Cornish circumstances.[45] It is often argued that in seeking devolved powers or greater self-determination, nationalists want to isolate their country or region. Such isolationism was no part of Richard and Ann Jenkin's philosophy and a year later *New Cornwall* again stressed that Cornwall did not exist in a vacuum, but needed to be viewed in relation to her sister Celtic countries, to England, and to the world.[46] Quangos based across the Tamar and the media have historically been viewed as unsympathetic to Cornish aspirations, and articles such as Peter Pool's 'Is the BBC West Region anti-Cornish?'[47] and Professor Anton Hilckman's 'Cornwall through continental eyes'[48] were welcome contributions to the debate.

On 1 April 1960 the BBC West Region broadcast Denys Val Baker's *Cornwall for the Cornish: 1966 and All That*, which the regional edition of the *Radio Times* described as '[t]he story of how in 1966 the Duchy of Cornwall decided to secede from the United Kingdom' and 'Cornwall's historic struggle for the right to run its own affairs'. It was clearly a spoof aimed at Mebyon Kernow, but the Cornish have become accustomed to being a target of fun over the years and, as *New Cornwall* pointed out, even this sort of programme was evidence of 'something stirring in Cornwall'; as one listener had remarked, one couldn't poke fun at a movement that didn't exist.[49] Richard himself would sometimes use humour to introduce or make a serious point. 'Cornwall: England's first and last colony', a piece written as Pasco Trevyhan, is an example. There was always the danger, though, that the humour – here, the news that Redruth Bacon Factory was now selling faggots and black-puddings to cater for the large and increasing number of settlers from the north of England and the Midlands – would be misconstrued. While the *Cornish and Devon Post* saw the article fairly objectively as a continuation of *New Cornwall*'s 'history of steady fighting in defence of Cornwall's Celtic heritage against "foreign" domination,'[50] another local newspaper regarded the whole article as 'facetious', viewing the edition of *New Cornwall* in which it was published as being 'for all of those "20,000 Cornishmen" who are so patriotic – and maybe for some of those who take it with a pinch of salt'.[51]

Some *New Cornwall* readers, too, were critical of its nationalist stance. One, 'mid-Cornishman', wrote to the editors about the editorial of the 150th anniversary edition of the *West Briton* – in particular its 'digs' at 'those Cornish Nationalist people' who rashly spoke of Cornwall as a nation and advocated Home Rule. 'It is amusing such a "silly idea" can be such an issue for the editorial (not the first),' he concluded. 'A "silly idea" which seems to be causing quite a headache to some.'[52] The 'some' in question was presumably meant to include the editors of *New Cornwall*! Part of a letter from another reader who was critical of the magazine's pan-Celtic stance was reproduced in the February-March 1961 issue: 'Although I like to see NEW CORNWALL,' he or she wrote, 'I detest with all my soul any Celtic racial get-together business. So un-Celtic! When did Celts want to be anything but separate? The nationalist spirit and racial pride have led to enough evil for my life time.'[53] The 'gist', as Richard described it, of his measured response shows what a careful and logical thinker he was. Yet another critic aired her views following the publication, in the very last issue of *New Cornwall*, of an editorial entitled 'The harvest is plenteous but the labourers few'. This looked at the numerous 'strong and ever-increasing forces' threatening Cornwall and the Cornish way of life, including 'a rash of speculative building of second homes, holiday flats and retirement homes for English immigrants' while many Cornish people still lacked first homes. This particular concern was reinforced by a timely article entitled 'Populations of Cornwall and of Great Britain' which compared the populations of both between 1801 and 1971.[54] Writing to Richard in order to renew her subscription, Dr—— was sorry to see him objecting so vigorously to 'retirement homes for English immigrants to Cornwall'. She had resigned her membership of the Celtic League on account of a similar statement to the press earlier that same year concerning overspill to Camborne. Dwelling at some length on the debts on both sides, she was of the opinion that if the English owed much to the Cornish, the Cornish owed as much to the English.[55] Richard began his reply by writing that he was unsure in which capacity he should write – as editor of *New Cornwall*, as president of the Celtic League [by which he meant the Celtic Congress], chairman of Mebyon Kernow or Deputy Grand Bard. He continued:

> Perhaps I had better make a personal answer and bind no-one else to my views. First, the vexed question of English settlers in Cornwall. It is pleasant to welcome foreigners who come to Cornwall and take an intelligent and unpatronising interest in Cornwall and its culture, but you know that the vast majority have no interest and bring their own brand of society with them. This might be accommodated if it were not for the vast numbers. Of the present population of Cornwall some 20 to 25% at least are immigrants. I'm sure that if 25% of the population of London was Cornish or Welsh the native Londoners would complain.

They complained enough about the small coloured population and one could not compare the effects of the few thousands of Cornish people amongst the millions of London with that of tens of thousands of settlers in the 300,000 of Cornwall. 'How can the Cornishness of Cornwall be kept,' he continued, 'if the Cornish are outnumbered in their own homeland and this, if present trends continue, is likely to happen before the end of the century. In the past we have assimilated settlers and Cornishized them in a generation or two, but now they are so many they are indigestible…'[56]

One of Richard Jenkin's most cogent analyses of Cornish Nationalism and its place within a wider framework, 'Nations and Nationalism Today', appeared in the first issue of the redesigned *New Cornwall* in January 1964. For Harri Webb, editor of Plaid Cymru's *The Welsh Nation*, its 'sensitive analysis' of the subject could not have been bettered.[57] Over the next decade, Richard would continue to write articles which explored the twin themes of Cornish identity and individual freedom. During this period the idea of regionalism became popular in the political arena and beyond, and was challenged by him in such editorials and articles as 'Regionalism and Cornwall', 'Thou Shalt Not Covet', 'Unite and Unite' and 'Creeping regionalisation'. The regional idea was only of value, he thought, if true devolution of power was considered, as opposed to what he called 'administrative devolution', which was seen by some politicians as a means of escaping responsibility by granting the appearance of local control while withholding the reality of power. 'Cornwall,' he concluded, 'has shared many experiences with England, some pleasant, others unpleasant, but Cornwall originated in a different tradition from that of England and after a thousand years the Cornish community is still determined to remain Cornish. To be amalgamated with English territory makes Cornwall less able to be herself. There must certainly be co-operation, but equal co-operation preserves identity while merging destroys it. Cornwall must refuse or resist anything which does not leave her identity intact or allow her people to follow their destiny in their own way. Cornwall is the territory of a nation and Cornwall is the only 'Region' for the Cornish.'[58]

In 1969 the Maud Report proposed a restructuring of local government and, with the subsequent White Paper that followed, the prospect of a new Tamarside authority consisting of St Germans Rural District Council and the boroughs of Torpoint and Saltash looked a distinct possibility. In 'Thou Shalt Not Covet', Richard berated those Plymouth councillors who for years had cast covetous glances over the Tamar, dreaming amongst other things of 'turning Saltash into a suburb of Plymouth'. For him – as for Mebyon Kernow and many other organizations – these schemes could not be allowed to succeed. Furthermore, it was essential 'to impress on the Government that Cornish people of all shades of opinion will not accept the transfer of any part of Cornwall to any non-Cornish local authority, and that we are prepared to do more than issue protests'.[59] In the penultimate issue of *New Cornwall*, 'Creeping Regionalisation' provided numerous instances of the amalgamation or absorption of Cornish organisations or bodies with or by Devon and Cornwall or South-West alternatives. For Richard, Cornwall was always a nation, or – to put it in the mildest and most neutral of terms – 'a recognisable area with a strong sense of identity'. As such it was a stumbling block to the bureaucratic mind which preferred a smooth, grey uniformity throughout Britain. Consciously or unconsciously, bureaucrats tended to put forward policies which would reduce the individuality of Cornwall. Creeping regionalisation was 'a cumulative poison' and Cornwall had reached the limit of toleration.[60] Particularly appreciative of Richard's leading article were local members of Mebyon Kernow's Cowethas Flamank group who, in a meeting that summer (1972), were in complete agreement that it gave a timely warning concerning 'the continual and insidious erosion of our control of essential services' which represented one of the most serious problems facing Cornwall just then.[61]

The freedom of the individual was another aspect of identity, and the state's curtailment of the greater good of the community was, for Richard, a constant concern. In 'Compulsion', for instance, he looked at the Compulsory Purchase Order, the overriding criterion of the necessity for which should, he felt, be the need of the community as a whole, not the profit of the community. Those who wielded power inherent in such orders should be 'men with a strong sense of justice and a tender conscience in matters of equity' if they were not to be corrupted by power into an arrogant autocracy'.[62] In 1968 the euphoria of the Prague Spring was crushed by Soviet invasion and led Richard to write 'Freedom', a passionate defence of the freedom and dignity of individuals and nations and of constitutional democracy.[63] It is reproduced in this volume.

A Cornish approach to Cornish history

The need for a Cornu-centric history of Cornwall was something that the editors of *New Cornwall* championed both within the magazine and in the Cornish movement generally. Early in 1958, for instance, having been contacted by a reader who commented on how little Cornish history was then taught to Cornish children by comparison with her own schooldays, they devoted much of an editorial to the subject. The main problem was the lack of a suitable textbook – something that made it difficult for most people to get a clear idea of the sequence of Cornish history. Fairly soon, though, they hoped to print as a supplement to *New Cornwall* a time chart showing the important dates.[64] Later that year the subject was again raised on the back of some discussion both in *New Cornwall* and in the Cornish press. Work on the time chart was said to be 'in progress' and it was hoped that it would appear before the end of the year. Although Richard maintained a notebook in which parallel chronological events in Cornwall and the other Celtic territories were recorded, the mooted time chart never saw the light of day. In the autumn of 1971, though, Pasco Trevyhan's 'Here and There' column carried a report of an initiative that showed the changing attitude to Cornish studies – namely a course on 'Cornwall and the Cornish' at the Education Authority's Teachers' Residential Centre.[65] And two decades later – between 1989 and 1992 – Ann Jenkin took over as co-ordinator of *Cornish Studies for Schools*, a ring-binder which contained essays by various writers on such subjects as 'The Great Migration' (Philip Payton), 'Cornish Place-Names' (Oliver Padel), 'The Arms of the Duchy of Cornwall' (Richard Jenkin) and 'Celtic Links' (Ann Trevenen Jenkin) and which was circulated to all schools.

Another prerequisite that was viewed as essential if Cornwall was to be seen as a distinct territory was some form of higher education and early in 1963, Robert Dunstone, the then chairman of Mebyon Kernow, contributed to *New Cornwall* an article entitled 'A University for Cornwall is Possible'. Having explored the financial benefits that such an establishment would bring to Cornwall, he emphasized that it would enrich her cultural life, with the prospect of many fields of study which could be very Cornish in direction being offered.[66] Richard followed this up with a report which in turn emphasized how widely Mebyon Kernow's appeal had been circulated, publicized and welcomed across Cornwall and beyond. He again reiterated the enriching effect of a university on all aspects of Cornwall's life – cultural, social and economic.[67]

In 1963 the then Deputy Grand Bard of Cornwall, Francis Cargeeg (*Tan Dyvarow*), read a paper to the Closed Gorsedh entitled 'A Cornish Approach to Cornish History'. This was duly published in three issues of *New Cornwall* in July, September and November that same year. Cargeeg concluded his masterful analysis of Cornish history and oppression with a forthright and passionate rebuttal of those who accused the Cornish of apathy and neglect where their heritage was concerned:

> No! Our Nationhood, our Language and our Celtic culture did not die of neglect at the hands of boorish peasants, tinners and fishermen as our Very Superior Anglicised Critics would have us believe. It died on the field of battle, and by persecution, and the Hangman's Noose, and finally by the brainwashing of the Educationalists, the Ad-men and the P.R.O. Boys of the English Establishment.

Without a Cornish approach to Cornish history all the labour and enthusiasm of the Celtic Revival would have been merely '"a gathering of the fragments" – antiquarianism tinged with nostalgia and romanticism'. For him, the remarkable revival of the Cornish language could not in itself provide a basis for Cornwall's claim to nationhood – and certainly not while some Cornish-language scholars were guilty of adopting a thoroughly English approach to Cornish history. The neglect of our history was, for him, 'the greatest defect of our Revival'.[68] Cargeeg's paper was widely praised. Peter Hourahane of Cardiff expressed his admiration for the author's approach, writing that he would be very surprised to see 'such strong stuff' from the pen of a Gorsedd leader in Wales. If the Welsh and Cornish were to be true to themselves, they needed to realise what was significant in their past.[69] Another enthusiast was John Legonna, who praised *New Cornwall* for publishing 'quite the truest treatment of Cornish history yet penned'. Cargeeg had boldly presented 'a new appreciation of the Cornish heritage' and – in the case of Michael Angove, the St Keverne blacksmith put to death at the end of the 1497 uprising – one 'through whose dawning light we see ANGOVE a name to mark, with Glyndwr and Bruce, with Boru and Pearse and many another ineradicably dauntless Celt'.[70]

'Is our Cornish really necessary?'
From the earliest days of their editorship, *New Cornwall* was seen by the Jenkins as an open forum which would publish articles by people of varying opinions. In short, they were never afraid to be controversial and the July 1963 issue which contained the first instalment of Cargeeg's seminal paper also featured a short, provocative piece entitled 'Is our Cornish really necessary?' With his first 'Here and There' column in November 1955, Richard had given due prominence to the Cornish language, proficiency in which had earned him his bardship eight years previously. In addition to featuring regularly in 'Here and There', the language was the subject of articles by both Richard and other writers. The latter included Arzel Even's 'A Breton's study of Cornish'; 'The Cornish Paradox' by E.G.R. Hooper; 'The Little That is Left – Cornwall's last living toehold upon its mother tongue' by Kenneth MacKinnon; Richard Gendall's 'Cornish as an optional subject in schools'; and Philip Payton's 'Language Revival'.[71] As well as writing occasional pieces about topics such as bi-lingual Cornish and English signage and initiating and contributing to the Cornish-language column 'Urth an Besont' (Order of the Bezant) which itself first appeared in October 1967 hard on the heels of the idea of a badge for Cornish speakers ('Arweth rak Kernewegoryon/A badge for Cornish-speakers'), Richard included his own paper for the 1965 Celtic Congress entitled 'Modernising Vocabulary', itself reprinted here. Other related contributions were Dr Ceinwen H. Thomas's 'Education in Welsh', which looked at Welsh-medium teaching and its position in Wales in the late 1950s, and the anonymous 'The Position of Gaelic in Scotland/Welsh in Wales' early in 1960.[72]

It was a brave move, then, to publish Joan Evason's article in which she began by asking, as many others have done and still do, if it was not a waste of time for Cornish children to be taught Cornish – or, for that matter, for Irish and Welsh children to be taught their mother tongues. In a short introduction, the editors described the author as 'a sincere and intelligent Englishwoman living in Cornwall' and, as well as providing a partial answer to her question in the form of a reprint of the petition of the Scandinavian professors to UNESCO, invited *New Cornwall* readers to submit other arguments which they thought would convince the writer of the desirability and importance of learning

Cornish.[73] The response was immediate! Christine Morton Raymont, daughter of the Cornish-language scholar Robert Morton Nance, argued that Joan Evason's point of view was utilitarian rather than cultural, and that Cornish had the potential to provide children with both a greater understanding of their surroundings – Cornish-language place names were all around them – and an interest and understanding of other languages. Rejecting the "By Jove, we will teach our own children Cornish!" approach, Archy Macpherson's was one in which he argued that asking which language should be used to teach children their own language was the crucial consideration. One's mother tongue was 'the very fabric of our thoughts and personality' and the lack of success in the revival of Irish compared with that of Hebrew underlined the fundamental differences in approach.[74] Citing his annoyance for the fact that his reply was 'badly put', 'jumbled' and ultimately 'childish', Richard Gendall lambasted Ms. Evason as yet 'another English person [who] does not see why anybody should want to bother with Cornish'. Surely it was best left to rot in musty old books, or 'fossilized in "quaint" placenames to charm ice-cream suckers' or to 'queer cranks'. Given that we were all supposed to know that anything English was superior to anything Cornish, why didn't we 'clear up some of these untidy Cornish names and substitute some really nice English ones like Chipping Sodbury, Shoreditch, Yapton, Piddle Hinton and so on? So much pleasanter sounding and easier to understand! After all we are already improving the native strain by settling Cornish homesteads with English people, and civilising some of those awful depressing beaches with a few nice lavatories, cafes, beach-huts etc.' Cornish had the potential to give its speakers all they needed for ordinary life and happiness, were it possible to make it widely known once again. '[M]ust we Cornish also judge the worth of everything by how useful it is?' he asked. He appealed to fellow Cornishmen not to be put off by what others – particularly English people – said against the Cornish language and ended his letter in defiant, fighting fashion:

> Fellow Cornishmen, you must not be put off by what people say against the Cornish language… You yourself may not wish to relearn your mother tongue, but if you are ashamed of it you have no right to consider yourself Cornish. We know what to think of the fellow who "makes

good" and becomes ashamed of his family.

Fellow Cornishmen, do you realise that Cornish people have never been more docile than since the Cornish language fell sick? We rebelled against what we did not like, several times, in the days when the language was truly in the people's mouths. Never since. <u>Of course</u>, the French deliberately try to squash the Breton language; <u>of course</u> the English deliberately tried to squash the Irish language. A language is a badge of independence...[75]

Strategically positioned below Richard Gendall's letter was a small advert for Peter Pool's recently-published *Cornish for Beginners*!

'Piskey Trade'

In 'Pymp Hernen', the short piece that he wrote for *New Cornwall* concerning the dual-language Cornish-English name to be seen on the Five Pilchards public house in Porthallow, Richard Jenkin made it clear that he was not advocating wider use of Cornish as a mere tourist gimmick[76] – or, as Richard Gendall had put it, 'to charm ice-cream suckers'. Indeed, it is clear that his attitude – and that of *New Cornwall* – to tourism was at best ambiguous and often hostile. In this same piece he judged the tourist trade to be then Cornwall's third or fourth biggest industry. A decade earlier he had contributed the poem 'Almost any Cornish town' to Dick Gendall's fledgling magazine, and its simple warning of the devastating effect that tourism invariable has on the demographics, housing and cultures of most countries – and, nearer home, particularly the Celtic countries – is still relevant, even if some of its language is inevitably dated. More amusing, though arguably less effective, is his early 1970s' poem 'Hurrah for the tourist trade'.[77]

For Richard, tourism was – at least in the late 1950s – at best a part-time money maker. Incredibly, given the subsequent population growth in Cornwall brought about by in-migration, he felt that not enough people were aware of the problem of de-population and the drift from the land. While the importance of new industries was beginning to be realised, more were needed in villages and market towns where local people could be employed.[78] The very idea that tourism could get out of control and that it should in some way be reined in may strike the reader as laughable in the second decade of the 21st century when the industry in all its manifestations – cultural tourism, heritage tourism, green tourism et al – is considered sacrosanct, but the 'bucket and spade' tourism of the 1950s and 1960s could often be a pretty tacky affair. 'New Piskey Trade', for instance, deals at length with the introduction of a new gimmick. 'Not content with piskies washed in the "Lucky Wishing Well",' wrote its unnamed author, 'they [some of the "pisky" shops] have jointly produced A Passport to Cornwall.' Purporting to be issued by Merlin on behalf of King Arthur of Tintagel and valid in forty-eight participating towns, the "passport" would be endorsed with a "visa" at specified piskey shops. 'He would be a brave passport-holder who asked for a visa without making a purchase,' commented the writer, almost certainly Richard Jenkin. Obtaining all the visas guaranteed the passport holder 'Honorary Membership of the Round Table and Court of King Arthur, certified on a parchment scroll, on payment of 5/- to a pisky shop in Newquay'. The potted account in the passport of each of the forty-eight participating places was sometimes ludicrously inaccurate. 'This is not a passport to the land of King Arthur,' he concluded, 'but to that of Joan the Wad, Queen of the Piskies, and its emblem is not a chough but a rook. How many will be gulled into tearing up and down to find forty-eight pisky-laden tourist traps? A more serious matter is the effect on the discerning visitor who will be sickened by such crass commercialism.'[79] The distinction between 'the discerning visitor' and his less discerning equivalent who could presumably be expected to lap up the passport idea, is unfortunate. Arguably, the cultural tourist is more of an elephant in the room than his 'bucket and spade' equivalent, for many not only visit, but – eventually – come back to settle.

Two issues later, *New Cornwall* drew attention to the litter problem that resulted from tourism. One remedy, felt the again unnamed writer, would be to 'reduce' the dependence of Cornwall on tourism. Was it really so vital? The need was for more light industries which would give 'round the year' employment for those who wanted it.[80] Fifty years later, of course, tourism is virtually an all-year-round industry. The *New Cornwall* editorial for April-May 1960 again looked at 'the flooding tide of tourism' which each summer rose higher, frantically encouraged by advertising campaigns. Many people were beginning to wonder if this was in the best interests of Cornwall. Among them was Denys Val Baker who had himself written in the 11 April issue of the *Western Morning*

News of the rush to cash in on holiday makers getting a little out of proportion. Town councils, he thought, should put the needs of their residents first. Echoing Richard's own thoughts on the subject, he called for the development of old and established industries and the encouragement of new ones, with a planned effort to put Cornwall's economy on a stable basis, in case the holiday trade bubble burst. 'We should certainly consider seriously whether the holiday trade in Cornwall has now reached saturation point,' concluded the editors.

Although tourism was never a major topic in *New Cornwall*, it is interesting to read between the lines and see how differently an industry which is now seemingly regarded as sacrosanct in official circles was viewed by the 'nationalist' minority in the middle of the 20th century.

'What every Cornishman should know'

At various stages in its existence *New Cornwall* featured a number of influential series designed to help Cornishmen and Cornishwomen understand both Cornwall's position vis-à-vis the world and themselves. Although 'What every Cornishman should know' was itself a relative latecomer as a series, with No. 1 'The Arms of Cornwall' gracing the pages of the revamped magazine in January 1964, its largely unsigned or pseudonymous essays over the next five years on subjects such as 'Trelawny', 'Michael Joseph and the events of 1497', 'The Cornish Chough', 'Cornwall's Flag' and 'The origin of the name 'Cornwall'' – this latter by Charles Thomas – endeavoured, as one local newspaper put it, 'to ensure that its patriotic readers are well acquainted with the background and history of their fatherland'.[81]

The longest-running series by a long chalk was 'Cornish Societies' which saw the light of day early in 1957, largely as the result of a suggestion from a reader. The initial article on 'The Royal Institution of Cornwall' was followed over the years by eighteen or more on the aims and achievements of bodies as diverse as the Federation of Old Cornwall Societies, the Cornish Branch of the Celtic Congress, The Morrab Library, Mebyon Kernow and the Cornwall Brass Band Association. These were mainly unsigned and therefore, presumably, the work of the editors or, in some cases, a collaboration between them and a representative of the society in question.

On 15 October 1964 the Cornish writer Anne Treneer wrote to Richard to renew her subscription to *New Cornwall* and to thank him for his note on the artist Peter Lanyon in the current issue. 'You express what we all feel,' she continued. 'Won't you write at length when you have opportunity? It is so important that those who have personal knowledge should write.'[82] In point of fact, Lanyon had been the first subject of another influential series which had appeared six years earlier. It was penned by Elizabeth Trewren (i.e. Ann Jenkin) who, in an introductory note, explained that although the series would be concerned primarily with contemporary Cornish artists, the link between the traditional Cornish craftsmen and contemporary ones was close.[83] Other artists featured in this series included Jack Pender, John Wells, Robert Morton Nance and Mary Jewells.

In an editorial early in 1963, Ann and Richard Jenkin wrote of their intention to publish from time to time articles on some of the smaller peoples of Europe who were barely mentioned in the national press. Comparing the problems of these lands with those of Cornwall, they hoped to gain a greater insight into both.[84] Richard had attended the Congress of the Federal Union of European Nationalities (FUEN) in Cardiff in 1955 and clearly retained an interest in the organisation's work, publishing a report of its 15th Congress in the October 1965 issue of *New Cornwall*. For 'The Catalans', the first in the Peoples of Europe series, he used the recently-published 'Report on the Cultural Situation in Catalonia' by FUEN and the writings of Professor Guy Herand of the University of Strasbourg as the basis for his article, while acknowledging its expression of opinion as his own.[85] Subsequent portraits of 'The Frisians' and 'The Basques' were unacknowledged, while David Hamblyn wrote those about 'The Czechs' and 'The Slovaks' and Gunnar Nissen penned 'The Land of the Wends'.[86]

There were, of course, other subjects which featured regularly in the pages of *New Cornwall* and Richard – as Pasco Trevyhan – used to the full his first-hand knowledge of and extensive contacts with the wider Celtic world to keep his long-running 'Here and There' column fresh and current. Again, the Jenkins' central place in so many Cornish and Celtic organisations enabled them to bring their readers first-hand reports of the activities of, for instance, the Cornish Gorsedh and the Celtic Congress. While its editors' ability to keep abreast of developments both inside and outside Celtic Cornwall guaranteed that *New Cornwall*'s coverage was extremely wide-ranging, they could not have managed without a substantial input from the magazine's readership. '[T]he success of "New Cornwall" depends on you,' its new editors wrote in their second editorial in 1957[87] and the concept of the magazine as an open forum for debate and reader engagement was always at the heart of its philosophy. It is time, therefore, to look more closely at how *New Cornwall* was perceived and sometimes moulded by those readers.

'Gesture of faith, pennant of promise…': New Cornwall and its readers
'Hurrah, that NEW CORNWALL grows, increases! NEW CORNWALL! – Gesture of faith, pennant of promise aloft before our Cornish eyes and hearts and deeply ineradicable national memories! So much so, that scarcely is it too much to say – Cornwall can never be the same again…'[88] This was how John Legonna began his Easter 1964 letter of congratulations to the magazine's editors. Legonna, with fellow students who included Richard Jenkin, had formed a new patriotic organisation called The Young Cornwall Movement at Exeter College, Oxford either in the latter part of 1943 or early in 1944. Eighteen years later he would write of how 'thrilling [it was] to think that our small group at Oxford has produced so fine a Richard of Cornwall' and of how encouraged he was to find the old spirit taking new wings.[89] Although Legonna would not return to the place of his upbringing, in the sense of settling there, until 1967 and then quite possibly for health reasons, he clearly saw himself as being just as engagé in Cornwall as he was in Wales. He wrote to *New Cornwall* on a number of occasions, contributed a review or two, and in 'The Forerunners' made a plea for the contribution made to Cornwall by pioneers such as Edward Lhuyd, A.S.D. Smith (*Caradar*), Francis Cargeeg (*Tan Dyvarow*) and Robert Morton Nance (*Mordon*) to be recorded for posterity.[90] Legonna's brand of strident nationalism will not have appealed to every *New Cornwall* reader and does not sit easily alongside Richard Jenkin's measured philosophy. More representative, perhaps, of the readership was an anonymous correspondent who in 1961 wrote of the publication as warming his heart 'with its freshness and sincerity, its strongly pro-Celtic and pro-Cornish blend of culture, economics, news, book reviews, humour, local news and combined fight for language and freedom'.[91]

Items contained in a packet of material relating to *New Cornwall* in the

Jenkin family archive reveal that many of the forty-four subscribers to the first issue in October 1952 came from places as diverse as Wolverhampton, Canada, Pennsylvania, Hull, Chelsea, Wales, Scotland and Plymouth. Free copies were despatched to many libraries, museums, newspapers, Celtic societies and Cornish societies across Cornwall and well beyond. The Institut für Keltologie und Irlandkunde Univerität Würzburg took four copies, while Roderick Macleod of the Gaelic student magazine *An T-Oileanach* revealed that in 1965 there were issues in the Edinburgh University Nationalist Club. From the magazine's early days under the editorship of both Dick Gendall and Helena Charles, it published letters from correspondents in Germany, France, the United States and Canada, as well as from those in Cornwall and across Britain and Ireland. Not everyone, of course, agreed with everything that was published. Without a range of perspectives, there would have been no debate. The writer has already explored, for instance, the heat generated in July 1963 by Joan Evason's 'Is our Cornish really necessary?' Seven years earlier, out of the many letters welcoming the reappearance of *New Cornwall* at the end of 1956, four commented unfavourably on former editor Helena Charles' article 'Suez and Hungary' which criticised the 'gunboat diplomacy' of the ill-fated Franco-British seizure of the Suez Canal that October.

The magazine either found its way to – or, as is more likely, was sent to – organisations which were mentioned in its pages. In 1961, for instance, Francis James, Information Officer for the BBC West Region, wrote to Ann and Richard Jenkin disputing their contention in the April-May issue that the large amount of airtime being given to Cornish subjects just then was perhaps partly due to the BBC getting in first before the Pilkington Committee recommended local broadcasting stations. Any possible action by the Committee on Local Broadcasting, he argued, had nothing to do with the tour of Cornwall on the programme 'Tonight' which had happened quite fortuitously to coincide roughly with the opening of a new television studio in Plymouth to serve Devon and Cornwall.[92] That same number of the magazine contained two pieces by M.C.V. Stephens, one of which 'Dre Wedrow Kernewek (Through Cornish Spectacles)', gave his frank opinion on some of the things he had read in *New Cornwall* recently, criticizing 'both sides [Cornish and English] without partiality'.[93] Richard – as Pasco Trevyhan – replied robustly to what he saw as Mr Stephens' accusation of hypocrisy in *New Cornwall* castigating centralisation on the one hand, while suggesting a Planned Economy for Cornwall on the other. Defending his Economic Plan for Cornwall published some months earlier, Richard wrote:

> What does Mr Stephens want? He seems to be advocating an anarchist system in which no-one makes any rules. "Rugged independence of spirit" is fine emotional talk, but I was considering practical possibilities…
>
> A healthy economic system is as necessary to a country as good health to an individual. Neither can be attained or maintained by a policy of neglect. Planning of some sort is necessary and, as far as possible, planning for Cornwall should be in Cornish hands. Surely even individualistic Cornishmen can work together for the good of their country without falling into "the evils of centralisation and bureaucracy"! Advocating more interest in planning in Cornwall for Cornwall is the very reverse of "advocating more Anglicization of Cornwall".

He also rejected Mr Stephens' contention that he had referred slightingly to King Arthur. What he did despise was the prettification of the historical Arthur in the name of crass commercialism.[94]

A mention of just a few articles and the debate they occasioned will suffice to show that its editors' vision for *New Cornwall* was more than realized. The unsigned 'Why not a folk museum for Cornwall?' brought constructive replies from Charles Thomas, then Lecturer in Archaeology at Edinburgh University, and W.F. Dalton, Curator of Helston Museum.[95] The following year, the debate centred on Stephen Fuller's 'The Neglected Youth of Cornwall'. Two responses – those of Peter Pool and his future wife Audrey Humphris – were printed in *New Cornwall*, but as the article's author revealed in his rejoinder 'Sad News for the Neglected Youth of Cornwall', the topic had caused quite a stir, with several Cornish letters and one from Scotland agreeing with his views and two – those printed in *New Cornwall* – against. 'We are… extremely lucky in Cornwall,' he wrote in his introductory comments, 'in having a medium such as this magazine where serious matters like this can be discussed.'[96] That same edition contained a response from Clifton Pender, Chief Fishery Officer, Cornish Sea Fisheries District, to Richard's front-page article 'Has fishing a future?' which

Mr Pender described as 'very clearly and fairly written' before commenting on one or two points.[97]

Another subject about which many Cornish men and women were passionate and which was embraced by Mebyon Kernow in the 1960s was the need for a memorial to the Cornish martyr Michael Joseph An Gof. Following the publication in *New Cornwall*'s series 'What every Cornishman should know' of an article about the events of the 1497 uprising, an appeal by J.R.C. Finlayson in support of a memorial appeared in several subsequent editions. By the autumn of 1966, enough money had been raised by the Cornish Movement and the winter issue could describe at length how on Saturday 22 October St Keverne was the scene of 'a great assembly from all over Cornwall and beyond' for the unveiling of the memorial. Messages of support to the then secretary of Mebyon Kernow from A.L. Rowse and from Harri Webb on behalf of the National Executive of Plaid Cymru were also published.[98] The following month (March 1967), John Legonna wrote to provide a free translation of Webb's Welsh verses on the occasion and to express in his own inimitable way his feelings about their message which had, he felt, 'a touch of historicity about it':

> It is likely to have been one of the first, if not the very first, [message] of vibrant national spirit from Wales to Cornwall since Cai bade the Celtic troops, "Yna y cyfodes Cai ac y dywawd: pwy bynnag a fynno canlyn Arthur, bid heno yng Nghernyw gyda ef. Ac ar nis mynno, bid yn erbyn Arthur..." "Then Cai rose and said: Whoever would follow Arthur, let him tonight make for Cornwall. And who would not, let him be against Arthur..."[99]

The topic which appears to have given rise to more debate than any other in the history of *New Cornwall* was that of a flower which would be emblematic of Cornwall. This began in March 1964 when, writing as sole editor, Richard Jenkin asked in 'A National Flower for Cornwall?' for readers to submit suggestions, his own favourite candidate being the Cornish Heath (Erica Vagans), a true native species. One of the first to take up the challenge was Richard Gendall whose own 'A National Flower for Cornwall' presented the various merits and claims of five contenders, namely valerian, the crocus, the lily of the valley, furze and the Cornish Heath. His own preference was the latter, '[l]ogically by far the strongest claimant'. That August Richard devoted his editorial to the subject and three further opinions were published, with *Morgelyn* of Towednack conceding that she doubted much progress would be made in making a final choice, 'as no one will agree with anyone else'. Richard Gendall effectively closed the debate in the following issue, concluding that the Cornish Heath had won the day. 'It is heartening to see such a ready response from readers of NEW CORNWALL,' he continued, 'and from what has been said it really does look as though people by and large have already decided that this [the Cornish Heath] stands for Cornwall, which is the correct way to reach a decision of this kind.' A late-comer to the debate was Roy Jennings of St Ives who, in agreeing with the verdict, remembered discussing the matter with the late Robert Morton Nance who had said that he would like to see Erica Vagans adopted – as, indeed, it has been by the Cornish Gorsedh – as the national flower for Cornwall.[100]

Support for *New Cornwall* was, then, essentially positive and the fact that it looked forward and outward as well as backward ensured that the support was broad. Writing to Richard to renew his subscription in October 1967, Charles Causley praised the tone of the last issue he had received, presumably that summer's.[101] However, feedback was not, as we have already seen, always positive. On the magazine's tenth anniversary an unidentified local newspaper thought that it still took 'a rather gloomy view of things',[102] while early in 1964 another or possibly the same paper described it as 'sombre, foreboding, detached' as it pursued 'its dogged way towards a new Celtic dawn'. While appreciative of the new smarter appearance of the first issue of volume 12, it questioned whether, in an area which boasted a premier school of mines, it was necessary to, as it put it, lift from another journal what it saw as an outdated article on tin prospecting.[103] The article in question was from the September 1963 issue of *New Scientist* and is very general, but *New Cornwall* used material from other publications very rarely and if any criticism is due, it could be directed at the small typeface and clarity of the article, by comparison with the usually-clear text.

Of course, roneoing was a very crude method of reproduction and the criticism of Crantock-based C.L. Williams of Gold and Base Metal Mines of Nigeria Ltd. is only justified if *New Cornwall* is compared to a commercial publication, which it was not. However, as others thought the same as he did, it is only fair to air his criticism. He wrote to Richard on 17 July 1966, so the issue with which his letter was concerned was the spring one. Having been lent a copy by a fellow member of the Nigerian Cornish Association, he had no doubt that he would be very interested if he could read it. 'The standard of printing is appalling,' he continued, 'the map of Cornwall with Cornish place names, for instance, is almost completely illegible, a big disappointment to me as I feel strongly about this matter of place names in Newquay many of the good old Cornish names have been replaced by 'furrin' ones...' He would be very happy to subscribe to *New Cornwall*, even at an increased subscription rate, if it could be made readable. Despite his harsh criticism, he went on to wish Richard 'every success in producing a very interesting and useful periodical'.[104] Williams' criticism of the map provided to accompany Kenneth MacKinnon's article 'The Little that is Left' is certainly justified and it has to be said that the juxtaposition of a full-page printed advert for Denys Val Baker's relaunched *Cornish Review* and a page of *New Cornwall* does not do the latter any favours. But this has always been something of a quandary for magazine editors in Cornwall and elsewhere. Do you sacrifice content to style and presentation in order to generate advertising income? The challenge was greater in the Jenkins' day, of course, because roneo as a method could not compete in terms of quality with commercial printing. A number of Cornish magazines have lost their way over the years because they compromised or sacrificed the integrity of their content in the search for increased revenue and wider readerships. *New Cornwall* remained true to its ideals and put content and a discerning readership before style or, as is so often the case nowadays, lifestyle.

'The harvest is plenteous but the labourers few'
The May 1969 issue of *New Cornwall* contained a letter from Coweth Solabrys who, despite having in the past enjoyed reading the magazine, wondered if the need for it had passed. All the various Cornish societies, he or she argued, now had their own publications, with, for instance, *Newodhow an Orseth* updating bards of the Gorsedh; *Old Cornwall* catering for the Federation of Old Cornwall Societies; *Cornish Nation* for Mebyon Kernow; *An Lef Kernewek* for Cornish speakers; and *Celtic News* for the Celtic League. Both the *Cornish Magazine* and the *Cornish Review* were aimed at the general reader, although the former actu-

ally ceased publication later that year. 'All in all,' Coweth Solabrys concluded, 'I don't think *New Cornwall* has a market left to appeal to and is redundant.' Conceding that he or she had a point of view, Ann and Richard Jenkin pointed out in an editorial note appended to the letter that some of the publications mentioned were limited to members of a society and wondered how many Cornish people subscribed to or could afford to subscribe to all the publications listed. *New Cornwall* had always aimed to provide a wide view of the whole Cornish movement. Nevertheless, they would be very interested to have their readers' response to the views of Coweth Solabrys. If there was either large-scale agreement or a deafening silence, they would have to reconsider the position of *New Cornwall*, although they had not noticed any dropping off in subscriptions.[105] Nearly nine months passed before the next issue appeared, with the editors citing in their apology for the delay the fact that they were also reporters, sub-editors, typesetters, printers, staplers, distributors and business managers. Of five letters printed, four were responses to Coweth Solabrys. Geoffrey Procter felt that the need for *New Cornwall* was much greater than when it was first produced in 1957. Then it had been difficult to interest people in Cornwall's special needs and MK could count its membership in tens, not thousands. Never was there a greater need for the accurate information on mid twentieth-century Cornwall which *New Cornwall* had always supplied. He subscribed to the *Cornish Magazine*, the *Cornish Review* and *Cornish Nation*, but *New Cornwall*'s much longer continuous production was to him proof of the need for it. It had been born with the new spirit that had made itself felt in Cornwall in the 1950s and had presented and represented that spirit ever since. 'If *New Cornwall* should cease publication what becomes of that spirit?' he asked. For the late Ted Chapman *New Cornwall* was still the nearest thing Cornwall had to a nationalist publication. The growth of other publications, he argued, did nothing to make it redundant. On the contrary, in some ways they made *New Cornwall* even more necessary. D. Cowtan considered it indispensible, keeping him well informed about his chief interest professionally and personally, the Cornish language. Finally, John Legonna, in uncharacteristically plain language, felt Cornwall needed not fewer journals where she could be written about, but more.[106] Ironically, this endorsement by what was admittedly a handful of subscribers coincided with the announcement that henceforth the magazine would only appear as and when material was available and ready.

In many ways, the four issues which make up volume 17 of *New Cornwall* contain some of its most trenchant articles, with the final two numbers giving a tantalising glimpse of the direction it might have taken had it survived. In addition to the splendid editorial entitled 'Creeping Regionalisation', the penultimate number in the summer of 1972, for instance, contained the interesting 'Thoughts of a Bourgeois Ratepayer' in which the anonymous author expressed at some length his views on the introduction of comprehensive education throughout Cornwall – a move he summed up as not so much an educational reform, but an attempt at social engineering.[107] Given Richard's aversion to totalitarian regimes, his championing of individual freedom in such pieces as 'Freedom' and 'Compulsion', and his professional background in the teaching profession, it is safe to conclude that he was the 'Bourgeois Ratepayer' author of the article! A stinging response, in the form of a letter from 'Socialist Ratepayer, R[oyston].G[reen]. (Redruth)' was published in the very last issue of *New Cornwall*. 'Bourgeois Ratepayer's' immediate response and defence of his views rather gave the game away and was followed immediately by 'Thoughts of a Bourgeois Nationalist'. This dual criticism of socialism and exploration of the differences between socialist nationalists and non-socialist nationalists bears all the hallmarks of Richard Jenkin's political thinking. The concluding paragraph reads as follows:

> It is greatly to the credit of the Scottish National Party and Plaid Cymru that they are not socialist-controlled and put their countries before any party dogma. Co-operatives rather than nationalised bureaucracies are seen as the best answer to their nations' problems. In the same way, Mebyon Kernow includes members of many different political ideas but the interests of Cornwall over-ride any other consideration. I hope and believe that this will continue and unity will be maintained in the struggle for the proper recognition of the nationhood of Cornwall and its embodiment in local self-government for Cornwall.[108]

There would be no further numbers of *New Cornwall*. The Jenkin family archive contains the following letter from Richard Jenkin to subscribers, dated June 1976. It is a fitting, if poignant, epitaph to a fine publication. The 'renaissance of the Cornish nation in all its manifestations', of which *New Cornwall* was an integral part, would and does continue, and others will take up the challenge.

<u>New Cornwall</u>

FAREWELL

It is necessary to face hard facts and with this we suspend the publication of NEW CORNWALL sine die. It is a sad end to a venture which began in October 1952 and which the present Editors took over in December 1956.

There are two main reasons for the inability to continue. One is the ever-increasing postal charges and rising costs which mean that for the magazine to be economic, it would be necessary to charge a subscription which we feel the public would be unwilling to pay for a duplicated production. The other is even more overwhelming. For the last five volumes of issues, the editor has not only written a large part of the material, he has also typed each stencil; rolled off each page; collated all the sheets of each copy; inserted every staple; addressed and posted every envelope. This is no longer something which can be attempted in the limited spare time available for it. It has also resulted in longer and longer intervals between issues. This is not fair to our loyal and patient subscribers.

If, as seems unlikely at the moment, it ever becomes possible to resume publication, the present subscribers will be notified. The possibility is being considered of issuing from time to time pamphlets or booklets on Cornish topics. These will be priced to be non-loss-making. The amount remaining of your present subscription will be credited towards the cost of the first such booklets, or will be returned on request. A note at the bottom of this page will tell you how much of your current subscription remains to your credit.

The editors thank our [sic] subscribers for their interest, sustained over so many years of publication. To those who do not already take CORNISH NATION we would recommend that magazine as the nearest to NEW CORNWALL as it used to be.

May we all continue to serve Cornwall as best we can.

Richard G. Jenkin

Notes

1. *New Cornwall*, no. 1, October 1952.
2. Cutting from [*Sunday*] *Independent*, 15 March 1970, in Jenkin family archive. In future notes, all the cuttings referred to are in the Jenkin family archive.
3. *New Cornwall*, no. 12, September 1953.
4. *New Cornwall*, vol. 5, no. 1, December 1956-January 1957.
5. *New Cornwall*, no. 2, November 1952.
6. *New Cornwall*, vol. 2, no. 11, August 1954 and vol. 3, nos. 6-7 [i.e. 10-11], July-August 1955.
7. *New Cornwall*, vol. 2, no. 1, October 1953.
8. *New Cornwall*, vol. 2, no. 4, January 1954.
9. *New Cornwall*, vol. 5, no. 1, December 1956-January 1957.
10. *New Cornwall*, vol. 5, no. 2, February-March 1957.
11. Bernard Deacon, Dick Cole and Garry Tregidga, *Mebyon Kernow and Cornish Nationalism*, Cardiff: Welsh Academic Press, 2003, p. 34.
12. *New Cornwall*, vol. 5, no. 4, June-July 1957.
13. Unidentified newspaper cutting, dated 5 October 1964.
14. *New Cornwall*, vol. 12, no. 5, October-November 1964.
15. Undated *Cornish and Devon Post* cutting; issue of *New Cornwall* referred to is vol. 12, no. 2, March 1964.
16. Cited in *Mebyon Kernow and Cornish Nationalism*, p. 38.
17. *New Cornwall*, vol. 6, no. 1, December 1957-January 1958.
18. *New Cornwall*, vol. 6, no. 2, February-March 1958.
19. *New Cornwall*, vol. 6, no. 4, June-July 1958.
20. Reproduced using a Roneo duplicating machine.
21. Unidentified newspaper cutting, dated 11 September 1958.
22. Unidentified newspaper cutting, dated 5 February 1959.
23. Cutting from [*Western?*] *Independent*, 10 May 1959.
24. *New Cornwall*, vol. 8, no. 2, February-March 1960.
25. *New Cornwall*, vol. 9, no. 7, December 1961-January 1962.
26. *New Cornwall*, vol. 8, no. 4, June-July 1960.
27. *New Cornwall*, vol. 11, no. 1, January 1963.
28. Cutting from *Cornish Times*, 25 [?] December 1959.
29. Cutting from *Western Morning News*, 13 September 1961.
30. Undated cutting from *Cornish and Devon Post*; issue of *New Cornwall* referred to is vol. 10, no. 4, July 1962.
31. Undated cutting from *Cornish and Devon Post*; issue of *New Cornwall* referred to is vol. 11, no. 1, January 1963.
32. Undated cutting from *Cornish and Devon Post*; issue of *New Cornwall* referred to is vol. 9, no. 5, September 1961.
33. 'Dasserghyn!', *New Cornwall*, vol. 17, no. 1, Winter 1970-1971.
34. *New Cornwall*, vol. 15, no. 1, May 1967.
35. Cutting from *Cornish and Devon Post*, 1 February 1964.
36. See Derek Williams, 'John Legonna 1918-1978', *An Baner Kernewek/The Cornish Banner*, no. 133, August 2008, pp. 12-16.
37. *New Cornwall*, vol. 12, no. 3, May-June 1964.
38. Ibid.
39. *New Cornwall*, vol. 12, no. 4, August 1964.
40. *New Cornwall*, vol. 15, no. 1, May 1967.
41. *New Cornwall*, vol. 17, no. 1, Winter 1970-1971.

42   *New Cornwall*, vol. 17, no. 4, Summer[-Autumn] 1973.
43   'The Common Market', *New Cornwall*, vol. 10, no. 6, November 1962.
44   *New Cornwall*, vol. 5, no. 3, April-May 1957.
45   *New Cornwall*, vol. 6, no. 1, December 1957-January 1958.
46   *New Cornwall*, vol. 7, no. 1, December 1958-January 1959.
47   *New Cornwall*, vol. 7, no. 4, June-July 1959.
48   *New Cornwall*, vol. 8, no. 3, April-May 1960.
49   Ibid.
50   Undated cutting from *Cornish and Devon Post*; issue of *New Cornwall* referred to is vol. 9, no. 7 [i.e. vol. 10, no. 1], December 1961-January 1962.
51   Unidentified and undated cutting.
52   *New Cornwall*, vol. 8, no. 5, August-September 1960.
53   *New Cornwall*, vol. 9, no. 2, February-March 1961.
54   *New Cornwall*, vol. 17, no. 4, Summer[-Autumn] 1973.
55   Letter to Richard Jenkin, 30 December 1973, Jenkin family archive.
56   Letter dated 4 February 1974, Jenkin family archive.
57   Harri Webb, 'From Across the Severn Sea: a View of Cornwall', *New Cornwall*, vol. 12, no. 2, March 1964.
58   'Regionalism and Cornwall', *New Cornwall*, vol. 12, no. 5, October-November 1964.
59   *New Cornwall*, vol. 16, no. 4, January-February 1970.
60   *New Cornwall*, vol. 17, no. 3, Summer 1972.
61   Letter from John Fleet to Richard Jenkin, 28 August 1972, Jenkin family archive.
62   *New Cornwall*, vol. 13 (1965), no. 2.
63   *New Cornwall*, vol. 16, no. 2, October-November 1968.
64   *New Cornwall*, vol. 6, no. 2, February-March 1958. Interestingly, Thurstan C. Peter's *History of Cornwall for Schools* had appeared in 1907, three years after Cornwall was accepted as a Celtic nation by the fledgling Celtic Congress.
65   *New Cornwall*, vol. 17, no. 2, Autumn 1971.
66   *New Cornwall*, vol. 11, no. 1, January 1963.
67   *New Cornwall*, vol. 11, no. 2, March 1963.
68   *New Cornwall*, vol. 11, no. 6, November 1963.
69   Ibid.
70   *New Cornwall*, vol. 12, no. 3, May-June 1964.
71   These five articles appeared respectively in *New Cornwall*, vol. 8, no. 1, December 1959-January 1960; vol. 9, no. 2, February-March 1961; vol. 14, no. 1, Spring 1966; vol. 16, no. 1, June 1968; vol. 17, no. 3, Summer 1972.
72   *New Cornwall*, vol. 6, no. 6, October-November 1958; vol. 8, no. 2, February-March 1960.
73   *New Cornwall*, vol. 11, no. 4, July 1963.
74   *New Cornwall*, vol. 11, no. 5, September 1963.
75   *New Cornwall*, vol. 11, no. 6, November 1963.
76   *New Cornwall*, vol. 13 (1965), no. 2.
77   *New Cornwall*, vol. 17, no. 1, Winter 1970-1971.
78   *New Cornwall*, vol. 5, no. 5, August-September 1957.
79   *New Cornwall*, vol. 7, no. 4, June-July 1959.
80   *New Cornwall*, vol. 7, no. 6, October-November 1959.
81   Undated cutting from *Cornish and Devon Post*; issue of *New Cornwall* referred to is vol. 13, no. 5, November 1965.
82   Letter in an envelope relating to *New Cornwall*, Jenkin family archive.

83 *New Cornwall*, vol. 6, no. 6, October-November 1958.
84 *New Cornwall*, vol. 11, no. 1, February-March 1963.
85 *New Cornwall*, vol. 13 (1965), no. 2.
86 *New Cornwall*, vol. 13 (1965), no. 3; vol. 14, nos. 2 and 3, Summer 1966; vol. 13 (1965), no. 4, October; vol. 13, no. 5, November 1965; vol. 15, no. 1, May 1967.
87 *New Cornwall*, vol. 5, no. 2, February-March 1957.
88 *New Cornwall*, vol. 12, no. 3, May-June 1964.
89 Letter to Richard Jenkin from London, 7 August 1961, Jenkin family archive.
90 *New Cornwall*, vol. 15, no. 4, March 1968.
91 *New Cornwall*, vol. 9, no. 3, April-May 1961.
92 *New Cornwall*, vol. 9, no. 4, July 1961.
93 Ibid.
94 'Hep Gwedrow vyth-oll (No Glasses at All)', *New Cornwall*, vol. 9, no. 5, September 1961.
95 *New Cornwall*, vol. 9, nos. 5 and 6, September and November 1961.
96 *New Cornwall*, vol. 9, no. 7 [i.e. vol. 10, no. 1], December 1961-January 1962; vol. 10, nos. 2 and 3, March and April-May, 1962.
97 *New Cornwall*, vol. 10, no. 3, April-May 1962.
98 *New Cornwall*, vol. 14, nos. 4 and 5, Winter 1966.
99 *New Cornwall*, vol. 14, no. 6, March 1967.
100 *New Cornwall*, vol. 12, nos. 2, 3, 4, 5 and 6, March, May-June, August, October-November, and 31 December 1964.
101 Letter dated 2 October 1967 in an envelope relating to *New Cornwall*, Jenkin family archive.
102 Unidentified and undated cutting; issue of *New Cornwall* referred to is vol. 10, no. 6, November 1962.
103 Unidentified cutting dated 28 January 1964.
104 Letter dated 17 July 1966, Jenkin family archive.
105 *New Cornwall*, vol. 16, no. 3, May 1969.
106 *New Cornwall*, vol. 16, no. 4, January-February 1970.
107 *New Cornwall*, vol. 17, no. 3, Summer 1972.
108 *New Cornwall*, vol. 17, no. 4, Summer[-Autumn] 1973.'Breathing the fire of Cornish patriotism': *New Cornwall*.

Election impressions

Richard G. Jenkin

During the General Election Campaign I had the opportunity of meeting many hundreds of ordinary Cornish people on their own doorsteps and discussing with them Cornwall's problems. My main impression is of the politeness and sympathy with which I was received. There were very few unpleasant characters to be found.

Everywhere, and among people of all political opinions, there was the feeling that Cornwall had been badly neglected. There were two main issues which caused concern to most people. Firstly, the lack of opportunities and the general low level of wages in Cornwall which mean the continued emigration of many of our young people. Secondly, entry into the Common Market and the problems it will bring to our housewives and farmers. Most had managed to convince themselves that the parties they supported would eventually recoil from this step in spite of public pledges.

There was also general resentment about Plymouth's plans for expansion at the expense of Cornwall. This is evidence that more and more people have come to think in terms of Cornwall and their own Cornishness. This growing awareness of Cornish individuality and nationhood, which has developed during the last twenty years, had its effect on the other candidates who had to give greater emphasis in their campaigns to Cornwall's needs and less to their parties' general policies. In many instances they were forced to defend Cornish interests against their own party lines.

In the end we won just under 1,000 votes – 2% of those who voted. It must be

PUT CORNWALL FIRST

PUBLIC MEETING

AT ZODIAC BINGO HALL, REDRUTH

7.30 pm TUESDAY 9th JUNE 1970

COME AND MEET RICHARD JENKIN YOUR M.K. CANDIDATE

VOTE MEBYON KERNOW FOR A CORNISH POLICY FOR CORNWALL.

Unemployment in Cornwall is twice the average for Britain and wages are amongst the lowest in Britain. This situation has continued under successive governments and will continue as long as they carry on with their present policies. The people of Cornwall need fresh consideration of their problems and therefore we intend to bring home to Parliament that the people of Cornwall are determined to see new policies employed.

Published by L. Truran, Trewolsta, Trewirgie, Redruth.

M.K. does not promise you any flyabouts, carry ons, let gos, better tomorrows, or all our yesterdays. We offer a man who will put Cornwall before Party.

Mebyon Kernow flyer for a meeting during the 1970 General Election

remembered that all these were voting Mebyon Kernow for the first time in a Parliamentary election and presumably had supported other candidates in the past. If we had been able to make more personal visits the figure would have been much higher.

Incidental gains in the election campaign were that every household in Falmouth-Camborne had the opportunity to learn more accurately what Mebyon Kernow stands for; that Mebyon Kernow has shown it is capable of mounting an election campaign; and that Mebyon Kernow policy appeared daily in the local press. Here we must thank the local daily and weekly papers which gave Mebyon Kernow equal space with the other candidates in the constituency. Of course, the English papers, radio and TV were denied us. The major parties weight the scales against any other contenders.

We were fortunate in having devoted helpers who gave up time and money for the sake of Cornwall. I should like to thank my agent, Leonard Truran, and all those who addressed envelopes, canvassed, put up posters, gave the use of their cars, contributed to the funds and helped in any way with our campaign.

This first campaign is only a beginning and we must use it as a stepping stone to greater efforts and achievements. With experience gained, more workers and more organization, we can greatly improve our position at the next election – which may be sooner than people expect now. We must start now to build up the machinery and finances for the next time when we can again put Cornwall's case before the electorate with even greater impact.

[*Cornish Nation*, vol. 2 no. 1, September 1970]

Vote Mebyon Kernow, vote Jenkin

Dick Cole

Richard Jenkin was, without question, Mebyon Kernow's most consistent and most dedicated champion, serving at the heart of the party for over fifty years.[1]

A founder member of Mebyon Kernow, Richard played a leading role in building the party into a formidable force in the 1960s and 1970s. He became MK's first General Election candidate in 1970 when he contested Falmouth-Camborne, and polled over 10,000 votes as MK's candidate for the European Parliament in 1979.

Richard rose to become Chairman of the organisation between 1973 and 1983, but also served in a myriad of roles at all levels in MK. He served as Vice-Chairman between 1968 and 1973 and again after 1983, as well as the organiser of Helston and District branch and the Chairman of the Falmouth-Camborne constituency party. He even continued as a member of the MK National Executive until the early 1990s.

He remained true to Mebyon Kernow through both good times and bad, always working hard for the cause of greater Cornish self-government, and in 1998 was rightly honoured with the award of Life Presidency of the party.

Growing up in Manchester, the son of an exiled Cornishman, Richard Jenkin was determined to explore his Cornish identity from an early age. As a teenager, he made frequent visits to the city's Central Library to 'look at anything about Cornwall and Cornish.'[2] While this was an extremely isolated introduction to his Cornishness, when he enrolled in Oxford University for a twelve month period in 1943, in advance of joining the army, he met a number of individuals who shared his interests in Cornwall.

Indeed, Richard Jenkin and others including John Legonna, David Balhatchet and Mary Foss formed the short-lived Young Cornwall movement, which was based on Guiseppe Mazzini's Young Italy. A precursor to Mebyon Kernow, the movement focussed both on cultural issues and the 'political stances' it could take on the problems facing Cornwall. The organisation also accepted the goal of self-government.[3]

Following his military service between 1944 and 1948 in Egypt, Greece, Iraq and Palestine, Richard's family returned to Cornwall, though he himself spent most of the next four years at the universities of Manchester and Exeter. Nevertheless, it was in this immediate post-war period that a number of Cornish patriots came together to explore building an embryonic nationalist movement, with Richard Jenkin at the heart of the discussions.

The major catalyst was the 1950 Celtic Congress, held in Truro at the Royal Institution of Cornwall. The event brought together a range of like-minded individuals, many of whom took part in a Cornish language performance of *Bewnans Meriasek* at the Congress. Richard Jenkin himself recalled how refreshing it was to be able to 'meet all of the leading figures of the Cornish movement of the time... some who became leading figures later on, and people from other Celtic countries.'[4] After the Congress, a series of meetings was held which led directly to the founding of Mebyon Kernow, with Plaid Cymru's Professor Ambrose Bebb providing considerable encouragement and guidance from Wales.

The formal launch of Mebyon Kernow took place at Oates' Temperance Hotel in Redruth on Saturday 6 January 1951. Thirteen people were in attendance at the meeting, including Richard and his future wife Ann Trevenen. The names of eleven of the participants are known from the minutes, as well as the names of the six individuals who sent apologies.[5] This meeting certainly brought together an impressive group of individuals from the Cornish revivalist movement, four of whom later became Grand Bards of the Cornish Gorsedh. The group included Helena Charles (Chairman), Lambert Truran (Secretary), George Pawley White (Treasurer and future Grand Bard), E. G. Retallack Hooper (future Grand Bard) and his wife Bertha who ran their own Cornish language school, Charles Thomas who became a Professor of Archaeology and the first Director of the Institute of Cornish Studies, and talented craftsman Francis Cargeeg.

This historic meeting agreed seven core aims for MK, which included 'to study local conditions and attempt to remedy any that may be prejudicial to the best interests of Cornwall by the creation of public opinion or other appropriate means,' support for the Cornish language, the encouragement of the study of Cornish history from a Cornish point of view, and 'by self-knowledge, to further the acceptance of the idea of the Celtic character of Cornwall, one of the six Celtic nations'.[6]

Although ostensibly a cultural movement at this point, it was obvious that members of the new organisation were also committed to political reforms. In September 1951, the aims were modified to include 'to further the acceptance of the Celtic character of Cornwall and its right to self-government in domestic affairs in a Federated United Kingdom'.[7] When he marked the 25th anniversary of the founding of MK, Richard himself recalled that constitutional change was at the heart of the new movement:

> Those of us who were there met in a spirit of endeavour – nothing less than the re-awakening of the whole Cornish nation to its continuing identity and the need for constitutional change to safeguard its future existence.[8]

For the first ten years, progress was relatively slow. Under the leadership of the mercurial Helena Charles (1951-1956), there was frequent discord but, following her resignation, Major Cecil Beer (1957-1960) oversaw a period described by Richard Jenkin as a time of 'quiet but steady' growth.[9]

Richard Jenkin's role in these very early years was relatively limited, because he was not resident in Cornwall, teaching at schools in Devon and South Wales,[10] though he attended several Inter-Celtic Youth Camps at Pantyfedwen, arranged by the Urdd, in the 1950s.[11] His main contribution was, from 1957 onwards, to edit *New Cornwall* with the support of his wife Ann, which evolved from being an 'MK magazine' into something geared to the serve the whole Cornish movement.[12]

In February 1960 Cecil Beer handed over the chairmanship of Mebyon

Kernow to Robert Dunstone. At this time, MK was still a small force but importantly it had survived its formative years and was well positioned to grow and enhance its influence into the 1960s. It is also telling that it was Richard Jenkin, once again resident in Cornwall from January 1960, who was a driving force behind moves to ensure that MK members were more proactive and met more regularly. At the 1960 AGM, he was recorded as proposing that the main meetings of the organisation 'be held every half-year instead of once a year only',[13] and then at the 1962 AGM he suggested that meetings be held 'quarterly instead of half-yearly'.[14]

These meetings considered a range of issues including the Cornish fishing industry, tin mining, changes to 'planning regions', but there was still a significant focus on cultural concerns with a large chunk of business taken up with 'discussion of calendars, Christmas cards, serviettes, Cornish language classes and proposals for things like the Cornish kilt'.[15]

Writing in 1965, Richard and Ann Jenkin argued that the emergence of Mebyon Kernow 'had been one of the most promising signs that Cornwall will continue to exist as a Celtic country',[16] while MK's campaigning style under Robert Dunstone, often described as continued 'patient, persistent, and polite lobbying',[17] led to a growing confidence within the movement and inspired a greater willingness to lead public campaigns. MK was prominent in opposition to the closure of railway branch lines which led to the formation of the Cornwall Transport Committee, demanding an integrated transport system for Cornwall. Mebyon Kernow also led calls for the setting up of a Cornish university.[18]

A range of external factors also galvanised the growing confidence within MK. These included the widespread opposition to the amalgamation of the Cornish police force with that of Devon, and Overspill – the attempt by the Greater London Council to ease overcrowding in the English capital by relocating thousands of Londoners into Cornwall through town development schemes in Bodmin, Launceston, Liskeard and the Camborne-Redruth area. Mebyon Kernow led the fight against Overspill, which helped to foster a rapid expansion in the size of the Party and its influence, and this coincided with the first wave of concentrated of electoral activity from 1965 to 1970.[19]

Although still a pressure group that did not exclude members of the Conservative, Liberal or Labour parties from being members, Mebyon Kernow started putting forward official Mebyon Kernow candidates. There were a number of successes with councillors returned in Hayle, Illogan, Liskeard, Padstow and Penzance, while in April 1967 Colin Murley became MK's first official councillor on Cornwall County Council at St Day and Lanner when he narrowly defeated Ken Stead, a well known local Liberal who had consistently supported Overspill talks.

This growing self-belief also manifested itself in the launch of a regular magazine *Cornish Nation*,[20] and the publication in September 1968 of the pamphlet *What Cornishmen Can Do*. As noted in *Mebyon Kernow and Cornish Nationalism*:

> It was the most comprehensive manifesto for Cornwall produced to date. Its proposals included some long standing MK grievances but also anticipated much of what has since become mainstream thinking. In *What Cornishmen Can Do* MK called for 'real' development based on Cornwall's natural resources, together with secondary industries that utilised those resources and took advantage of the 'technical genius' of the Cornish people. Other proposals included more emphasis on food processing, support for small farmers, the creation of a University of Cornwall, quality tourism with greater overseas marketing and the expansion of renewable energy through the construction of tidal barrages.[21]

There was a clear intensification of MK activity, with Richard Jenkin also edging himself towards a much more prominent leadership role. He made numerous presentations to a wide range of bodies in order to promote the organisation and in 1967, for example, spoke to St Ives Rotary Club about the 'movement's strong opposition to regional development which would include Cornwall in a West of England area administered from as far away as Bristol.'[22] At the 1968 Annual General Meeting, Len Truran was elected Chairman, with Richard Jenkin as his Vice-Chairman,[23] an enduring partnership that would last until 1980.

This period of significant progress followed the by-election successes of Gwynfor Evans[24] and Winnie Ewing, who respectively won Carmarthen for Plaid Cymru in 1966 and Hamilton for the SNP in 1967, and MK members decided to press ahead with preparations to contest the next General Election.

The National Executive Committee was instructed to prepare a list of prospective candidates. Richard was approved as a prospective parliamentary candidate in 1968[25] and, later in the year, he was chosen to contest the Falmouth-Camborne constituency.

It was developments such as these which offered greater credibility to the movement and the non-political *Cornish Review* even pondered:

> Along with its bigger brothers in Wales and Scotland, Mebyon Kernow has recently received wider support than hitherto. Wales has already returned the first Welsh Nationalist MP, and Scotland might well do likewise – is it too much to envisage that one day Cornwall's own party might achieve a similar success? Without wishing to take sides in an age-old controversy, the *Cornish Review* feels that no harm, and, indeed a great deal of good, would surely be done by having someone with a firm Cornish background up at Westminster to speak, with Cornish knowledge, for Cornish interests. After all, which of our 'Cornish' MPs is a native of the county?[26]

Writing in *Cornish Nation*, Richard set out the importance of his parliamentary campaign:

> I am greatly honoured that I have been chosen to be the one to carry Mebyon Kernow's fight for Cornwall into the parliamentary field. Cornwall needs a voice at Westminster, a voice that will speak for Cornwall alone and will not be compromised by suspicions of serving London party politics. Almost daily Cornwall suffers new blows caused by ignorance and apathy in Whitehall about her problems and needs. Cornwall must speak up for herself.
>
> Even now plans are being made to alienate Cornish territory: to subject her to a distant regional authority: to strip powers from the lesser Cornish authorities. We cannot allow any part of our historic Cornish land to be stolen, nor shall we find any advantage in dealing with London through Bristol or elsewhere.[27]

But there was significant discord within Mebyon Kernow at this time and in July 1969 several members who were unhappy that MK was not being transformed into a political nationalist party, formed the Cornish National Party. The dissidents claimed that MK's broad and varied membership held 'every imaginable view from extreme nationalism to the exact opposite' and that 'it has proved impossible to agree on a consistent, workable policy of nationalism'.[28] The dissidents argued that they could be members of both the CNP, a political party, and Mebyon Kernow, which they considered to be a cross-party pressure group. However the wider organisation did not agree and sixteen prominent members within the movement were expelled.[29]

Richard remained loyal to Mebyon Kernow, its growth and more gradual evolution into an overtly political organisation. In the 1970 General Election, he fought an energetic campaign on a platform of 'internal self-government' and the proposals outlined in the *What Cornishmen Can Do* pamphlet. His election leaflet hit out at the Government's 'ignorance of conditions in Cornwall' and its desire to 'centralise all power of decision in London so that even a zebra crossing cannot be put in Falmouth without the special permission of the Ministry in Whitehall'.[30]

He presented a total of eight key policies:[31]

1. Industrial development that will encourage factories giving work to Cornishmen at wages equal to those in other parts of Britain.
2. Improved communications with special emphasis on the railway and the A30 main road.
3. A taxation policy to encourage mining.
4. A farming policy to support our small farmers.
5. No entry into the Common Market under present conditions.
6. Development of all levels of education in Cornwall, with the eventual provision of a university.
7. No transfer of any part of Cornwall to non-Cornish authorities.
8. Greater powers within Cornwall to decide and carry out policies of internal Cornish affairs.

Richard managed a total of 960 votes, or 2% of the total, and although MK achieved fewer votes than had been hoped for, party members put a brave face on the results. Comparisons were made with the result achieved by Plaid

Cymru's first foray into Westminster politics in 1929 and, according to Len Truran, the MK campaign meant that 'We had an enormous effect on the election in Cornwall. We suddenly had 15 candidates speaking like Cornishmen.'[32]

The formation of the CNP just a few months before the 1970 General Election had in Richard's own words acted as a 'distraction' which 'prevented the campaign from being as effective as it might have been'.[33] It was also the case that he was up against prominent Liberal John Davey and Conservative David Mudd, who were both actually members of MK.

There was certainly a sense of uncertainty within the movement that followed the split of 1969 and the result in the General Election of 1970.[34] MK's research and lobbying group Cowethas Flamank, set up in the early part of 1970 by John Fleet, summarised the situation as 'an unhappy malaise' and a 'general lack of confidence,'[35] which partly helps to explain the lack of explicit electoral activity in the early 1970s.

In spite of this, Mebyon Kernow was a growing organisation. By 1969, the *Western Morning News* was reporting that the Falmouth Branch had 'coming on for 1,000 members' with 'hundreds more in the Camborne, Redruth and St Day branches,' and that there was a 'militant branch in Hayle'.[36] By 1971, MK was claiming that it had over 3,000 members[37] and a promotional leaflet from this time lists the reports produced by MK on a wide range of topics including railways and an integrated transport policy, a university for Cornwall, the Cornish fishing industry, broadcasting, education, local government reform and mining development and taxation.[38] Mebyon Kernow members were also increasingly active in numerous campaigns, which ranged from opposition to Concorde booms to objections to the South West Economic Planning Council's economic region, while speaking out against the imposition of Plymouth (PL) and Exeter (EX) postcodes on mid and east Cornwall.

One priority for MK in the early 1970s was the Crowther (later Kilbrandon) Commission, which had been set up to take evidence about the case for devolution, following the progress made by Plaid Cymru and the SNP. In May 1971, Richard Jenkin was part of the MK delegation which gave evidence to this Commission and demanded Cornish self-government. It has been recorded that they were listened to with 'polite disdain', but at least placed on record the Cornish case in this major review of constitutional arrangements.[39]

Richard was elected Chairman of Mebyon Kernow at its 1973 Annual General Meeting, with Len Truran taking on the role of National Secretary,[40] and Richard was soon to the forefront in condemning the Kilbrandon Report. While the report did acknowledge the 'special status of Cornwall', Mebyon Kernow were extremely aggrieved that the Commission did not go far enough. In a statement on behalf of the party, Richard Jenkin said:

> Mebyon Kernow maintains that the survival of a Cornish Cornwall requires, as the minimum, the establishment of internal self-government similar to that enjoyed by the Isle of Man and now recommended for Scotland and Wales ... Cornwall must not become part of any English region ... for Cornwall, government from Bristol or Exeter is no improvement on government from Whitehall.[41]

In early 1974, the Prime Minister Ted Heath called a snap election, which once again brought MK's uncertainty about its electoral strategy into sharp focus. MK took the decision that there was inadequate time to organise a proper campaign in the Falmouth-Camborne constituency, as they had originally planned, though in the Truro constituency James Whetter went forward as an official MK candidate. And when a second General Election was called for October 1974, MK again failed to contest Falmouth-Camborne, preferring to openly support an Independent Liberal candidate.[42]

Throughout 1974, Richard Jenkin also found himself having to deal with increased disagreements within MK and a worsening public perception of the party, caused in part by its perceived views on Irish republicanism. *Cornish Nation*, edited by James Whetter, was becoming increasingly strident and there was growing concern about the sympathetic coverage of the activities of Sinn Fein. Problems came to a head when the magazine published a photo of a dead Irish hunger striker, Michael Gaughan, describing him as a 'Celtic hero'.[43] This was picked up by the media and further publicised during a period of intense concern about IRA bomb attacks on the British mainland, which triggered a press statement from senior MK officers, distancing themselves from 'the extreme views' expressed in the magazine, and apologising for any offence caused.

These disagreements led directly to James Whetter challenging Richard

Jenkin's leadership of MK. At the May 1975 AGM, James Whetter failed to secure the Chairmanship of the party, although it has been reported that the 'margin of victory was small'.[44] James Whetter soon after resigned from MK to form the Cornish Nationalist Party, claiming that 'MK was not equipped to become a positive nationalist movement'.[45] Whetter also declared the CNP would look to an all-embracing electoral strategy, but its outlook was otherwise almost indistinguishable from that of MK.

In hindsight, it appears that the 1975 split and associated disputes hastened the increased politicisation of Mebyon Kernow under the leadership of Richard Jenkin, which was assisted by an influx of a younger generation of activists into the party. Richard Jenkin had already made, in March 1975, a statement that Mebyon Kernow hoped to contest every General Election seat in Cornwall and, to do this, the party set out to form a series of constituency associations. Writing in *Cornish Nation* after his re-election as MK Chairman in 1975, Richard Jenkin linked himself wholeheartedly with an improved electoral strategy:

> But more important than what we have achieved is what still needs to be achieved. Mebyon Kernow must continue to develop and grow into an effective political means of defending Cornwall's nationhood. To retreat from this into a pressure group within the general Cornish movement would be a regression – a betrayal of the spirit in which Mebyon Kernow was [46]

By February 1976, Len Truran had been duly adopted as prospective parliamentary candidate for the St Ives constituency and by April Richard himself had been selected as the candidate for Falmouth-Camborne. A year later, Richard Jenkin resigned as candidate in Falmouth-Camborne to concentrate on his leadership role within the party so that Len Truran could move over to contest the Falmouth-Camborne constituency, with Colin Murley duly adopted in his stead at St Ives.[47]

The ambiguous political position of MK was further clarified at the 1976 Spring Conference, when a resolution was carried to exclude members of other parties, and MK members once again started to contest local elections as official MK candidates. Six members stood for the new district councils in 1976, with Neil Plummer and Roger Holmes winning Stithians and Liskeard respectively,

Mebyon Kernow leaflet for the European Assembly Elections, 7 June 1979

and in 1977 seven candidates stood for Cornwall County Council.

With three parliamentary candidates in place well in advance of the actual election, Mebyon Kernow was actively raising its profile. MK showed its support for the Cornish fishing industry by holding rallies at Penzance and Falmouth, calling for a 50 mile exclusion zone for Cornish boats, and other campaigns included opposition to government policies which were driving up unemployment locally, and opposition to the possibility of nuclear dumping in Cornwall. MK members also continued to focus on Cornwall's distinctive identity by organising the first St Piran's march at Truro.

In 1979, over 4,000 people voted for Mebyon Kernow in the General Election.[48] It has been noted that 'although activists were disappointed it was not higher, the St Ives result was higher in percentage terms than Plaid Cymru's performance in 14 of the 36 Welsh constituencies, the Falmouth-Camborne result higher than 12'.[49] In the local elections, MK's nineteen district council candidates polled in excess of 10,000 votes with both Neil Plummer and Roger Holmes re-elected. Numerous members were also elected to their local parish councils.[50]

But the election highlight for MK in 1979 was the candidacy of Richard Jenkin for the combined Cornwall and Plymouth constituency in the European Parliament. Ironically, there was considerable prevarication, spread over a number of Executive meetings, as to whether MK should contest the seat. One resolution to leave the matter on the table was only rejected on Richard Jenkin's casting vote as Chairman, and it wasn't until March 1979 that it was agreed to stand Richard Jenkin as MK's Euro-election candidate.[51]

Mebyon Kernow had consistently demanded European representation that recognised Cornwall as a single unit, but the eventual placing of Plymouth in a cross-Tamar constituency allowed MK to focus significant attention on border-blurring and to argue for a Cornish Constituency, with the strap-line 'Campaign for Cornish Recognition'. Richard was described on his election material as 'A Voice for Cornwall in Europe', and his election leaflet stated:

> Don't you think that Cornwall should have its own representative in the European Parliament? Most people in Cornwall do, yet Cornish opinion was ignored by the Government. It included Plymouth in the constituency even though it was allowed by the EEC to vary the numbers in a constituency for geographical reasons. It has done so in Northern Ireland, also, the number of voters per member is about the same as the number of voters in Cornwall.
>
> Even the local Liberal, Labour and Conservative associations supported a Cornish constituency but now their party leaders have accepted the boundaries and have chosen non-Cornish candidates whose interests are in Plymouth or London. The only way to get reconsideration of the constituency is to have a massive vote for a candidate pledged to keep campaigning for recognition of Cornwall's rights, as I will do.[52]

Following on from the enormous amount of campaigning undertaken by MK members in the late 1970s – and with less pressure to vote tactically – 10,205 people voted for Richard Jenkin, which equated to 'as much as 9 or 10 per cent of the Cornish vote'.[53]

It was certainly an outstanding result for MK at that time. Colin Murley, who served as election agent, recalls how Richard Jenkin was the 'natural' candidate, who gave the campaign 'a sense of unity and clear purpose', and that he was the driving force that allowed the short campaign to achieve such a positive result.

According to Colin, 'Richard brought a sense of we're in this together for Cornwall... there were no disputes, everybody wanted to do something and be in on the act... the message was simple, if you're Cornish, be Cornish and vote Jenkin'.[54]

The editorial of the *Cornish Nation* which followed the election was certainly upbeat:

> ... 1979 has proved to be the year when Cornwall began to awake and assert its nationhood; a year of remarkable significance, rooted not in defeat, nor in despair, but in a superb start to MK's first serious attempt to achieve multi-level representation from Parish Councils to the European Parliament.[55]

The view was positive and forward-looking:

> 10,000 Euro-votes and 10,000 District Council votes, in addition to the Parliamentary and Parish Council votes, were but the tip of an iceberg because for every voter who found the conviction and self-confidence to vote the MK way, there were several more who almost voted for us but whose nerve failed at the last moment as they conformed to the Lib-Lab-Con brainwash that has been beamed at us since cradle days.[56]

Sadly for MK, there were soon disagreements concerning demands for 'an up-to-date constitution, a full investigation of MK's financial set-up, better communications within MK, a policy document, and an investigation into the feasibility of having a headquarters,[57] as well as the role of certain individuals. This meant that the modest but genuine electoral progress made in 1979 was not built upon, and the push for a more decentralised organisational structure became mired in growing personal disputes.

Tensions came to a head at the 1979 AGM which was held in Truro in October. Pedyr Prior challenged Len Truran for the post of National Secretary, and although Len Truran won the vote by 53 votes to 40,[58] it was undoubtedly a 'pyrrhic victory' for him, with many members struggling to find common ground with each other.[59]

These personal disputes were also compounded by ongoing debates about policy. Richard Jenkin had always taken the view that Mebyon Kernow should not restrict its appeal in any way and once told an MK Conference that he was a 'flag-waving, libertarian, Cornish patriot' and that the vision 'founder-members had of Mebyon Kernow was of an organisation which could be supported by all Cornish people who recognised the national identity of Cornwall…'[60] But this view was not shared by many in the late 1970s who believed that MK needed to develop more detailed, left-of-centre policies on a range of economic, environmental and social issues. One member, for example, argued that 'it is not enough to seek a self-governing Cornwall and then to work for economic and social justice. The two must go hand in hand.'[61]

In May 1980, Len Truran resigned from the post of National Secretary and from the National Executive, blaming 'unrestrained personal attacks' on himself, 'Trotskyite extremism' and the fact that he had lost the 'Chairman's confidence'.[62] Within a matter of days, MK was attracting a significant amount of extremely unwelcome UK-wide press coverage, with Mr Truran claiming that there was a 'middle-class clique [of] Trotskyites' that wanted to see Cornwall as a 'socialist republic'.[63] The disputes were covered in UK newspapers, with the headline in the *Guardian* stating 'The Reds blight Cornish dawn'.[64]

As a level-headed and largely cohesive influence on the party, Richard Jenkin did his utmost to combat the claims and to protect MK from the controversy. He certainly made great efforts to challenge Len Truran's claims, time and again describing Mebyon Kernow as a 'middle of the road' movement and one that was 'broad-based'.[65]

He was unable to prevent a large swathe of resignations from the party, which sapped the enthusiasm and morale of remaining activists. There were some meaningful political actions taken by MK at this time with party members, for example, taking a leading role in the campaign against a nuclear power station in Luxulyan, with one drilling rig occupied by MK members in a non-violent direct action protest. But overall, there was a significant downturn in political activity. In terms of elections, MK put forward nine candidates for the 1981 Cornwall County Council elections and this fell to seven for the 1983 district council elections – a third of what was managed in 1979. Penwith bucked the trend, where there was considerable activity, but this was not replicated elsewhere, with only one candidate east of the district of Kerrier.

At one point, Richard even attempted to use the good will of his Euro-elec-

RICHARD JENKIN
SOME PERSONAL DETAILS:

Son of a Mousehole man, Richard Jenkin and his wife Ann and four children have lived at Leedstown since 1960, when he became a teacher at Helston School. He is a Parish Councillor

A founder member of Mebyon Kernow, Richard Jenkin is now its Chairman and was its candidate in the European Elections. He has always been involved in many Cornish organisations including being Grand Bard from 1976 to 1982.

VOTE FOR

on THURSDAY JUNE 9th
VOTE FOR

Published by J.N. Plummer, New Road, Stithians, Truro. Tel: Stithians (0209) 860574.   Printed by Helston Printers, 12 Wendron St., Helston.

Mebyon Kernow flyer, General Election, 9 June 1983, when Richard stood in Falmouth-Camborne

tion campaign to re-energise and unite the party, with the launch of a new 'Campaign for Cornish recognition.' In a speech to the National Executive in October 1980,[66] he attempted to reach out to individuals, both inside and outside of MK, by concluding:

> Each and every one in Cornwall can make a contribution to this campaign for the recognition of Cornish identity. I want to see us, one and all, expressing in our lives and actions our sense of Cornishness. Only in that way can the Cornish people survive. Our message to the Cornish people must be:– On the foundation of your Cornish identity build yourselves a Cornish future.

Richard Jenkin was also the prospective parliamentary candidate for Falmouth-Camborne by 1982.[67] But as the election approached, it was again Richard who had to take the lead in tackling inaction at the heart of MK. There had been limited active campaigning to promote his candidacy and it was necessary for him to write to all members in the constituency to cajole them to follow through with their decision to fight the election:

> My personal view is that we ought to contest the election if possible. MK is not supporting its aim of self-government if it does not try to win places in all the authorities that at present control Cornwall. Not to contest the elections will be considered a retreat and there seems no plausible excuse to offer the public for this ... the success or failure of MK depends on the commitment of the members.[68]

Leading from the front, he fought a traditional MK campaign which reflected his views on what MK should represent to the people of Cornwall. He told his adoption meeting:

> Governments of every kind have always neglected Cornwall's needs and problems. Even their local politicians have put party interest before that of Cornwall. Here at the edge of Britain, we are considered of no account unless we stand up and speak for ourselves...
>   Cornwall needs a voice in Parliament which would speak up for Cornish interests irrespective of party advantage: which would not necessarily be pro- or anti- whatever government was elected but would

Richard Jenkin leads the memorial service to Cornish martyrs at St Keverne, 8 July 1983 (copyright Paul Yockney, Helston)

always be pro-Cornwall. We want to introduce a new dimension into politics in Cornwall. We are asking people to put Cornwall first and vote Mebyon Kernow. Anything else will not serve Cornwall but only the parties with their eyes on power in London.[69]

Richard Jenkin polled 582 votes (1.2%), a dramatic but unsurprising drop from the result in the previous General Election campaign. It was consistent with the decline in the MK vote in the neighbouring St Ives constituency – the only other seat contested by the party in 1983.

This was also the year in which Richard stood down from the leadership of the party after a decade in the role. During this time, he had provided a sense of continuity with earlier decades, he had stabilised MK after the disruptions of the period around 1980, he had guided MK through its evolution from a pressure group into a political party and consolidated MK as a progressive, left-of-centre party, even though this was not necessarily the vision that he himself had of the organisation. But such was Richard's commitment to the party, he continued in the role of Vice Chairman from 1983 and Vice-Chairman West from 1984 onwards.

In the latter half of the 1980s, there was temporary shift in emphasis within Mebyon Kernow. It should be acknowledged that many MK members were putting significant effort into local pressure groups such as the bi-annual Conference on Cornwall and Cornish Alternatives to the Structure Plan in preference to electoral politics, though in 1988 MK itself was able to lead a fresh campaign for Cornwall to have its own European parliamentary constituency. It forced the Boundary Commission into holding a Local Inquiry on the matter,[70] and then put forward Colin Lawry as a candidate for the European election to the Cornwall and Plymouth constituency in 1989, when he called for a 'Westminster bypass'.[71]

But it could not be denied that the party was in crisis.[72] Membership had fallen to a precarious level and the party was contesting very few elections. In the Cornwall County Council elections of 1985 and 1989, there were only three official MK candidates. And in 1987, when over 200 district council seats were contested, MK managed just two candidates. That year, the party also failed to nominate candidates for the General Election.

In the second half of 1989, Loveday Carlyon resigned from the leadership of MK, leaving the party with no-one at the helm and with no sense of direction. An emergency meeting was held in 1990 to consider whether MK wished to 'continue as an organisation at all',[73] which allowed the *Western Morning News* to colourfully ponder that 'as Eastern Europe celebrates the springtime of nationalist movements, the flower of Cornish nationalism – Mebyon Kernow – may be wilting and could fold and die'.[74] Richard Jenkin was a prominent presence at the meeting and told other members that he would 'always see that there is an MK.'[75] He was delighted when Mebyon Kernow reaffirmed its commitment to continue as a political party at a follow-up meeting in September,[76] when his daughter Loveday was elected as MK's ninth Party Chairman.

The re-emergence of Mebyon Kernow as a political force was not immediate and in 1992 it failed to contest any seats at the General Election. But by the mid-1990s, MK was fighting more local elections than at any time since 1979. Even more importantly, MK was starting to win seats on principal local authorities.[77] MK also fought the Cornwall and West Plymouth seat in the European elections in 1994 and, in 1997 it fought parliamentary elections for the first time since 1983.

Richard continued to be heavily involved with Mebyon Kernow. He was a fixture at party conferences and meetings, and he also supported a range of initiatives from MK and the wider Cornish movement, such as the protest against the closure of South Crofty tin mine in 1998[78] and the launch of the cross-party Cornish Constitutional Convention in 2000.[79] Most importantly of all, he was a willing and generous source of advice for new members of the party, encouraging one and all to build a strong nationalist movement for Cornwall.

In 1998, MK members came together to bestow the honour of a Life Presidency of MK onto Richard Jenkin, in recognition of his 'dedicated service to both our party and Cornwall'.[80] It was a most fitting tribute to Richard's life-long commitment to Mebyon Kernow and the wider Cornish nationalist movement and never was an award more deserved.

Richard Jenkin's last speech as Life President was at MK's 50th anniversary celebration at Redruth's Penventon Hotel in 2001. In an inspiring address, he called on the party to redouble its efforts to win an Assembly for Cornwall and more:

50 years ago, it took a lot of idealism and determination to think the unthinkable and say it out loud in public. In those early days, all Mebyon Kernow policies were there in black and white or embryo, and the great and the good in Cornwall thought them laughable nonsense or subversive politics.

Fifty years on, we have not yet achieved all our aims but what we have done is to make them subjects of serious discussion among Cornish people. And more and more are accepting these are the best way ahead for Cornwall.[81]

Describing Mebyon Kernow as the 'only party whose sole existence is to put Cornwall first', he acknowledged that he was unlikely to be present at any future anniversary celebrations but warned those MK members present:

If we don't have a Cornish Assembly up and running and a Cornish University and a prosperous economy in Cornwall, I'll come back and haunt you. Give it everything you've got and all can be achieved. Success to Mebyon Kernow and our country, Cornwall.

The speech was made during an extremely exciting time for Mebyon Kernow, with people from across the political spectrum backing MK's Declaration for a Cornish Assembly campaign. Richard died in October 2002, but he lived to see over 50,000 people sharing his dream and signing individual declarations, which proclaimed that 'Cornwall is a nation' and demanded greater self-government for Cornwall. Presented to 10 Downing Street in December 2001, these declarations remain an outstanding statement of intent from the people of Cornwall about their aspirations for their future.[82]

It must be our hope that Richard Jenkin would be heartened by the continuing growth of Mebyon Kernow and the strength of its ongoing campaigns, such as those to defend the territorial integrity of Cornwall, to secure fair funding, to protect Cornwall and its public services from savage and unnecessary government cuts, and to deliver proper local-needs housing while fighting to protect the countryside of Cornwall from over-development.

We trust that he would have been greatly cheered by MK's ability, over the last decade or so, to win seats on principal local authorities in communities as diverse and far-flung as Penzance, Porthleven, Crowan and Wendron, Camborne, Illogan South, St Enoder, Treverbyn / Penwithick and Boscoppa, Bodmin, Bude and Callington, as well as numerous seats on town and parish councils.[83]

But most of all, he would have been extremely proud of how his immediate family is continuing his work. His daughter Loveday was Chairman of MK between 1990 and 1997, and stood in the 1994 Euro-elections and the 2009 General Election in the Camborne and Redruth constituency. She has also been a Crowan Parish Councillor since 1995 and served on Kerrier District Council between 1995 and 2009.[84] She is the present member for Crowan and Wendron on Cornwall Council, having won a by-election in 2011 when she out-polled Conservative, Labour, Liberal Democrat and Independent opponents.[85] Re-elected in May 2013, she achieved 55% of the vote.[86] His youngest son Conan has meanwhile contested numerous local election campaigns in Camborne and Truro, fought the Truro and St Austell seat at the 2001 and 2005 General Elections and has been a member of Truro City Council since 2007.[87]

Following in the footsteps of their father, both siblings were also candidates on the MK list, when the party contested the south west seat to the European Parliament in 2009 and polled 11,534 votes in Cornwall – MK's best-ever electoral achievement.[88]

Notes
1. This chapter reuses some material from Bernard Deacon, Dick Cole and Garry Tregidga, 2003, *Mebyon Kernow and Cornish Nationalism*.
2. Interview with Richard Jenkin, 14 February 2000, Cornish Audio Visual Archive (CAVA); Bernard Deacon, Dick Cole and Garry Tregidga, 2003, *Mebyon Kernow and Cornish Nationalism*, p. 27.
3. Bernard Deacon, Dick Cole and Garry Tregidga, 2003, *Mebyon Kernow and Cornish Nationalism*, pp. 27-28.
4. Interview with Richard Jenkin, 3 October 2001, Cornish Audio Visual Archive (CAVA); Bernard Deacon, Dick Cole and Garry Tregidga, 2003, *Mebyon Kernow and Cornish Nationalism*, p. 29.
5. Minutes of inaugural meeting of Mebyon Kernow, 6 January 1951; Dick Cole, 2011, *The Story of Mebyon Kernow*, pp. 4-5.
6. Minutes of inaugural meeting of Mebyon Kernow, 6 January 1951.
7. Richard Jenkin, *40 Years of Mebyon Kernow*.
8. Richard Jenkin, Chairman's Notes in *Cornish Nation*, Vol. 3, 3, (Winter 1975).
9. Richard Jenkin, *40 Years of Mebyon Kernow*, p. 4.
10. Richard Jenkin, hand-written autobiographical note in papers held by MK. Richard Jenkin worked as a teacher at Devonport High School 1952-53, Bedwellty Grammar School, Monmouthshire 1953-1956, King Edward VI School, Totnes 1956-1959.

11 Richard Jenkin, hand-written autobiographical note in papers held by MK.
12 MK launched *New Cornwall* magazine in 1952. The first ten issues were actually edited by Richard Gendall, under the pseudonym 'R. Morris', and then by Helena Charles until her resignation from the post of MK chairman in 1956. It continued until 1973.
13 Mebyon Kernow Annual General Meeting, 27 February 1960.
14 Mebyon Kernow Annual General Meeting, 10 March 1962.
15 Bernard Deacon, Dick Cole and Garry Tregidga, 2003, *Mebyon Kernow and Cornish Nationalism*, p. 46.
16 Richard and Ann Jenkin, 1965, *Cornwall: The Hidden Land*, p. 27.
17 Bernard Deacon, Dick Cole and Garry Tregidga, 2003, *Mebyon Kernow and Cornish Nationalism*, p. 47.
18 Robert Dunstone, February 1963, 'A university for Cornwall is possible' leaflet.
19 This was the first of MK's three main electoral phases; (i) 1965-1970 (ii) 1976-1983 and (iii) from 1993 to the present day. Richard Jenkin himself only once stood for election to a principal local authority, which was the first election to Kerrier District Council in 1973. He did not stand as an official MK candidate, but mentioned his role in MK and the wider Cornish movement in this election leaflet. He was also a member of Crowan Parish Council from 1964 until 1995.
20 *Cornish Nation* magazine was first published in a duplicated form in 1967 by Len Truran. It was soon after relaunched as 'Cornwall's first truly national newspaper' under the editorship of Derek Tozer. The magazine appeared until 1982 and the editors included James Whetter (1970-1975), Donald Rawe (1975-1977), Julyan Holmes and Pedyr Prior (1978-1980), Julyan Holmes (1980-1981) and Neil Plummer (1982). *Cornish Nation* was relaunched in 1993. It was initially produced by Conan Jenkin and more latterly Dick Cole. This second series continues to the present day.
21 Bernard Deacon, Dick Cole and Garry Tregidga, 2003, *Mebyon Kernow and Cornish Nationalism*, p. 53.
22 *St Ives Times and Echo*, 2 June 1967.
23 Minutes of Mebyon Kernow Annual General Meeting, Truro, 18 May 1968.
24 Gwynfor Evans, 1996, *For the Sake of Wales*, 68; Gwynfor Evans twice visited Cornwall to speak at a short series of meetings organised by Mebyon Kernow, when he stayed with Richard Jenkin.
25 *Western Morning News*, 1 January 1969.
26 *The Cornish Review*, 6 (Summer 1967).
27 *Cornish Nation*, Vol. 1, 8 (November 1969).
28 Letter from Len Trelease and Roger Holmes to MK National Executive, July 1969: MK Collection. This was the first of three major splits in the organisation at roughly five year intervals – 1969, 1975, 1980 – two of which led to alternative Cornish nationalist parties.
29 *Independent*, 6 July 1969.
30 Richard Jenkin General Election leaflet, 1970.
31 Richard Jenkin General Election leaflet, 1970.
32 *Sunday Independent*, 21 June 1970.
33 Richard Jenkin (1991), *40 Years of Mebyon Kernow*.
34 *Kevren*, 1 (1971).
35 *Kevren*, 1 (1971).
36 *Western Morning News*, 1 January 1969.
37 *Cornish Nation*, Vol. 2, 5 (September 1971).
38 Undated MK promotional leaflet, c. early 1970s.
39 *Cornish Nation*, Vol. 2, 5 (September 1971).
40 Report on MK AGM 20 June 1973 in *Cornish Nation*, Vol. 2, 13 (September 1973)
41 MK press release, 2 November 1973.
42 Bernard Deacon, Dick Cole and Garry Tregidga, 2003, *Mebyon Kernow and Cornish Nationalism*, p. 64.
43 *Cornish Nation*, Vol. 2, 17 (September 1974).

44 *Forward*, 4 (June 1975). This was a short-lived publication produced by Bert Boyd and MK members in the Illogan area.
45 *An Baner Kernewek*, 1 (1975).
46 Richard Jenkin, Chairman's Notes in *Cornish Nation*, Vol. 3, 3 (Winter 1975).
47 Bernard Deacon, Dick Cole and Garry Tregidga, 2003, *Mebyon Kernow and Cornish Nationalism*, p. 68.
48 Colin Murley polled 1,662 votes (4.0 per cent) in St Ives, Len Truran polled 1,637 votes (3.0 per cent) in Falmouth-Camborne and Roger Holmes managed 865 votes (1.7 per cent) in Bodmin.
49 Bernard Deacon, Dick Cole and Garry Tregidga, 2003, *Mebyon Kernow and Cornish Nationalism*, p. 68.
50 *Cornish Nation*, 37 (Summer 1979).
51 Minutes of meetings of MK National Executive, 16 February 1979, 23 February 1979, 16 March 1979 and 30 March 1979.
52 Richard Jenkin election leaflet for European election, 1979.
53 Bernard Deacon, Dick Cole and Garry Tregidga, 2003, *Mebyon Kernow and Cornish Nationalism*, p. 71.
54 Statement from Colin Murley reproduced in full elsewhere in this publication.
55 *Cornish Nation*, 37 (Summer 1979). The editorial was jointly written by Pedyr Prior and Len Truran.
56 *Cornish Nation*, 37 (Summer 1979).
57 *West Briton*, 18 October 1979.
58 Minutes of MK Annual General Meeting, Truro, 13 October 1979. At this meeting Colin Murley stood against Richard Jenkin for the chairmanship of MK. Richard was easily returned with 68 votes to the 25 achieved by Colin Murley, while the minutes record that 'Mr Murley said he thought it important all elections are contested and this is why he allowed his name to go forward. He wished to make it clear there was absolutely no animosity between himself and Mr Jenkin.'
59 Bernard Deacon, Dick Cole and Garry Tregidga, 2003, *Mebyon Kernow and Cornish Nationalism*, p. 73.
60 Original speech held by MK, believed to date from 1981.
61 Julyan Drew (1980) 'The Way Forward' in *Tributaries*. This was an occasional publication from the magazine *An Weryn*, which included a series of articles from activists on the future direction of the Cornish movement. Two issues appeared; the first in 1980 and the second in 1986.
62 Letter from Len Truran to Richard Jenkin, 20 May 1980. Held by MK.
63 *Western Morning News*, 31 May 1980.
64 *The Guardian*, June 3 1980.
65 *Western Morning News*, 31 May 1980; *The Guardian*, 3 June 1980.
66 Speech to National Executive Committee, 17 October 1980, reproduced in *Gwyn ha Du* 1, November / December 1980.
67 Minutes of meeting Falmouth-Camborne Constituency Association, 14 June 1982.
68 Richard Jenkin, letter to MK members in the Falmouth-Camborne constituency, 9 May 1983.
69 Richard Jenkin adoption address for 1983 General Election in Falmouth-Camborne.
70 Bernard Deacon, Dick Cole and Garry Tregidga, 2003, *Mebyon Kernow and Cornish Nationalism*, p. 88.
71 Colin Lawry election leaflet for European election, 1989.
72 Bernard Deacon, Dick Cole and Garry Tregidga, 2003, *Mebyon Kernow and Cornish Nationalism*, pp. 81-85.
73 Letter from MK's London Branch inviting members to an emergency meeting, which took place on 21 April 1990.
74 *Western Morning News*, 20 April 1990.
75 Minutes of MK emergency meeting at Murdoch House, Redruth, 21 April 1990.
76 Invitation to meeting held in Truro on 8 September. Sent out on 28 July, it stated that the meeting would consider options such as 'to become a pressure group,' 'remain as a political party' or 'to become a more flexible political movement;' Bernard Deacon, Dick Cole and Garry Tregidga, 2003, *Mebyon Kernow and Cornish Nationalism*, pp. 90-91.

77 Colin Lawry, first elected in the 1980s, continued to represent MK on Cornwall Council (Penzance South) and Penwith District Council (Penzance Central), Tom Tremewan was elected to Carrick District Council (Perranporth) in 1994, Loveday Jenkin won a seat on Kerrier District Council (Praze) in 1995, while John Bolitho and Dick Cole were elected to North Cornwall District Council (Bude) and Restormel Borough Council (St Enoder) in 1999.
78 Dick Cole, 2011, *The Story of Mebyon Kernow*, p. 25.
79 *Cornish Nation* second series 18 (Summer 2000).
80 Report of MK Conference, 10 October 1998, in *Cornish Nation* second series 11 (Autumn 1998).
81 *Cornish Nation* second series 21 (Spring 2001).
82 *Cornish Nation*, second series 24 (Winter 2002); Cole, 2011, *The Story of Mebyon Kernow*, p. 26-27.
83 Dick Cole, 2011, *The Story of Mebyon Kernow*, pp. 32-35. See www.cornwall.gov.uk for recent election results.
84 Dick Cole, 2011, *The Story of Mebyon Kernow*, pp. 22-23, 28-32.
85 *Cornish Nation*, second series 61 (January 2012).
86 *Western Morning News*, 4 May 2013.
87 Dick Cole, 2011, *The Story of Mebyon Kernow*, pp. 28-29.
88 *Cornish Nation*, second series 52 (July 2009). The 'south west' constituency comprised Cornwall, South West England and Gibraltar. Mebyon Kernow polled a total of 14,922 votes, which included 3,380 in South West England and eight in Gibraltar.

The first UK European Election of 1979: The Cornwall and Plymouth Constituency

Colin Murley

The selection of a candidate for Mebyon Kernow seemed to naturally support Richard Jenkin, the Grand Bard. Richard gave our campaign a sense of unity and clear purpose. I easily fell into the legally-required post of agent, having been a former Mebyon Kernow County Councillor.

Somehow, Richard brought a sense of 'we're in this together for Cornwall'. My job was easy. There were no disputes; everybody wanted to do something and be in on the act. I particularly remember driving Richard all over Cornwall and even to Plymouth – that is, to the BBC there. We fixed up a loud speaker on the car. The message was simple: if you're Cornish, be Cornish and vote Jenkin.

Everything seemed to just happen the way it should. Even the weather was onside. No aggro from the other contestants. On our travels, on one occasion we landed up in Camelford only to find two volunteers, Malcolm Williams (from St Just) and Pedyr Prior (from Porthleven) in the middle of the town on the job canvassing. The sense of duty engendered by the process was inspiring.

Richard was a natural with the BBC. Of course, Cornwall should be a separate Euro-Constituency. Remote control from London was not democracy. I'm sure Richard invented the word 'devolution'. We could only manage one leaflet and there were not many posters to be seen on our travels. The main thing was knowing that we were doing the right thing, and that kept us going with confidence.

We certainly did not expect a five-figure result. I can still see Richard on the stage at the count smiling and giving our MK group the thumbs up when the result was announced.

'Wales'

Richard G. Jenkin (Pasco Trevyhan)

For me there is magic in Wales
Where I walk as though in dream
And all is familiar, yet strange,
As the waters of some slow stream
Will stir and shiver and change
The image of some loved face.
The very sounds of the name
Of each little wayside place
Loudly and surely proclaim
The kinship of Cornwall and Wales.

Wherever I go in Wales
Some fleeting image recalls
A Cornish memory sweet –
A cottage with stone built walls,
The grouping of men in the street,
A whisper of Welsh in the crowd
Like a ghost of the Cornish speech –
And my heart is full, and proud
Of the truth these memories teach –
The kinship of Cornwall and Wales

[*New Cornwall*, vol. 13 (1965), no.3]

Whegh Bro Un Enef/Six Countries One Soul

Ann Trevenen Jenkin

Introduction
A study of Celtic matters and his involvement with them played a major part in the life of Richard Garfield Jenkin, perhaps only superseded by his dedication to Cornwall. Almost as soon as he discovered as a teenager in Manchester that Cornwall had its own language, he also learnt that Cornish was one of six Celtic languages and that it had especially close links with Welsh and Breton, and a more distant correlation with Manx, Scots Gaelic and Irish. These familial relationships were stimulating and exciting, both through their similarities with and differences from Cornwall.

The 1940s
Richard Jenkin spent the year 1943-44 at Exeter College, Oxford, reading chemistry. Here he helped to establish a Young Cornwall Movement with fellow Cornish people, who included, among others, Mary Foss, David Balhatchet and John Legonna. The last two became language bards of Gorsedh Kernow, and Mary and David married. Richard described in rather flowery teenage prose what the Young Cornwall Movement at Oxford was all about:

> The YCM was started by some young Cornish people with the object of retaining and furthering the spirit of Cornwall, and so preventing the

loss of its individuality and saving it from a degraded uniformity with the rest of Britain, in which it would be neither Cornish nor English, but an irredeemably soulless hotch-potch of the two.[1]

One can already see, however, the broad vision of an eighteen year old who wanted so much for his beloved Kernow. After failing to reach the required standard in his first year examinations in 1944 – possibly because of spending too much time on Cornish matters and trying to gain support from A.L. Rowse, then a junior lecturer at Oxford – Richard had to take part in National Service in Britain and the Far East. And between 1944 and 1948 he worked with the Forces Broadcasting Service and the British Military Mission to Greece. One of his delights was to read some of his own Cornish poetry and that of others over the airwaves.

In 1948, he returned to Manchester, where his parents were living, to complete his degree, and found time to follow up some of his research and also to widen links with the Celtic world. In 1948, for instance, he joined Kelgh Keltek (Celtic Circle), which had been established in Cornwall by Kathleen Rowe, the wife of Ashley Rowe. Together the Rowes had already set up links with a Friends of Brittany group among those Bretons who had escaped – often by fishing boat – from France in the 1935-45 war and were living in west Cornwall. Kelgh Keltek was originally established under the auspices of the Friends of Brittany, but later linked up with the Cornish Branch of the Celtic Congress.[2]

The aims of Kelgh Keltek were to link young Cornish writers with others in the six Celtic countries who were interested in the development of minority cultures, language and identity, and to exchange news, books and information. Apart from Kathleen Rowe, the leading lights in Cornwall were Margaret Norris and Lambert Truran, secretaries, and Daphne Allerton, librarian. All later became language bards.[3] Other writers in Cornwall involved in some measure were Francis Cargeeg, E.G. Retallack Hooper, and P.J. Courtney, an Irishman working in the still room at Tregenna Castle. In Brittany there was François Ters, later a controversial figure as archdruid in the Breton Gorsedd, and Yann Piette who later lived and worked in Aberystwyth for many years with his Welsh wife. They were indefatigable writers, and M. Omnes from Plougrescant, Brittany arranged Celtic gatherings for these young Celts at his boarding house. Tomas MacNeacail, then living in Newcastle, and from Wales, Dr Ceinwen Thomas and Gwennant Davies who worked for the Urdd (Welsh Youth Movement), also gave Richard Jenkin a wider Celtic perspective and linked him with many lifelong Celtic friends. However, after the death of Kathleen Rowe in 1950, the organisation faltered and then failed, although many personal Celtic links remained.

From about 1948, when in Cornwall he first met Helena Charles with her broad knowledge of several languages including Hebrew and Breton, Richard was ready for further exploration. His perspective widened even more through contact with Celtic groups in Cornwall. For instance, the large Irish community in St Ives, where there was a strong branch of the Gaelic League, was closely linked with Father Delaney, the Irish-speaking priest from the local Catholic Church. Other Cornish people such as Helena Charles and Ann Trevenen lent their support and learnt Irish dancing, while Helena taught the Irish some Breton dances and the Cornish Furry Dance.

In April 1949, there was an Inter-Celtic Festival in St Ives, with numerous events arranged, and although Richard was not present, he knew all about the new developments from his friends who did attend. There was Irish dancing, Celtic literature, games and competitions as well as an Open Exhibition of Cornish Crafts, for which the town and arts elements worked very closely together. Exhibitors included Robert Morton Nance, his sons Robin and Dicon, Guido Morris, Bryan Wynter, Bernard Leach and Marion Grace Hocken. This early effort was another stirring in the development of Cornish and Celtic liaison.[4]

Richard later established links with the European group FUEN (The Federal Union of European Nationalities) and attended one of their conferences in Europe, but family responsibilities in the fifties precluded him from attending many. He also helped from 1949 onwards with a correspondence course in Cornish for the Celtic Society at the University College of the South West at Exeter, as it was then, and many students, including the undergraduate Ann Trevenen, took advantage of his teaching.[5]

Stepping stones
The earlier foundation stones were already established for Richard Jenkin with

his discovery of Henry Jenner's paper 'Cornwall: a Celtic Nation', which he had read before the Pan-Celtic Congress at Caernarfon in 1904, thus paving the way for Cornwall to be admitted as a full member of the Celtic Congress. This was published in the *Celtic Review* in 1905, and reprinted in *Henry and Katharine Jenner* a century later.[6]

Secondly, in 1932, the first regular Celtic Congress was held in Cornwall, and the practice of making honorary bards from other Celtic countries was introduced, a custom that has continued up to the present day. The Gorsedh ceremony to welcome the Celts was held at the Merry Maidens, St Buryan, close to Boscawen-Un, an important place in Welsh and Cornish ideology.[7] Honorary bards that year included Professor Agnes O'Farrelly, M.A., International Secretary of the Congress and Professor Douglas Hyde, (Ireland); Rev. J. Mackechnie (Scotland) ; Professor Mary Williams and Rev. G. Hartwell Jones (Wales); Percy Kelly B.A., (Mann); and François Gourvil (Brittany). Two other honorary bards were created: the Master of Sempill, who was also from Scotland and arrived wearing his kilt, and Ethel Paynter of Boskenna, St Buryan. It is not known if they were members of the Congress, nor exactly why they were added to the list.[8]

A third foundation stone was the publication of Robert Morton Nance's 1943 paper 'The Spirit of the Celtic Movement'. For some of the background to Celtic aspirations in Cornwall at the time see 'Re-awakening Cornwall's Celtic Consciousness',[9] and the full text of Nance's paper in *Setting Cornwall on its Feet: Robert Morton Nance,1873-1959.*[10]

However, the greatest influence was the Celtic Congress, later known as the International Celtic Congress, for had Jenner not said in 1904 that a Cornishman was 'as much a Celt... as any Gael, Cymro, Manxman or Breton'.[11] And Nance had added in 1943:

> One thing, too, is shown as found among them all [the Celts] and that is the capacity to blow on patiently until below dead ashes a kindling spark is reached again.[12]

This is very much what did happen to Celtic aspirations in Cornwall.

The 1950s

Helena Charles' family were Cornish and had lived in the Helston area for generations, although she herself had been born in India and had spent many years working in London during the Second World War. When, therefore, she returned to Cornwall to live, she met many like-minded Cornish people who had similar aspirations for Cornwall as part of the Celtic world. These included George Pawley White and E.G. Retallack Hooper and a distant relative, Ann Trevenen, then living in Redruth. Richard Jenkin was still not living in Cornwall at that time, but met with Helena Charles, Ann Trevenen and others on his frequent visits.

Although he had two years previously already attended a preliminary meeting held to publicise a Celtic Congress in Cornwall,[13] his first close contact with the Celts of Kernow and other nations was the 1950 Celtic Congress in Truro. An even earlier proposal to hold the Celtic Congress in Cornwall in 1939 had had to be abandoned because of the outbreak of the Second World War.[14] The then Congress secretary Ashley Rowe and others introduced Richard Jenkin to the Cornish Branch of the Celtic Congress, whose President was Grand Bard Robert Morton Nance. As Richard had become a bard in 1947 through study of the Cornish language, there were circles within circles. Very Celtic! This again provided a stimulus to his rapidly-growing interest in Celtic matters.

There is a photograph of the 1950 Celtic Congress[15] outside the Royal Institution of Cornwall in Truro. Cornish members, apart from Robert Morton Nance, who were at some of the events, but not all present for the photograph included Ann Trevenen, Helena Charles, Richard Jenkin, Joan Stott, Ashley Rowe, chairman, Audrey Humphris, who had taken over as assistant secretary after the death of Kathleen Rowe, and Lambert Truran. The vice-chairman for that Congress was Canon R.H.W. Roberts, a Welshman and Dean of Truro Cathedral. Among the visitors from the other Celtic countries were Archdruid Cruwys of Wales, and Brian Fitzpatrick and Frank Willis from Ireland. Also from Wales was the general secretary of the International Celtic Congress, Dr Ambrose Bebb, who later helped advise Mebyon Kernow on its foundation as a political movement in 1951.[16] Richard Jenkin was one of those who worked together with Dr Bebb on that, and these closer links with Wales, both political and cultural, were a further influence on his own political and cultural aspira-

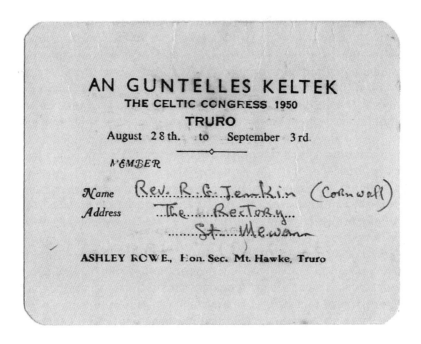

Rev (sic) Richard Jenkin's ticket for the Celtic Congress, Truro, August-September 1950

tions. David Craine attended from the Isle of Man, and the Rev. T.M. Murchison from Scotland. A close friend of Cornwall who came over from Ireland was Oscar Macuilis/MacUileas, who was in the enviable position of speaking and understanding all six Celtic languages, including Cornish – a goal for other Celts to aim for. The most outstanding event of that Congress was an illustrated talk by Sir Cyril Fox, from the National Museum of Wales, on 'Celtic Art'.[17] That event was chaired by His Honour Judge Scobell Armstrong from Cornwall.

After that Congress, visits to other Celtic countries by Richard Jenkin were very much the norm. He became a faithful supporter and, indeed, quickly a leader in Celtic matters in Cornwall. From 1950 to 2002, the year of his death, he attended forty-three Celtic Congresses, a record among delegates. He became, too, a well-known speaker for Cornwall, was almost always a Cornish delegate, and after his marriage in 1956 to Ann Trevenen and the birth of his children from 1957 onwards, the whole family also attended on many occasions. In Cornwall he held many executive positions, among them Branch Secretary and, later, President, but he was also International Secretary from 1955 to 1960, Vice President between 1969 and 1971 and International President from 1971 to 1976. That year he was one of the few to be made an Honorary Life President for services to the International Celtic Congress.

Meanwhile, back in 1950s' Cornwall he attended the Isle of Man Congress in Ramsey two years into the decade. A group photograph shows many of the then members, including Richard Jenkin, Oscar McUilis and Per Denez, a charismatic, academic, Breton-speaking leader and activist. They were photographed on a visit to Tynwald, the site of the Manx Parliament, a scene which would have resonated with Richard Jenkin's developing political sympathies.[18]

Also that year – together with many other young Celts and some not so young – he attended Gwersyllt Celtaidd, an inter-Celtic camp at Pantyfedwen, Borth, Ceredigion arranged by Urdd Gobaith Cymru (The Welsh League of Youth). For the same event in 1953, Richard helped Cornwall provide a photographic exhibition of Cornish Life, through the good offices of the then Cornwall County Council and Cornwall Youth Service. Richard Jenkin attended with Lambert Truran, Ann Trevenen and possibly others, and the Cornish delegates also took part in the talks on 'Our National Heroes', and in reading a selection of Cornish literature. Other Celts present included Aled and Urien Wiliam from Wales, Brian Stowell and Bernard Caine, teenage schoolboys from the Isle of Man who attended with Leslie Quirk, and Tomas MacNeacail from Scotland. Social contact through songs, dancing, outings and films gave Richard and other young Cornish Celts an inkling of what could one day be achieved in Kernow with funding and support.[19]

Unable to attend the 1953 International Congress in Glasgow, he sent a telegram in Cornish. The following year, though, he was present at the Congress in Dublin, where the Chairman of the Irish Branch was the Chief Justice of Ireland, Conchubar Macguire. David Craine from the Isle of Man was now International President. In Dublin Richard and his wife to be, Ann

CELTIC INTERNATIONAL YOUTH CAMP

CASTLE GOTHA, PORTHPEAN.

ISSUED BY THE

CORNWALL COUNTY YOUTH SERVICE

COUNTY HALL, TRURO

Cover of Celtic International Youth Camp brochure, August-September 1956

Trevenen, met Per Denez from Brittany – Ann for the first time – and were themselves enthused by his energy and enthusiasm. He remained a lifelong family friend. One of the main topics for discussion in 1954 was 'The Position of Celtic Language Publishing'. Richard Jenkin spoke for Cornwall and stressed that little had been done since the war, but that it was hoped to do better in the future. There were no state or government funds in either Cornwall or Brittany.[20]

In fact, it is only in the last twenty years or so that Cornish-language publishing has really taken off, so it has taken fifty years to become well established, with many books of a high standard now being produced in Cornish. Richard Jenkin would have been proud to see this development, and also the growth in spoken Cornish. Again, the enviable position and number of Irish publications was noted and admired at the 1954 Congress. When Richard returned to Cornwall afterwards, he and others helped to re-establish and revitalise the Cornish Branch of the Celtic Congress. This was necessary to counteract the effects of the abortive, schismatic Congress held in Brittany in 1951 under Per Mocaer, which was disallowed by the International officers. Ashley Rowe had attended unwittingly, and was caught up in the backlash. However, with the support of G. Pawley White, E.G. Retallack Hooper, Helena Charles, R. Morton Nance, Richard Jenkin and others, and with public lectures and discussions, the Cornish branch became active again and increased its membership.[21]

In 1955 a delegation went from Cornwall to the Congress in Brest, Brittany, where they took a full part in the proceedings. The Cornish delegates were Helena Charles, Ann Trevenen, Richard Jenkin and Denis Trevanion, who was accompanied by one of his sons. One of the highlights of the Congress was the production of a short extract in Cornish from *Gwreans an Bys*, entitled 'Adam and Eve and Death'. Richard Jenkin was Adam, Ann Trevenen was Eve and Helena Charles played Death. Ann and Richard were by now engaged, so perhaps it was appropriate casting – at least for them! It was the first time that a Cornish play had been performed in Brittany in modern times and the Bretons found the Cornish understandable. It was at that Congress, too, that Richard Jenkin was elected International Secretary.[22]

The following year the Celtic Congress returned to Cornwall on its usual six-

Celtic Congress delegates, Ramsey, Isle of Man, 1952; Richard far left

year cycle. It was again held in Truro, with two joint secretaries, Togo Chetwood-Aiken and Audrey Humphris, and Robert Morton Nance as chairman. Some of the Breton delegates were reputed to have sailed to Cornwall in a fishing boat.[23] Among the visitors from the other Celtic countries were Conchubar Macguire and Michael Yeats, son of the poet W.B. Yeats, who was accompanied by his wife, a singer and harpist. Richard Jenkin and others had visited them in Dublin in 1954 and were pleased to meet them again in Cornwall.[24] One of the innovative events associated with the Celtic Congress in

Cornwall that year was a Celtic International Youth Camp at Castle Gotha, Porthpean, from 25 August to 8 September. This was Cornwall's first attempt to copy the well-established youth camps in other Celtic countries, particularly in Wales. Members of the Congress and bards of Gorsedh Kernow visited the camp, which was under the supervision of Jon West, Cornwall (County) Youth Organiser. About twenty young people from the camp came to join in with the Congress events in Truro, the aim being to encourage all young people of whatever background to reflect on, study and be proud of their Celtic heritage.[25] Richard and Ann Jenkin had recently married in Redruth, Cornwall and on returning from their honeymoon in southern Ireland, attended the 1956 Congress and actively supported these two events.

In 1957, Richard Jenkin as International Secretary and accompanied by his wife, visited the Welsh National Eisteddfod at Llangefni, Anglesey. He went specifically to encourage the revival of the Welsh Branch of the Celtic Congress which had collapsed. In a letter dated 26 July to the Misses M. and P. Roberts he expressed the hope that they would help the Congress in the work of International Celtic co-operation. As a Cornishman, he was 'most anxious to see our Welsh cousins again taking a leading part in The Celtic Congress'.[26] He was successful in this, encouraging 'Miss Roberts' by writing to her again and by sending lists of addresses he had gathered at Llanfefni.[27] He spoke for Cornwall in Cornish at the Welsh National Eisteddfod Gorsedd ceremonies. This again was a pattern of future links, for Richard Jenkin was never a narrow-minded Cornishman and would speak at Welsh eisteddfodau on many future occasions as a representative of Kernow.[28] Four months later, Morwenna his first daughter was born. She later became a Cornish, Breton and Welsh scholar and teacher in her own right.

At the Isle of Man Congress in 1958, Richard Jenkin spoke for Cornwall on 'The Rights of Small Nations in an Atomic Age', giving a quick review of the position of Cornwall and lamenting the fact that it did not have an institution like the Tynwald.[29] On his return, he gave a talk about the Isle of Man to the Cornish Branch. He continued to support the re-activated Welsh Branch, advising Miss Roberts on how best to write a secretary's report.[30] The decade ended with Richard Jenkin as International Secretary leading a 12-strong Cornish contingent to Edinburgh. Another play – *An Try Brogh* – was performed in

Cornish, an exhibition of Cornish books was on display and Dick Gendall entertained with Cornish songs. Once again, Cornish delegates demonstrated the value of Kernow as a small Celtic nation.[31]

Late in 1959, with his wife and two small daughters, Richard moved back to Cornwall, where he was to remain for the rest of his life. Finally, a dream realised! There he taught chemistry for many years at Helston Grammar School and then other sciences at Helston Comprehensive School.

The 1960s

Although he did not attend the first Celtic Congress of the new decade at Aberystwyth in 1960, he continued as International Secretary until the following year when he was succeeded by Eluned Bebb.

In August 1962, Richard Jenkin and his wife and their two daughters (Loveday had been born in 1959, just before the family returned to Cornwall to live), Hugh and Joan Miners, and other members of the Cornish Branch flew to Brittany to attend the Celtic Congress there. This was an inspiring and lively Congress held in Landreger (Treguier), where four-year-old Morwenna managed to get her first taste of Breton cider. Many of the Congress delegates stayed in Plougrescant with M. Omnes, a former member of Kelgh Keltek. Teenager Alan Cochevelou, who would later become famous as Alan Stivell, played stirring Breton songs to charm and uplift the souls of the Cornish delegates. In addition, there was Breton processional dancing through the streets of Landreger until about 2am. The illuminated stained glass windows of the local church provided a magical backdrop for all the concerts, which also featured numerous other young Breton musicians, many of whom, such as the Keraod family, became friends. One of the most famous who entertained was Glenmor.[32] That autumn Richard and Ann Jenkin arranged a coffee morning at Leedstown to raise funds for the impending Celtic Congress in Carbis Bay in the spring of 1963. The amount raised – a grand total of £21 5s – was considered a satisfactory profit in those days![33]

1963 saw the introduction of a raffle – Gwary Dall dhe Sen Pyran/Grand St Piran's Day Draw – in aid of the Celtic Congress in Cornwall and promoted by Stephen Fuller. All the Branch members helped with sales to raise more funds for Carbis Bay.[34] At that Carbis Bay Celtic Congress Dr Charles Thomas, a

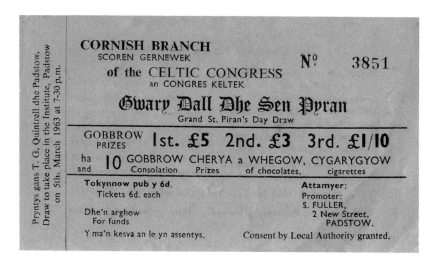

Ticket for Grand St Piran's Day draw, Celtic Congress, March 1963

young lecturer in archaeology at Edinburgh University, came back to chair the whole event, with which Richard Jenkin was, of course, deeply involved. Charles Thomas spoke on 'The Cornish Revival 1903-1963', which was well received; other speakers also praised the revival in Cornish language and culture since the end of the Second World War.[35]

Richard Jenkin was one of those early visionary revivalists, not always obviously seeking the limelight, but working quietly and conscientiously as a mover and shaker. He had recently been made Joint Vice-chairman of the Cornish Branch. Many motions presented to the full Congress were in support of the proper recognition of the Breton language and Breton history, education and culture, and it is interesting that about fifty years later, the International Congress was asked to support similar motions in respect of Cornish. It did take fifty years for Kernow to begin to catch up with the other Celtic nations, partly because Cornwall was still seen as an 'English county' by many.

In 1964, Richard attended the International Celtic Congress in Douglas, Isle of Man and the following year was one of six people representing Cornwall in

Glasgow. On 18 August he spoke for Cornwall at the Congress symposium on 'Modernising Vocabulary', outlining the special circumstances surrounding the Cornish language. Furthermore, in 1966 he was interviewed in Cornwall by a team from Wales who were collecting material about the Cornish language for the Welsh-language programme, *Heddiw*.

The following year the whole Jenkin family attended the Congress in Cardiff, and there is a photograph of all of them with Richard – Gawen had been born in 1963 – on a visit to what is now St Fagan: National History Museum, which is itself another fascinating example of a Celtic initiative which Cornwall might one day be able to emulate.[36] These family visits to Celtic countries became the norm, and the Jenkin children were fortunate to attend many Congresses throughout their childhood, to meet children from other Celtic countries and to absorb the history, culture, language and music of these other small nations. This was also an enduring legacy of Richard and Ann Jenkin's lifelong involvement in Celtic matters.

1968 saw them all in Fougères in Brittany, where one of the highlights was the outdoor concert in front of the stunning castle, with Christine and Mary Truran, daughters of Leonard and Joan Truran, singing movingly in Cornish. On Wednesday 21 August, Richard Jenkin spoke for Cornwall on 'The Present Situation in the Celtic Countries'.[37] At the Congress at Kenegie, Gulval, near Penzance the following year, he led a discussion on 'The Economic Situation and its Social Effects in the Celtic Countries'. He also took a Cornish-language service at Gulval Parish Church, a practice which was strengthened when he first became Deputy Grand Bard of Gorsedh Kernow in 1972, and which continued for the rest of his life.[38]

The 1970s
In 1969 Richard Jenkin had been invited to become International Vice-president, a post created because the current President, Rev. T.M. Murchison from Scotland, could not attend owing to his having been elected President of the Methodist Conference and the clash of dates that this brought about. For the Isle of Man Congress at Douglas the following year, therefore, Richard took on the role of Acting President, and in 1971 became President in his own right, a post he held for the next five years, finishing at Port Erin, Isle of Man, in 1976.

In that year he became Grand Bard of Gorsedh Kernow, which resulted in more commitments in Cornwall. With the birth of Conan, their fourth child, in 1969, and with four children to raise, his wife Ann could not always manage to attend every Congress.

Those six years between 1971 and 1976 were extremely active ones for the new President, and Richard discharged his duties and obligations with charisma, always speaking Cornish on official occasions, and always stressing the importance of the little land he represented, as well as Cornwall's need for the support and friendship of the other Celtic nations. In 1971 he was in Stirling where he contributed to the symposium on Celtic Art. From that year, he was also Chairman of the Cornish Branch. Ahead of the 1972 Celtic Congress, which was held in Bangor, north Wales, he wrote as President to a Mr Roberts (presumably Hywel Roberts, the Secretary of the Welsh Branch) concerning a forthcoming meeting to choose the Cornish delegates and clarifying the arrangements which the host country normally put in place:

> We are not yet sure how many of our family will be with us – probably all of them... The youngest is three which is an awkward age, either to bring or to leave![39]

The 1973 Congress was held in Blessington, Eire.

During these years, Richard Jenkin had some tough assignments, as by now young people – particularly in Wales and Brittany – were becoming more politically active. In essence, one of the problems is that the Celtic Congress is non-party political, and yet so much of what the Celts need can be on the fringes or, indeed, at the centre of parliamentary action. In Nantes, Brittany in 1974, for instance, a great number of young Bretons arrived wanting political action, and despite the fact that he himself as an individual was sympathetic to their views – he was, after all, a founder member of Mebyon Kernow – no party political action could be taken, although statements on economic and cultural diversity were, of course, 'political' with a small 'p'. In fact, at Nantes, a Declaration of Cultural Rights was agreed and published, the theme of that Congress being 'The Cultural Rights of Human Communities'. The speakers were expected not only to deal with the situation in their respective countries, but also primarily to state what cultural rights were, in their view, fundamental for the development of their own (Celtic) culture.[40] As chairman, Richard Jenkin described to the Congress Annual Business Meeting that a committee of three had 'worked through the night' to produce a draft of the proposed Declaration.[41]

The Declaration, which each country took back to publicise in any way possible, included discussion on Education, Literature, Mass Media, Administration, Cultural Destruction and Culture and the Economy. There was also an addendum, strongly supporting the rights of Bretons to expect a more positive status for their culture and language from the French Republic, and citing the European Convention on Human Rights. The Congress also asked that the British/English and Irish governments should support the special case for Brittany.[42] After the Congress, Richard Jenkin in his report spoke of its success, not only in the matter of the above Declaration of Cultural Rights, but also for the support for the revival of interest in the Brythonic languages, including Kernewek. The second inspiration for him '... was the interest and knowledge of Kernow to be found among our brother and sister Celts...'[43] This is interesting, as until the 1980s, Kernow was seen very much as the poor relation of the six Celtic countries; thereafter, though, support from the wider Congress helped to strengthen Cornwall's cultural diversity and language.

When the Congress came back to Cornwall in 1975, large numbers of young Bretons arrived at Carlyon Bay unannounced and without having booked accommodation. They again supported political action, so this was another fine line for Richard Jenkin to tread, which he did with tact and consideration for all views. The theme of this Congress was 'The Effect of Tourism and other Economic Developments on National Life'. Younger members, in particular, argued that politics was an integral part of the theme and should be discussed. At the end of the discussions, a statement was drafted condemning any *further* expansion of tourism as detrimental to the quality of life in the four countries which were not self-governing, although delegates accepted that tourism played some part in the economy of the Celtic peoples. They asked for close, effective control of the tourist industry and strict limits on its expansion in the future. It was also felt that it was better to channel resources into the creation of permanent employment. Priority should be given to preserving land and national resources for the benefit of the people of the Celtic countries, rather than allowing for exploitation by developers and others for purely commercial and selfish ends.[44]

One of the most heartening and impressive effects of that Congress was the greater use of the Cornish language for talking, announcing, singing, acting – in fact, using Cornish again as a spoken language. The Cornish language was just one subject of a long and interesting letter which Richard and Ann Jenkin wrote to Hywel Roberts, then Secretary of the Welsh Branch and Vice-chairman of the Celtic Congress, and his wife Glennis towards the end of 1975. Richard thought that the language movement was making good progress, with many more young Cornish people involved than formerly. One of the main difficulties was a shortage of good teachers. As far as the Congress was concerned, he was hoping for a quiet one in Mann in 1976. 'After Ireland, Brittany and Cornwall,' he continued, 'I am beginning to feel that my term of office might have been the noisiest presidency ever in the history of the Congress.' The Manx subject, 'The Future of my Country', could prove controversial, too. He hoped that Hywel would find his term as President 'easier, with a more constructive and less critical membership'.[45]

Port Erin in the Isle of Man was, then, the venue for the 1976 Celtic Congress. It proved to be another successful and profitable occasion, on which the chairman, Jack Keggin from the Port Erin Commissioners, welcomed everyone and said they could now see devolution in action – something that was not true of any other Celtic country. He was thanked by President, Richard Jenkin. The speaker from Cornwall, Julyan Holmes, spoke on the theme 'What does it mean to belong to the Celtic World today?' He emphasised that Kernow was at the start of a long road, especially as the Cornish had had to cope with a debilitating feeling of inferiority common to other Celts. In his opinion, '…the most aware Cornish men tended to be those who had emigrated, and now not more than 40% of Cornish living there, were of Cornish stock'. He went on to emphasise '…that now this obliteration of awareness had been reversed, he hoped the trickle would soon become a flood…'. There were now Cornish language classes in most major Cornish towns, although there was a shortage of trained teachers, and the standard was not yet good enough. However, there was a strong move to get back Cornish culture into the work of choirs, bands and folk groups.[46]

Thirty-five years later, many of Julyan Holmes's aspirations have come to pass, and for Julyan Holmes, Richard Jenkin and other Cornish delegates, some of the inspiration for improvement came from Congresses like that of 1976, where the highlight was visiting Tynwald, the seat of Manx government. However, Celtic countries were also beginning to look outwards to Europe and the European Economic Community for future development and inspiration.

It was at the 1976 Celtic Congress that Richard Jenkin was made International Life Vice-president in honour of his continuing work for the Congress, both abroad and at home in Cornwall. Hywel Roberts from Cardiff, the incoming President, paid the highest tribute to Richard Jenkin for six years of service as President. He also paid tribute to Ann Jenkin for all her loyal support to her husband in his Cornish and Celtic activities.[47]

In 1978 Richard Jenkin was the speaker at the symposium on 'Cornwall and the EEC', in Carmarthen, south Wales. Having spoken of the industries common in Cornwall at that time – market gardening, farming, some fishing, some mining – he came to the conclusion that EEC policy on many of the industries was not understood in a peripheral country like Cornwall. The advantages that could accrue from Europe were being stifled by being controlled and administered by the English government whose interests were not always the same as Cornish national interests. To him, this suggested the necessity for a direct channel of communication from Cornwall to the EEC through some form of government organisation of our own.[48]

The 1980s
From the 1980s onwards, Richard Jenkin was not only deeply involved in Gorsedh Kernow, Esedhvos Kernow and other cultural organisations in Cornwall, but also with Mebyon Kernow and Cornish politics. As a result, his work for the Congress was not continuous, although it never completely stopped and he continued to visit and support Congresses until 2002, attending his last one in Carmarthen just before his death. He spoke on several occasions, as did other members of his family. In 1984, 2000 and 2011 it was Dr Loveday Jenkin; in 1987, Conan Jenkin at a Youth Symposium; in 1980 Morwenna Jenkin spoke, and her husband Mikael Baudu was a speaker at Carmarthen in 2002. Ann Jenkin gave a talk in 1997 on 'The Effects of the Media on the Celtic

Cover of booklet to commemorate visit of Celtic Congress to Newquay, April 1988

Cover of booklet for Celtic Congress, Lesneven, Brittany, July 1989

World', and on 'Celtic Women in History' in 2004, so the Jenkin family was not silent for long! After learning Breton, marrying and moving permanently to Brittany, where she now teaches in the Diwan schools and trains Breton teachers, Morwenna has acted as a simultaneous translator for many years at Celtic Congresses, right up to the Guingamp one in 2012.

Cornwall continued to be extremely active in Congress matters generally in the 1980s, hosting the event in 1982 at Ponsandane, Penzance, and in 1988 in Newquay. An extract from the booklet published before the first of these conferences stresses this fact:

> Possibly because of our small size, the Cornish Celtic Revival is very outward-looking, taking inspiration and encouragement from our fellow Celts. The Celtic Congress, as the first international body to recognise our existence as a nation, is held here in special regard.[49]

When Richard Jenkin retired as a teacher in December 1981, he had more time to devote to Cornish and Celtic matters. A Congress photograph,[50] taken on the steps of St John's Hall, Penzance after a civic reception, of Richard Jenkin, Grand Bard, and Ann Jenkin, Congress secretary and recently-elected International treasurer, stresses this continuing involvement. Morwenna Jenkin, their eldest daughter, was that year teaching Welsh and Cornish at Rennes University in Brittany.

In 1984 Loveday Jenkin was the speaker for Cornwall, in Cork, Eire, on 'Benenes a Gernow/Women of Cornwall', and as an active young Cornish woman, she gave an impassioned speech on the importance of women in both Cornish and Celtic society. The speech was given in Cornish, with a written translation provided; her husband, Brian Webb was also an inspirational Cornish entertainer.

When the Celtic Congress met in Inverness, Scotland, in 1987, the theme was 'Growing up in a Celtic World'. Eighteen-year-old Conan Jenkin, the fourth child of Richard and Ann, had just left school and was one of the growing number of young people who stressed how hard it was to remain true to their roots in Kernow, where almost everything was dictated from central government, including Cornish children's English-oriented education. Conan, though, was one of the lucky ones to go to Camborne School where there was some respect for Cornish Studies, Cornish dancing and the Cornish language. Cornish plays were performed annually and some radio broadcasts and interviews were conducted in Cornish. A few candidates voluntarily took CSE Cornish, but most were not so fortunate. The visit to Scotland had again given Kernow the goals to aim for. Richard Jenkin was by now encouraging all young people, including his own, to be true to their Cornish and Celtic heritage.[51]

When the Congress returned to Cornwall in 1988, the theme was 'The Celtic Congress and the Sea'. Once again, many young people attended and took part at the Great Western Hotel, Newquay, overlooking a stormy coast.[52] Richard Jenkin welcomed the Celtic delegates to Cornwall and as the son of a Church of England clergyman and a staunch member of the church, he gave the sermon on:

> A clew ny pan grysys orthys
> Gans nep war vor yu peryllys.
>
> *O hear us when we cry to thee*
> *For those in peril on the sea.*

As always, his strong voice and powerful delivery made this sermon memorable, especially his references to the strength and destructiveness of the sea, by which Kernow is almost surrounded, and to the power of God to calm the raging storm. It was remembered, too, by his other Celtic friends in the congregation, many of whom did not know or understand the Cornish language, but could appreciate its poetry.[53] A small booklet, *Kernow ha'n Mor/Cornwall and the Sea*,[54] was published for that Congress by An Gresen Gernewek, the Cornish Language Centre set up by Dr Loveday Jenkin and her late husband. Richard Jenkin's contributions to the poems and other writings on the main theme were: 'Cornwall Recalled (at Volos Greece)', 'The Irish Lady' (under the nom de plume, Garfield Richardson), and 'The Mermaid' – all emotive poems full of the passion of love, the movement and power of the sea, and with a great sense of place.

The final Congress of the '80s took place at Lesneven, Brittany, in 1989. A

Richard and Ann Jenkin, Celtic Congress, Carmarthen, July 2002

photograph[55] shows that the members attending included Richard and Ann Jenkin, Morwenna and Loveday Jenkin, and Trystan, Loveday's son, so the next generation was becoming involved at an early age!

The 1990s
These were again busy years when Richard Jenkin, despite not very good health, was still involved in the Celtic Congress, especially with events in Cornwall, and sometimes those further afield. At Douglas, Isle of Man, in 1992, it was stated that 'the idea of self-appraisal of the Celtic Congress should be on a regular basis', as Richard and other Celtic leaders did not believe that the Celtic world should be backward-looking or stand still if its influence was to be expanded. He did not attend the 1993 Congress in Inverness, but was present in Falmouth the following year when another very successful Congress with a broad and inclusive programme was held.

Following on from previous Congresses such as that in Eire in 1991, where the emphasis had been to encourage young people to participate, youth-focused events in 1994 involved several youngsters from Cornwall. One of the innovations at that Congress was a celebrity auction, which raised several hundred pounds for the Cornish Branch.[56] In 1995 he travelled over to Lorient, Brittany, with a busload of Welsh friends, his wife – as Deputy Grand Bard of Gorsedh Kernow – being in the United States addressing the Cornish American Heritage Society conference.

In 1996 the Cornish Branch was pleased to welcome Larry Climo as only the second Cornish International President of the Congress, Richard Jenkin having been the first.[57] Twenty-five Cornish delegates took part in the Congress in Bangor, north Wales, that year, the theme being 'Celtic Literature and Culture in the Twentieth Century'. Richard and Alan Kent shared the floor for Kernow, with Richard talking about literature in the Cornish language and Dr Kent about Cornish literature in English. The two speakers complemented each other and their very full presentation was greatly appreciated. The papers were published, and are a helpful reminder of how much Cornish writing had been extended and developed by the 1990s. Richard Jenkin as poet, writer and lecturer, both in Cornish and English, had helped with that renaissance. The publication of the lectures also helped to raise the profile of Cornish cultural diversity in Cornwall itself, as well as among the other Celtic countries.[58] Richard, himself, had had several poems published in Welsh magazines, having as a young man in the early 1950s before his marriage lived and taught in Wales for a few years, and made many lifelong friends there.

In Dublin in 1997, when Ann Jenkin spoke for Cornwall on 'The Role and Influence of the Media', the International Celtic Congress supported publicly a vote of confidence in the Cornish march to London that May to commemorate 500 years since the original march by Michael Joseph 'An Gof'. It was impressed by the energy and determination of the Cornish to emphasise and enhance their own twentieth-century identity, a change from the early days of the Congress in Kernow. The Jenkins – particularly Ann, one of the main organisers – were deeply involved with that event, although Richard could not walk much of the route. He was, however, present at the start at St Keverne, when the marchers crossed the border at Launceston, and at the final day at Blackheath a month later – a measure of his continuing devotion to Cornwall.[59]

That September, a new poetry anthology was published by the American New Native Press entitled *Writing the Wind: A Celtic Resurgence*. Sub-titled *The New Celtic Poetry*, it was edited by Thomas Raine Crowe, with Gwendal Denez (Brittany) and Tom Hubbard (Scotland) as advisers, and featured poems from all six Celtic nations. Richard was one of the contributors from Cornwall.

He attended the Congress in Port Erin, Isle of Man, in 1998, but not the one in Glasgow the following year, although Ann Jenkin was present as one of the Cornish contingent.

2000 onwards

In the year 2000, the Congress once again returned to Cornwall and was held at Bude. Richard attended, partly to support Ann who by then was in her final year as Grand Bard of Gorsedh Kernow. That year she had met overseas Celtic women at their conference in Milwaukee in the USA, where she had been given the overall award as Celtic Woman of the Year, a great honour for Kernow and for the Jenkin family. Celtic roots were widening and deepening through the diaspora. Dr Loveday Jenkin spoke at Bude on 'Celtic Resurgence',[60] and Richard contributed some of his own poems at a Celtic poetry evening in the Falcon Hotel. He also took part in the Gorsedh Proclamation and enjoyed chatting to old friends and listening to the lectures.

Later he attended the first Dehwelans/Homecoming at Pendennis Castle, Falmouth, a conference chaired by Ann Jenkin to encourage the Cornish from overseas to come back to celebrate their Cornish and Celtic heritage.[61] This was a very successful innovation in the Cornish calendar and an event which was greatly enjoyed by Richard and others, helping re-establish global links. Richard, himself, had always had a huge correspondence with overseas bards and others, even though he did not travel overseas to meet them except to other Celtic countries. Many, though, sought him out in Cornwall when they visited friends and relations or attended Cornish events in the homeland.

Richard did not attend the Celtic Congress in Rennes in 2001, but the following summer he accompanied his wife Ann to his last Congress in Carmarthen, where, as always, he enjoyed meeting everyone and taking part in most of the programme. A photograph of him shows the same enthusiasm for life and the same good humour that had been there sixty years before.[62]

Richard Jenkin's contribution to the Celtic world

Richard Jenkin was a dedicated and faithful member of the Celtic Congress both in Kernow and beyond the Tamar for well over fifty years. His work was immeasurable and his support unwavering. He loved the wide links with the other five Celtic countries, especially Wales and Brittany. He left a lasting legacy to his family where all four children, to a greater or lesser degree, have been involved in supporting minority cultures, languages, history and education. He followed with the same enthusiasm the growth of interest in Celtic languages and culture of his five older grandchildren over the years; four others were born after his death in 2002. Three of these older children learnt to speak Breton from birth and two to speak Cornish. Three of the younger ones are now learning to speak Cornish from birth. He was an encourager and inspirational leader to both individuals and to groups, as well as to his family. His continuing support for Kernow and the Celtic nations was summed up for this writer in the following short poem – 'Whegh Bro, Un Enef/ Six Lands, One Soul' – which he had written some years previously:

> Whegh bro yndan an nef,
> Whegh corf, un enef,
> Whegh yeth, un lavar.
> Whegh cledha, un escar,
> Whegh bro a Geltya.

> *Six lands under heaven,*
> *Six bodies, one soul,*
> *Six languages, one speech.*
> *Six swords, one foe,*
> *Six lands of Celtia.*[63]

Postscript

In 2003, at the International Celtic Congress in All Hallows College, Dublin, there was a special commemoration of Richard Jenkin, emphasising his links through well over fifty years with the organisation's Cornish and International branches. It was a moving occasion for his family, several of whom were present.

In 2004, at the International Celtic Congress in Port Erin, Isle of Man, Ann Trevenen Jenkin, his widow, donated a Cornish copper plastron on behalf of his family for the use of succeeding Celtic Congress presidents in memory of Richard Jenkin and to commemorate his great achievements for Kernow and the Celtic world.

Notes
1 Jenkin family papers, Leedstown.
2 Celtic Congress records, the author, 1950.
3 Ibid.
4 Ibid.
5 Personal reminiscences, the author; University College of the South West Student Journal, March 1952; Exeter Celtic Society.
6. *Henry and Katharine Jenner: A Celebration of Cornwall's Culture, Language and Identity*, Derek R. Williams (ed.), Francis Boutle Publishers, 2004.
7 Gorsedh Kernow Archives.
8 *West Briton*, 15 September 1932.
9 *Setting Cornwall on its Feet: Robert Morton Nance, 1873-1959*, Peter W. Thomas and Derek R. Williams (eds.), Francis Boutle Publishers, 2007, pp. 248-270.
10 Ibid., pp. 271-276.
11 *Henry and Katharine Jenner*, p. 51.
12 *Setting Cornwall on its Feet: Robert Morton Nance, 1873-1959*, p. 276.
13 Celtic Congress records, the author.
14 Ibid., the author.
15 Photograph outside the Royal Institution of Cornwall, Truro, 1950, Celtic Congress Archives, Cornwall Record Office, Truro.
16 Bernard Deacon, Dick Cole and Garry Tregidga, *Mebyon Kernow & Cornish Nationalism*, Welsh Academic Press, 2003.
17 Undated press cutting, Jenkin family archive.
18 Photograph, Isle of Man, 1952, Celtic Congress archives.
19 Programme and press cuttings, the author; postcard Pantyfedwen, the author.
20 *Connacht Tribune*, 31 July 1954.
21 *Western Morning News* [?], 17 February 1955.
22 Per Denez, 'Richard Jenkin (1925-2002)', *Al Liamm*, (Tir na'n Og), no. 335, Kerzu 2002. See English translation by Morwenna Jenkin in this publication.
23 *Western Morning News*, [n.d.], 1956.
24 Photo taken outside the Royal Cornwall Museum, Truro, 1956, Jenkin family archive.
25 Cover design, the author.
26 Envelope marked 'Cyngres Celtaidd 1958/1959/60', Celtic Congress Archive (GB 0210 CELESS), National Library of Wales of Wales, Aberystwyth.
27 Ibid.
28 There is a striking photograph of him speaking to the Welsh National Eisteddfod, probably at Flint in 1969; at least, his style of dress suggests the late 1960s.

29 *Isle of Man Weekly Times*, 11 April 1958.
30 Letter from Totnes dated 29 July 1959, 'Cyngres Celtaidd 1958/1959/60', Celtic Congress Archive (GB 0210 CELESS), National Library of Wales of Wales, Aberystwyth.
31 *Cornishman*, 27 August 1959.
32 Photograph of stained glass window, Tréguier, the author.
33 Press cutting [Autumn, 1962], Jenkin family archive
34 Raffle ticket, 1963, the author.
35 *St Ives Times and Echo*, 19 April 1963.
36 Photograph, the author.
37 Personal memories, the author.
38 Jenkin family archive.
39 Letter dated 29 April 1972, buff box 'Additional material relating to the International Celtic Congress 1971-9... 8/16/1, Celtic Congress Archive, National Library of Wales of Wales, Aberystwyth.
40 *Kendalch Keltiek Newsletter* 1, Hor Yezh, c/o Yann Desbordes, Lesneven, Breizh.
41 [Minutes] of Annual Business Meeting in Nantes University, Brittany, 16 August 1974, envelope marked 'Cernyw 1969 and 1975', Celtic Congress Archive, National Library of Wales, Aberystwyth.
42 *Kendalch Keltiek* 5, text in different Celtic languages.
43 Report on the Congress, *Kendalch Keltiek* 7.
44 Report by Ann Trevenen Jenkin, Celtic Congress secretary, Kernow.
45 Letter dated Nadelek 1975, unmarked buff folder, Celtic Congress Archive, National Library of Wales, Aberystwyth.
46 *Manx Star*, 23 April 1976.
47 *The Cornishman*. 29 April 1976; photograph of Richard and Ann Jenkin, Port Erin, Isle of Man, in the *Manx Star*, 24 April 1976.
48 Copy of speech, Jenkin family archive.
49 Leaflet, Celtic Congress Archives, Cornwall Record Office, Truro.
50 Photograph, Jenkin family archive.
51 Newquay Congress, Jenkin family archive.
52 Ibid. 1988.
53 Ibid. 1988.
54 *Kernow ha'n Mor/Cornwall and the Sea*, Dr Loveday Jenkin (ed.), An Gresen Kernewek, 1988.
55 Photograph, Jenkin family archive.
56 Press report [n.d.], 1991.
57 *West Briton*, 8 August 1996.
58 *Celtic Literature & Culture in the Twentieth Century*, International Celtic Congress, 1997; Jenkin family archive; Cornwall Record Office, Truro.
59 Celtic Congress press release 1997, Ann Trevenen Jenkin, Celtic Congress press officer, Cornish Branch.
60 Celtic Congress Archives, Cornwall Record Office, Truro.
61 Dehwelans 2000 archives, the author.
62 Jenkin family archive.
63 Unpublished poems, Jenkin family archive.

Acknowledgements

Gorsedh Kernow Archives, Leedstown; Cornwall Record Office, Truro; Courtney Library, Truro; Celtic Congress Archive, Cornwall Record Office, Truro, and National Library of Wales, Aberystwyth; Dehwelans Archives

(Keskerdh Kernow); Jenkin family archive and photographs.

Thank you to Morwenna, Loveday, Gawen and Conan (our children) for their advice, help and support, as well as to many friends in Cornwall and the other Celtic countries, particularly Brian Stowell (Isle of Man).

'Cusk lemmyn, cuf-colon'/'Sleep now, sweetheart'

Richard G. Jenkin

Cusk lemmyn, cuf-colon.
Dege dha dheulagas squyth.
Vorow dans drok ny omglewyth.
Powes yv cosel, baby vy'an.

Cusk lemmyn, cuf-colon.
Dagrow tyn rak glyn cravys,
Bay mam a'n gwra-ef yaghhys.
Powes yn cosel, chyl vy'an.

Cusk lemmyn, cuf-colon.
'Ma puscas gwell whath y'n mor.
Ancof e, caf aral war nep cor.
Powes yn cosel, maghteth vy'an.

Cusk lemmyn, cuf-colon.
Dha wour tramor res eth;
Arta ef a dhe nep deth.
Powes yn cosel, ow myrgh sowyn.

Cusk lemmyn, cuf-colon/Sleep now, Sweetheart

Cusk lemmyn, cuf-colon.
An paynys a fy dhe'n fo.
'Ma dhys lemmyn dha flogh.
Powes yn cosel, ow myrgh gerra.

Cusk lemmyn, cuf-colon.
Cosoleth hyr y fyth dhys
Y'n beth bys gorfen bys.
Powes yn cosel, ow myrgh gerra.

Sleep now, sweetheart.
Close your tired eyes.
At morn you'll not feel toothache.
Rest calm, li'l babe.

Sleep now, sweetheart.
Sharp tears for a scratched knee,
Mam's kiss will make it better.
Rest calm, li'l child.

Sleep now, sweetheart.
There's better fish still in the sea.
Forget him, find another somehow.
Rest calm, li'l maid.

Sleep now, sweetheart.
Your man has gone abroad;
He'll come back some day.
Rest calm, my lucky daughter.

Sleep now, sweetheart.
The pains will flee away.
You've got your child now.
Rest calm, my dearest daughter.

Sleep now, sweetheart.
A long quiet rest you'll have
In the grave till the world ends.
Rest calm, my dearest daughter.

[This poem was commended in the Gorsedh Cornish Verse competition in 1999]

'Bedhen Breder Warbarth': Richard Jenkin and the Cornish Language

Jori Ansell

Early inspiration

A chance discovery of books on Cornish in Manchester library when he was a teenager whetted young Richard Jenkin's appetite to learn more. He was at the time on a visit from his Derbyshire home, where his father was training for the ministry. His awareness of his Cornish roots was all part of his upbringing and it was bolstered by regular visits to Mousehole with his father. From there he was able to visit the Morrab Library in Penzance and immerse himself in its collection of Cornish material.

Once he had decided to learn the language, he used Henry Jenner's *Handbook of the Cornish Language*, A.S.D. Smith's *Lessons in Spoken Cornish* and Morton Nance's *Cornish for All*, which were the principal books available at the time. On his arrival at Exeter College, Oxford, to read chemistry, he met several prominent Cornish people – A.L. Rowse, Nina Bawden, John Legonna (of Welsh/Cornish parentage) and others – who were instrumental in forming the Oxford University Cornish Society.

John Legonna writes in his diary for 11 February 1944 '...yn darllen 'Old Cornwall'. Ar ol hall gyda Jenkins yn gwneud Cernyweg' ['...*reading Old Cornwall. After hall with Jenkins (sic) doing Cornish*']. It should be noted that there is also a Dafydd Jenkins mentioned in the diary, but the references to studying Cornish are more likely to concern Richard Jenkin. On 16 February 'Yn yr

Union ar ol Cinio ac ar ol hall gyda Richard Jenkins yn gwneud Cernyweg' [*'In the Union after dinner and after hall with Richard Jenkins doing Cornish'*]. There are similar entries for 22 and 28 February. On 5 May he writes '… Ar ol cinio gyda Richard, Mary ac Alun gyda'r Cernyweg…' [*'… After dinner with Richard, Mary and Alun doing Cornish…'*].

As well as John Legonna, he also met David Balhatchet, who involved himself in the Cornish language movement and was received into bardship by examination in 1992. Richard was to work with David from the late 1980s as a tutor for Kernewek Dre Lyther.

Military service interrupted his university career but not his Cornish studies. He continued learning Cornish and was admitted to the Gorsedh by proxy in 1947 (Launceston) as he was in Greece at the time. His earliest teaching appointment, at Totnes Grammar School, was close enough to Cornwall to allow frequent visits to make contact with people in the language movement and to be able to take part in language activities. His appointment to the staff at Helston School brought him permanently into the midst of the Cornish movement.

The Cornish Language Board

In 1967, with interest in the language growing apace, Gorsedh Kernow and the Federation of Old Cornwall Societies co-operated to found the Cornish Language Board to take full responsibility for the development of the language which had theretofore been partly in the hands of individuals, partly in the hands of the Gorsedh and the Federation. Richard was a founder-member of the Board, first as Federation representative and later, from 1986 under the new constitution, as an elected member.

At the first meeting of the Board he was chosen to serve on the Publications Committee, which was instructed by the Board 'to proceed forthwith with the reprinting of the Cornish-English dictionary and the preparation of a Cornish record: …Jowan Chy-an-Horth on one side, Abram hag Ysak, the Lord's Prayer, the 23rd Psalm and the Creed on the other'. Richard was chosen as one of the five 'suitable voices' for the recording. The record was completed and there are later reports in the Board's minutes of very good sales.

At the second meeting of the Board, Richard suggested the adoption of a small badge to enable Cornish speakers to identify one another. He was asked to produce designs and the matter would be considered further. At the next meeting he proposed 'a plain gold bezant' and the Board asked him to obtain a quotation from a manufacturer for 200 badges. The quotation was 4s.8d. each (for 100) and the Board decided no further action be taken on grounds of cost.

Another initiative from Richard in the early days of the Board was to approach the television companies with a view to their putting out information about Cornish and broadcasting a short weekly reading. This was accepted and he agreed to draft the necessary letters. It was later reported that the approach had been 'sympathetically received but has as yet produced no concrete results'.

In 1970 the Board decided to establish an Education Committee, with Richard as one of the members. He was to be involved in arranging weekend and one-day schools, promoting liaison between schools and other educational establishments, compiling a list of teachers and assessing the demand for classes. When a day school was held at Helston School, nineteen students attended. Richard supported Richard Gendall in arranging the event and it is believed to have been the first time in the teaching of Cornish that modern, language-laboratory methods of teaching had been used. This was repeated a year later when twenty-one students took part.

Richard continued his work on the committees of the Board over the next few years until, in 1976, he became co-chairman on being installed as Grand Bard. At his first meeting in the chair he urged the publication of work in progress on the new dictionaries, as the project had been envisaged from the outset as a 5- to 6-year commitment. At the Annual General Meeting of the Board there was a full discussion on a paper prepared by Peter Pool on the possibility of a 'Cornish language society'. Richard chaired the debate and summarised the conclusions in a motion carried with just one vote against, setting in motion the process of founding Cowethas an Yeth Kernewek (The Cornish Language Fellowship), launched at the Fowey Kescows in March 1979.

From 1985 Richard was a tutor for Kernewek dre Lyther (KDL) the correspondence course set up and run by Ray Edwards under the auspices of the Language Board, where he eventually worked alongside his colleague from university, David Balhatchet, who passed his final examination and became a bard in 1992. Following the adoption by the Board of Kernewek Kemmyn in 1987, he continued tutoring those students who wished to continue with Unified Cornish. The new constitution for the Cornish Language Board came into effect in 1986 and Richard was one of the successful candidates for election to membership.

Discussion and division
Dissatisfaction with Unified Cornish had been emerging during the late 1970s. The writer of this article remembers an informal discussion at lunchtime during a Penseythen Kernewek (Cornish Weekend) at Carworgie Manor, near St Columb Road, when several speakers, Richard included, debated the shortcomings of UC and put forward their ideas for amending the orthography of Cornish. The discussion was curtailed by the start of the official timetable of classes and activities at 2 o'clock, but all present agreed to go home, do their research and publish their evidence and proposals. During the 1980s various papers and publications appeared with a wide range of ideas, from minor adjustments to a few words up to a full repositioning of the chronological base of the language.

A significant turning point was reached in 1986 with the publication of *The Pronunciation and Spelling of Revived Cornish* by Dr Ken George, proposing 'dhe wellhe Kernewek yn un ewnhe fowtow Mordon, ha dhe worra an gis-leveryans keffrys ha'n lytherennans war sel moy skiantjek' [*'to improve Cornish by correcting Mordon's errors and to put the pronunciation and the spelling on a more sound academic basis'*]. At an open meeting held in the Friends' Meeting House, Truro, on 13 June 1987, Richard was reported in the Board's minutes to have stated his position thus:

> Ny vynnaf assentya dhe janj dyen par dhe dowl Ken George. Da yu genev sevel neppyth le ynter tybyans Ken George ha furf an tavas del yua lemmyn: ny allaf-vy holya an forth noweth [*I cannot agree to total change such as Ken George proposes. I would like to make a more modest revision, somewhere between Ken George's idea and the form of the language as it is now: I cannot follow the new way*].

This meeting set the scene for several years of confrontation and sometimes unpleasant debate about the future of the language. Richard, however, always remained courteous and polite, distancing himself from more extreme statements, even those supporting Unified Cornish.

At a meeting of the Gorsedh Council in February 1988, Richard shrewdly made the following proposal:

> The Gorseth in recognising that no one person nor one body can enforce particular spelling or pronunciation of Cornish, resolves that (i) work in Cornish in any spelling system or pronunciation shall be acceptable in the Gorseth competitions; (ii) in its own ceremonies, services, official statements, letters and bardic names, it will continue to use Unified Cornish; (iii) it is recommended that this resolution shall be changed only by a majority vote at an AGM.

It was largely because of the high esteem and respect which Council members had for Richard – he had served three terms as Grand Bard, totalling nine years, and four years as Secretary in the 1960s – that the motion was adopted by a majority vote after an animated debate. This had the effect of raising the Gorsedh above potentially damaging arguments and the Grand Bard could offer his services as an honest broker, appeal for courtesy and reason in the debate and speak in confidence to bards who, in his opinion, had overstepped the mark. The Grand Bard during much of this time was *Gwas Costentyn* (Dr John Chesterfield, Grand Bard 1988-1991). He arranged a meeting of the proponents in the debate at his house in Chacewater to try to resolve the apparent deadlock, but without success. He declared at a Cornish Language Board meeting in January 1990 that there 'was no clear outcome' to the discussions. Subsequent Grand Bards were obliged to follow the same path of trying to 'pour oil on troubled waters' with varying degrees of success.

At the same Language Board meeting, Richard asked whether the GCSE would be in both Unified Cornish and Kernewek Kemmyn. The Board member responsible for the process, John King, replied that the South-West Examination Board would only accept one spelling form, which would be KK.

During all this time Richard continued to serve on the Board's various committees, principally Yeth ha Gerva (Language and Vocabulary) and Dyllans (Publication). He was re-elected to the Board in 1992 and continued until 1995, often a lone voice speaking up for Unified Cornish at meetings. To his great sadness he failed to gain re-election in that year. The Board sent him a letter of thanks for his long and valuable service and he replied that he hoped the Board would continue to co-operate with users of UC.

Personally this writer admired his courage in remaining for some years as the sole supporter of Unified Cornish on the Language Board, knowing that at each meeting he was in a minority of one. His low point was when he failed to be re-elected to the Board – he was, this writer believes, a victim of the atmosphere at the time – but he bounced back, as was his nature, and championed Cornish through Agan Tavas. His arguments over the language were always pursued with respect for the opinions of others and, as in his other activities, he always thought the best of everyone. A letter of 1996 from Richard Gendall to Richard Jenkin said that, after all, they were speaking the same language and he hoped for a good relationship and cooperation between followers of Unified and Modern (Late) Cornish.

In May 1989 a last-ditch attempt to find common ground was made at a meeting in the Royal Institution of Cornwall (RIC) arranged by Peter Pool and Richard, but without success. Ray Chubb has expressed the opinion that the current Standard Written Form with traditional graphs may well have been acceptable to users of Unified Cornish at that time, including Richard. But the SWF was still nearly twenty years in the future. Richard joined Agan Tavas in December 1989 when it metamorphosed from a society for fluent speakers into one dedicated to supporting Unified Cornish and immediately became a member of its Council.

Agan Tavas

Over the next decade he worked for Cornish within Agan Tavas. His series of literary journals entitled *Delyow Derow* ('Oak Leaves') ran to fifteen editions. It had two aims: to establish a regular publication in Unified Cornish and to provide a showcase for past entries in the Gorsedh competitions. He gave valuable assistance in preparing a revised edition of *Mordon*'s two-way dictionary and edited with Ray Chubb and Graham Sandercock the Unified edition of *Origo Mundi* which was published in 2001.

In 1995 Dr Nicholas Williams published his monograph *Cornish Today*, an analysis of traditional and revived Cornish and a suggested form for the lan-

Cover of the first issue of Delyow Derow, *Winter 1988*

guage in the future, which he called Unified Cornish Revised. In *Delyow Derow* No.15 Richard published a translation by Dr Williams of Tennyson's 'Death of Arthur' ('Ancow Arthur') to show to what extent his recommendations would affect the familiar spelling. He also expressed his own thoughts on the proposals:

> In my opinion, Dr Williams's suggestions are not alterations to Unified Cornish but rather extensions to our language, making it yet more flexible and expressive.

He went on to recommend the acceptance of Williams' spellings and new words, as well as grammatical forms and idioms from Tregear as 'valid alternatives' to Unified Cornish, 'not a difference in structure or in language but in style'. After Richard's death in 2002, Dr Williams went on to make further, more extensive changes to his spelling system. We can never know, of course, how acceptable they would have been to Richard, but we can be sure he would have scrutinised them and brought his many years of experience and knowledge to bear on the subject before expressing his opinion. He was made an Honorary Life Member of Agan Tavas at the Annual General Meeting in February 2002.

Sermons and prayers
Richard was born 'in exile' in Ilkeston, Derbyshire, because his father was there training for the Church of England ministry. Not only did he instil in the young Richard a sense of his Cornish origins, but also laid the foundations for a lifetime of involvement in the Church. His father later held livings at St Gennys, near Bude, and at St Mewan, near St Austell.

Once Richard had returned to Cornwall after military service and university, he preached in Cornish on many occasions. His nine years as Grand Bard gave him an opportunity to develop this talent and he became well known and well respected in the Cornish movement for his sermons. *Cornwhylen* (Fr Richard Rutt) considered him the best preacher in Cornish. This was mentioned at a conference at Perranporth when *Cornwhylen* was critical of some Grand Bards for delivering sermons at the annual Gorsedh Service that were lightly veiled nationalist speeches (the writer of this article must plead guilty to this charge!).

In 1982, when he finished his second term as Grand Bard, Richard published *Naw Pregoth* (*Nine Sermons*) which he had delivered between 1976 and 1982. These include his address at the bicentenary service in commemoration of the burial of Dolly Pentreath at Paul Church. In the introductory paragraph he says:

> Men cof Dolly, gans y eryow ancoth, o an kensa Kernewek gwelys genef ha my a-wruk ervyra dhe dhysky an yeth-ma, hy yeth ha'm yeth owhonen [*Dolly's memorial, with its strange words, was the first Cornish I had seen and I decided to learn this language, her language and my own*].

His sermon has three texts: from Revelation and Thessalonians 1 and 2, all of which have the exhortation to hold fast to traditions and what is good. Because of the occasion, this could be interpreted as 'nationalistic' but equally it was a challenge to those who too easily abandon principles in favour of the current trends.

He used his sermon at Camborne in 1981 to appeal for unity in the Cornish movement, including his translation of the well-known song 'You say tomahto, I say tomayto…':

> Ty a lever tahs ha my a lever taas,
> Ty a lever gwlahs ha my a lever gwlaas…

He likened these small differences to shibboleths, used to identify a friend or foe:

> Cryseugh, my a gas pys, bos re erel owth obery rak Kernow puponen yn y forth y honen ha dhe les ahanan-oll yn deweth. Bedhen breder warbarth [*Believe, I beg you, that others are working for Cornwall each in his own way and for the ultimate benefit of us all. Let us be brothers together*].

In his last Gorsedh sermon as Grand Bard – evensong in St James' Church,

Antony, on Sunday, 6 September 1987 – he preached on the subject of humility. There was no suggestion of nationalism here, just a plea to work diligently at whatever task is before us:

> ...y coth dhyn-ny dhe wul an ober us gorrys adheragon, gwella gyllyn-ny, nag owth-owna dyfygyans nag ow-quaytya sowynyans. Yma nanyl na'y gyla y'gan deudhorn-ny [...*we should carry out the task before us to the best of our ability, neither fearing failure nor expecting success. Neither the one nor the other is in our hands*].

Whilst it would be presumptuous in the extreme for a relative newcomer to say that Richard wrote excellent Cornish, this writer finds his writings clear and natural, not unduly arcane, and yet he uses a wide vocabulary and a range of grammatical structures that make his texts interesting and pleasurable to read (and, as live sermons, to hear). His public enunciation of Cornish, both from the pulpit and the Men-omborth of the Gorsedh, has been widely commended. The fact that students could actually understand what Richard said in a speech, reading or sermon in Cornish gave considerable encouragement to many. Ray Chubb has said that 'no-one would read a traditional play, making perfect use of the rhymes as did Richard'.

From its inception in 1975, Richard was an active member of the Bishop of Truro's Advisory Committee for Services in Cornish and translated many prayers, prepared services and either translated sermons for others or helped with and corrected their sermons, including for his wife *Bryallen* at a St Piran's Day service when she was Grand Bard. He was involved in the Bible translation project that began in 1977, but this stalled with the outbreak of arguments about spelling. He did not take part in the project which was initiated in 1996, as the intention was to publish mainly in Kernewek Kemmyn: copies in Unified were to be made available on request. Poignantly, the task he undertook just before he died was the translation into Cornish of some prayers for the wedding of his younger son Conan and his fiancée Emma, to take place in April 2003.

His activity within the Church and his use and promotion of Cornish were not simply cultural, but reflected a deeper faith. His sermons were serious and carried messages that would be thought-provoking in any language. He also carried out church duties for his community, as a member of Crowan Parochial

Church Council and as Deputy Church Warden at St James' Church, Leedstown. This combination of religion with the Cornish language and culture was a powerful force.

Research, writing and criticism

From his early years of involvement with the language he was always curious and enquiring about etymology, place-names and the medieval texts, carrying out research whenever he had the time. In his occasional literary magazine he published a series of articles entitled 'Nebes Geryow Adro dhe Eryow' ('A few words about words') showing his research on such diverse subjects as 'the origins of the place-name Nanstallon' (suggesting we have evidence for a word *stallon* meaning 'stallion'); 'is the Cornish word *conna* (neck) of Irish origin?'; 'what is the real meaning of the word *gwragh*?'; and the performance of the play *Bywnans Meryasek*.

His paper to a symposium arranged by the Celtic Congress in 1965 expressed his views on new vocabulary:

> It would help us greatly if three things could be achieved. Firstly, that Welsh and Bretons would co-operate with each other in their word-making; secondly, that lists of new Welsh and Breton words should be easily available for study; and thirdly, that we in Cornwall should ourselves circulate and publicize agreed lists of new Cornish words.

Sadly, none of these three ideas has been put into practice.

As soon as he had learned the language, Richard became a prolific writer both in prose and verse. Over a period of forty years he consistently won prizes in the Gorsedh competitions, probably more than any other bard.

Many of his early works were submitted under the pseudonym of Garfield Richardson and in *Delyow Derow* we find poems and prose with both attributions. In the Cornish verse competitions for the 4th Esedhvos Kernow of 1992, a poem by 'Garfield Richardson' was highly commended and one by 'Richard G Jenkin' was commended! Also published in *Delyow Derow* was a series of comical tales by 'Garfield Richardson', with 'John Stone' as the principal character and set in Newlyn.

In *New Cornwall* magazine he rebuffs Tim Saunders' complaints published in the Celtic League Annual 1972 about modern Cornish writers and he berates, in Cornish, Tim's own use of the language:

> ...res yw scryfa yn Kernewek sempel ha gwyr-Gernewek, heb geryow gwakhes ha daslytherennys dyworth Kembrek. Nyns yw man dhe les scryfa Kernewek na-yl bos convedhys gans Kernewegoryon ha skentyl ha dallethoryon [...*it is essential to write in Cornish that is simple and truly Cornish, without vacuous words that are respelled from Welsh. There is no point at all in writing Cornish that cannot be understood by all Cornish speakers, both advanced and learners*].

In the same edition of *New Cornwall* he gives a very favourable review (in English) of Richard Gendall's new book *Kernewek Bew*, showing he was very much prepared to move on from the older, more literary self-tuition books and embrace these modern methods of teaching.

Family and Community
Richard and his wife Ann used Cornish in their family life whenever possible and this was a strong influence on their young family. The earliest memory this writer has of Cornish things on television was seeing the Jenkin family sitting in their garden at Leedstown and speaking Cornish, probably in the early 1970s. This love of the language and determination to support its growth and development has been passed on to their children and grandchildren.

Apart from the instances already mentioned, Richard attended innumerable events in Cornwall and beyond, using Cornish in the community whenever the opportunity arose and participating in any way he could to support and promote the language. The following are some examples of his contributions:

- Having been one of the Cornish delegates to the Inter-Celtic Youth Conference organised by Urdd Gobaith Cymru at Borth, near Aberystwyth in 1953, Richard wrote a brief report in Cornish for *An Lef*. This shows how he used Cornish at every opportunity, regarding it as an integral part of the Cornish movement.[2]

- A report on a camp held for Cornish and Breton Guides at Chytodden

Farm, Troon, in the summer of 1970: '...Cornish was not neglected either, as the Leedstown Guides sang a couple of songs in Cornish – a Cornish Lullaby and the Cornish Grace, and at one Camp Fire Mr Jenkin, a Cornish language bard, read two poems in Cornish...'[3]

- 'Richard Jenkin translated into Cornish the resolution on tourism passed at the 1975 Celtic Congress at Carlyon Bay.'[4] (*West Briton*?)

- (First AGM of the Cornish Language Fellowship, Truro). 'Richard Jenkin said that as language was an integral part of any nation, it was essential that not only should the future of Cornish be safeguarded but that the language should be strengthened.'[5]

Conclusion

This writer has a strong attachment to the memory of *Map Dyvroeth*, having first met him in the mid-1970s at a language event in Helston when he himself was in the throes of learning the language. Having negotiated his bardic name with Richard in 1978, he was received into the Gorsedh by him at the Merry Maidens. In 1988 at Poldhu Richard installed his successor *Gwas Costentyn* as Grand Bard, who in turn installed *Caradok* as his Deputy. Then at Crowan Church in 2002, the writer had the great honour of delivering a tribute to him at his funeral. *Map Dyvroeth*'s contribution to the revival and advancement of Cornish covered over half a century and influenced every aspect from the academic to the mundane, from the literary to the religious and his work is widely respected throughout the movement.

Notes

1 'Let us be brothers together': from a sermon delivered by Richard Jenkin at Camborne, 1981.
2 *An Lef*, June 1953.
3 *New Cornwall*, January-February 1970.
4 Undated newspaper cutting [*West Briton*?].
5 *West Briton*, 13 November 1980.

Sources
An Lef, 1952-1961; *Delyow Derow*, Editions 1-15; extracts from the minutes of Agan Tavas, 1989-2002; John Legonna's Diaries 1944, National Library of Wales, Aberystwyth; minutes of Kesva an Taves Kernewek 1967-1995 and 2002; *Naw Pregoth / Nine Sermons*; *New Cornwall*, January-February 1970 and vol. 17 no.4, 1973; Jori Ansell, Tribute to Richard G. Jenkin at his funeral, 2002; *West Briton*, 13 November 1980; personal memories of Dr John Chesterfield, Ray Chubb, Rev. Brian Coombes, Fr Richard Rutt and Jori Ansell.

Modernising Vocabulary

Richard G. Jenkin

When speaking last in a symposium one is at a disadvantage because all one's best points have already been made effectively by the previous speakers. I do not wish to go over these again, but there are some special points to be made about Cornish.

There are two mutually dependent ways in which new words appear in a language – usage and invention. When old ways give place to new old words change their meaning, make new combinations, and express new ideas. This is done unconsciously in living speech. When a new thing is made a new name is found. Sometimes it is an old word reused, like engine, – more often it is a deliberate invention, like television. Even so, the deliberate invention depends for its life on usage by the people in their common speech. For instance in English, velocipede never caught on and was replaced by bicycle; kinematograph was transmogrified into cinema. Hardly anyone now says omnibus or influenza and few hesitate to write bus and flu.

However, the situation is rather different in Cornish than in most languages. In the last decade or so there has been an increase in fluency in the spoken language – perhaps due to the Summer School of Cornish that is being held for the third time this year. Nevertheless, Cornish is still more often written than spoken. Therefore invention plays a greater part than common usage. Also, Cornish passed out of common use in the 18th century, though there was never a time when there was no-one who could read or write Cornish, and during its last half-century as a language of the people it was practically confined to fishermen and labourers. Therefore new words ceased to be made about 150 years before our revival at the end of the last century.

So the special features of the situation in Cornwall are that Cornish at the beginning of this century lacked words for all the new things since about 1750 and that the formation of new words is left almost entirely to the writers. Since Cornish writing exists mainly in manuscript or in duplicated editions of small circulation it is common for different writers to invent different words. After all, if you need a new word in a hurry you make it, and put an explanation or else an English translation in brackets after it to make sure that your reader gets the idea. Unfortunately, there is no present means of telling the degree of acceptance of the various words used by different authors.

Then there is the fundamental question of the word-type:– whether, like most European languages, Cornish should adopt international forms such as telephone, or whether, like German, the word should be built up from native roots. Some maintain that if Cornish is to be a modern method of communication and not an antiquarian toy it must follow the example of other European languages and that 'fotograf' is no less Cornish because it is used by half a dozen other languages. On the other hand, some would reject this on the main ground that it is used in English, appearing to English speakers a direct loan, and that such words would make Cornish appear a bastard mixture – like the 'Franglais' which is arousing the ire of French Academicians. You can see that there are strong arguments on both sides, and so we are left with the choice between 'fotograf' and 'lughes-scryf'; and as we use 'pellweler' for telescope what are we to use for television – 'pellvyr' or 'pellwolok' or 'televu'?

A further important consideration in extending Cornish vocabulary is its relation to Welsh and Breton. The greater part of root words in Cornish are identical with those in Welsh and Breton. I think most Welsh and most Bretons will understand most words in this verse:–

>   Whegh bro yndan nef,
>   Whegh corf, un enef,
>   Whegh yeth, un lavar,
>   Whegh cledha, un escar.
>   Whegh bro a Geltya.

Now we wish to ensure that Cornish grows on parallel lines to Welsh and Breton and not on divergent lines; therefore we do try to consider what new words are used by Welsh and Breton before choosing our own – though sometimes we think we can do better. We prefer 'tanbrenyer' to 'matshen' or 'alumetezenn' for matches!

It would help us greatly if three things could be achieved. Firstly, that Welsh and Bretons would co-operate with each other in their word-making; secondly, that lists of new Welsh and Breton words should be easily available for study; and thirdly, that we in Cornwall should ourselves circulate and publicize agreed lists of new Cornish words. The Language Examinations Board of the Cornish Gorsedd has this among its duties, but as yet no list has been prepared.

[A contribution to the symposium at the International Celtic Congress held in Glasgow in August 1965; *New Cornwall*, vol. 13, no. 5, November 1965]

The Cornish-language Poetry of Richard Jenkin: a short survey

Donald R. Rawe

Richard Jenkin is unique among poets writing in Kernewek, in that his appreciation of natural surroundings is tinged, indeed suffused, with a sense of wonder and homecoming – the latter no doubt stemming from his consciousness of being born of Cornish parents outside his homeland (actually in Derbyshire). So even in the most intimate and playful of his verses there is a childlike or adolescent underlying joy of recognition. Other Cornish poets have written significantly of their sense of national identity (Henry Jenner, for instance, in his great Kernewek version of Trelawny). Jenkin, however, is always rather more subtle, challenging and reflective. For example:

Kernow, Gwlas Syns[1]

My a gan a Gernow, gwell-garadow,
Yu bro an moyha benygys y'n bys-ma.
'Ma omma lyes sans mas, hep falladow –
Moy 'es yu gwelys lemmyn y'n lys-na
May 'seth perlet py pronter an purcattys
Rak dewys dremas bones eglos-tasek –
Yn pup plu hanow noweth-flam yu parys
Ow-ry dhyn Martin yn le Meryasek.

Mes whath, A Dhew, an syns pur whek a'th pys
Ha ragon-ny ha rag an wlas ker-ma
Der oll an curow splan yn Paradhys,
Ha whath Dha vennath ny a wel omma.

[Cornwall, Land of Saints

I sing of Cornwall, well-beloved,
The most blessed country in this world.
Here without a doubt are many holy saints
More than are now seen in that court
Where sits a prelate or a pulpit priest
To choose a holy one to be a patron –
In each parish a brand-new name is ready
Giving us a Martin in place of a Meriadoc.
But still, O God, the gentle saints pray to Thee
Both for us and for this dear land
Through all the shining courts in Paradise
And still Thy blessing we see here.]

This is directly charming and a real assertion of faith, yet there is a subtle warning here: we must not forget our Celtic saints, substituting later and wider-known medieval ones, such as Martin for Meriadoc at Camborne. Would the latter have survived in popular memory without that pillar of the language, the play *Bewnans Meriasek*? Fortunately, the sterling work of Canon G.H. Doble has enshrined the stature of such holy men and women who might otherwise have been obscured and forgotten.

Jenkin's greatest poem of protest is without doubt 'Gwaytyans a'm bus'[2] ('Yet I have hope'), the first three stanzas of which read as follows:

Pyth wrons y dhe'm Kernow lemmyn?
Ow trehevel treven gans to
Pryleghennow; fen'stry ledan,
Tommys oll an chy dre dredan.

Whath gwaytyans a'm bus men ha leghen
Pella a bys 'es fosow bryk.

Pyth wrons y dhe'm Kernow lemmyn?
Ow tyswul keow, men ha men,
Rak dry ajy dhe barcow coth
Jyn-tenna hag aras tre dhyen
Dh'un gwel, rak gwaynya nebes moy.
Whath gwaytyans a'm bus bos arta
Blejyow gwyls y'n dascor a wun.

Pyth wrons y dhe'm Kernow lemmyn?
Ow trelya gwyffa-gol dhe werthjy
a vukkyas ha talgell puscas
Dhe vosty may lenk havysy
Ow myras orth an mor mostys,
Hag ynno dyscargys caugh-dre,
Ow nyja scon dhe'n treth fleghes.
Whath gwaytyans a'm bus teweth Gwaf
A gyf pup tra oll dhe'n downvor.

[*What are they doing to my Cornwall now?*
They're building bungalows with roofs of tile,
With picture-windows letting in the view
And all-electric central heating, too.
Yet I have hope that slate and stone outlast
The creeping concrete walls, pre-cast.

What are they doing to my Cornwall now?
They're tearing down the hedges of the fields,
Stone by stone, to get their tractors in
And send birds soaring by their strident din
While ploughing all the farmstead to one field,
To gain a few percentage more in yield.

Yet I have hope that wild flowers still will shoot
When gorse and heather flood back here to root.

What are they doing to my Cornwall now?
They're making sail-lofts into piskey shops
And cafes out of cellars by the quay
Where tourists stuff themselves and watch the sea,
And pump the sewage a mile into the bay
To float back on the beach where children play.
Yet I have hope that Winter storms will sweep
The whole damned lot away into the deep.]

There is an underlying anger here, restrained only by a politician's assessment of how we should go forward into the 20th and 21st centuries. The underlying message is, of course, "Beware – they'll exploit, submerge and ruin us if we don't become aware of what is happening". This is a clear statement of warning and opposition to recent modern developments. It directly implies "Can Cornish identity survive in this climate of economic so-called growth? Can the treasured ancient way of life of the Cornish be protected, and if so, how?"

As a politician, Jenkin was heavily involved, being Chairman of Mebyon Kernow (polling over 10,000 votes in the first European Parliament election in 1979), twice Grand Bard, and perennially active in numerous Cornish societies and movements.

In 'Gyllys dhe-ves' ('Gone away') he seems to be a Cornish voice speaking from the past, like the medieval Irish and Welsh poets:

Gyllys dhe-ves yu ef a gerys-vy.
Eghan! A callen-vy y weles ajy
Ow-'sedha unwyth arta ryp an tan.
A, blew y ben o maga tu 'vel bran,
Ha'y dhyns mar wyn avel an bluven-ergh;
Gyllys yu-ef ha'm joy-oll war y lergh.
Kens en-ny lowen omma y'gan chy
Mes hedhyu, 'ma saw anken dhymmo-vy;

Ow har caradow, ef yu gyllys dhe-ves
Ha ganso-ef yu kellys oll ow cres.
Solabrys kerensa gref a splanna
Mar dek 'vel howl y'n nef ha ny a gana
Kepar hag ydhyn y'ga nyth mar dom
Mes tewl yu lemmyn ha'gan chy yu lom
A wres kerensa. Gyllys yu-ef, ow har,
Nyns us y'n norvys bras-ma nefra y bar.
Pandra whyrfyth dhymmo heb an gour-na?
My yu kellys hebtho. Dres pup journa
My 'wra kyny, scullya dagrow tyn,
Ellas, A callen bos y'm beth mar yn!

[*Gone away is he that I loved.*
Ochone! If only I could see him inside
Sitting once more by the fire.
Oh, the hair of his head was as black as a raven.
And his teeth as white as the snow-flake;
He is gone and all my joy after him.
Once we were happy here in our house
But today, I have only grief;
My beloved dear, he is gone away
And with him is lost all my peace.
Once strong love used to shine
As fine as the sun in heaven and we used to sing
Like birds in their nest so warm
But it is dark now and our house is bare
Of Love's warmth. He is gone, my love,
There is never in this great world his equal.
What will happen to me without that man?
I am lost without him. Throughout every day
I mourn, shedding painful tears.
Alas, if only I could be in my narrow grave.]

One seems here to be listening to the voice of Taliesin or Fionn Mac Cumaill [Finn MacCool] whose laments still cry out of the lakes and hills of their homelands – a truly Celtic lament.

Jenkin could be childlike and charming, reflecting his love of children and enjoying their growing appreciation of the natural world about them:

Can fleghes dhe dykky-dew

> Tege' Dew.
> Splan dha lyw.
> Ke dhe-ves
> Dywar an pras.
> Haf 'wra mos.
> Gwaf 'wra dos.
> Ef a gergh
> Rew hag ergh.
> Tege' Dew,
> Ke dystough.
>
> [*Children's song to a butterfly*
>
> *Butterfly,*
> *Bright your hue,*
> *Go away*
> *From the lea.*
> *Summer is going,*
> *Winter is coming.*
> *It will bring*
> *Frost and snow.*
> *Butterfly,*
> *Go quickly.*]

Elsewhere Richard Jenkin wrote warmly this tribute to St Petroc, which fits the Welsh tune Ar Hyd y Nos (All through the night). Petroc, a royal Cambrian who came to Cornwall, founded Padstow (erstwhile Petrocstow), proselytised Cornwall and Devon (there are no less than twenty dedications to him across the Tamar, including one in Somerset) and presided over the dominant monastery at Bodmin for much of his ministry:

St Petroc[3]

Petrok, Tasek agan Plu-ny,
    Dynargh yu dhys,
Dh'agan pow ow-try an awayl,
    Gwyryon yn bys.
Bewnans hyr hag ober cales
Gans Bredereth cref ha huvel,
Dremas sans hag Abas skentyl,
    Dynargh yu dhys.

Dyndyl 'wrussys rag Dew Kernow,
    Dre dermyn hyr,
Sonys o an jeth pan dhuthys
    Huvel ha whar,
Gras a-ren a'th pregoth salow,
'gan hendasow dyskys ganso
Y a-wruk 'vel pow Dew Kernow,
    Dre dermyn hyr.

Ny a-worth an Sans hag Abas
    Gans canow prays,
Petrok nep a-dhros dhyn Jesus,
    Cref ny a'th prays.
Ha warlergh an Sans aragon
Ny a-brays an Arluth awos
Bos hembrynkyas Petrok ragon
    Dhe Dhew ha'y 'ras.

> [*Petrock, Patron of our Parish,*
>   *Greeting to thee,*
> *To our country bringing the gospel,*
>   *Righteous in the world.*
> *Long life and hard work*
> *With Brethren strong and humble,*
> *Holy good man and learned Abbot,*
>   *Greeting to thee.*
>
> *Win thou didst for God, Cornwall,*
>   *Through long time,*
> *Blessed was the day thou camest,*
>   *Humble and meek,*
> *Thanks we give for thy sound preaching,*
> *Our forefathers taught by it*
> *Made as God's country Cornwall,*
>   *Through long time.*
>
> *We honour the Saint and Abbot*
>   *With songs of praise,*
> *Petrock who brought to us Jesus,*
>   *Strongly we praise thee.*
> *And following the Saint before us*
> *We praise the Lord because*
> *Petrock was a leader for us*
>   *To God and his Grace.*]

It seems fitting to close this short survey of a great Cornish patriot's verse with 'Hayl dh'aga Mamvro',[4] his Kernewek version of 'Hail to the Homeland', which was written by A. Pearce Gilbert and is now sung at the Gorsedh and by male voice choirs across the Cornish world to Kenneth Pelmear's music:

> Hayl dh'agan Mamvro ! – Ker vur a'gan rythsys,
> Clew prest dha fleghes a-gan kerensa dhys;

Heb os dha splander – an flam Keltek golow,
On ny oll gothys a'n golewder a'th hanow.

Gweleugh an tekter – an cres war hal Bodmen,
Marghogeugh tarth mor wor'tu ha'n treth Sennen;
Chersyeugh gans dorn cref carrygy war Drencrom
Caneugh Trelawny Bras heglew gans colon dom.

Hayl dh'agan Mamvro ! – ahanas on ny ran,
Y'gan colonnow a rythsys golow splan;
Ynny ha hembronk gans gallos lanow ny,
Erbyn an jeth a drelyans roy dha nerth dhynny.

[Hail to the Homeland ! – great bastion of the free,
Hear now thy children proclaim their love for thee;
Ageless thy splendour – undimm'd that Celtic Flame,
Proudly our souls reflect the glory of thy name.

Sense now the beauty – the peace of Bodmin Moor,
Ride with the breaker towards the Sennen shore;
Let firm hands fondle the boulders of Trencrom –
Sing with all the fervour then the great Trelawny song.

Hail to the Homeland ! – of thee we are a part,
Great pulse of freedom in every Cornish heart,
Prompt us and guide us – endow us with thy power,
Lace us with liberty to face this changing hour.]

Notes

1   Richard Jenkin's poetic output, much of it unpublished, forms part of the family archive. Peter Harvey has generously had scans of the poems converted into text using optical character recognition (OCR). Although every effort has been made to correct any obvious mistakes, it is still possible that the resulting text occasionally differs from the typed originals. Unless otherwise specified, the English-language versions are almost certainly by Richard Jenkin.
2   Both versions were entered in the Gorsedh verse classes – the Cornish, under the pen-name Cothwas Coynt,

and the English using the name Garfield Richardson.
3   This Cornish version is a translation of 'St Petroc' by Ann Wherry, St John & St Petroc, Devoran. The literal English translation is Richard Jenkin's.
4   English words reproduced by permission of Marjorie Summers.

Cornish Literature in the Twentieth Century

Richard G. Jenkin

Lef y'n Nos

Ha my ow-crowedha y'm gwely,
Y clewys-vy lef whek y'n nos,
Ow-whystra yn cosel hag ysel:
"Ow herra, a vynta-jy dos
Dres anken hag ober hep deweth
Dhe bowes yn cres a buptra
A drobel dha vewnans gans drokter?
Y hyllyth-sy cuska yn ta
Hep covyon a dhregyn adro dhys.
Rak hunlef ha preder mar dhown
Y'th whythaf." "Pyu osta?" a gryys.
"A goweth, yth of-vy Annown."

(Richard Jenkin)

I suppose there are probably less than 2,000 people throughout the world who could understand that; and probably less than a 100 have read it. Literary writing in Cornish needs devotion and determination. To let you into the secret this is what it means:

Voice in the Night

As I was lying in my bed,
I heard a sweet voice in the night,
Whispering softly and low:
"My dearest, do you want to come
Beyond grief and endless work
To rest in peace from everything
That troubles your life with evil?
You can sleep well
Without memories of mischief around you.
From nightmare and care so deep
I will keep you." "Who are you?" I cried.
"O friend, I am Annwn."

(Annwn is 'the other side', the land of the dead)

Modern literature in Cornish is co-eval with the 20th century. Nothing was written in the 19th century and very little in the 18th century. However, there is more Cornish written and recorded in this century than remains from all previous centuries. Much of it is still unpublished and the various publications during the century are not all easily available even in libraries.

The first 20th century writer in Cornish was the initiator of the Cornish Revival Henry Jenner (*Gwas Myghal* to give him his bardic name). He had poems printed in *Celtia* at the turn of the century. From then until the 1930s poems, songs and hymns by Jenner, both original and translations, appeared from time to time in newspapers, magazines and songbooks. Nevertheless, opportunities for publication were limited and some of his work is still unpublished.

However, his work inspired those who learned Cornish from him. Jenner and R. Morton Nance (*Mordon*) founded the Federation of Old Cornwall Societies in 1922 and the magazine *Old Cornwall* in 1925. This magazine contained a story or poem in Cornish in every issue throughout Nance's long editorship and for a good while afterwards as long as unpublished stories and verses by Nance remained, and Cornish verse and prose by other writers have appeared intermittently since then.

Morton Nance was a fluent writer of both prose and verse and his vast knowledge of all pre-existing Cornish writings enabled him to compile his grammars and dictionaries. In his literary work he seems to have preferred to write versions of standard folk tales e.g. *Lyver an Pymp Marthus Seleven* (*Book of the Five Marvels of Selevan*) and to translate songs, especially Breton or Welsh folk songs. Can you recognise this?

Gwytha'n Gwaneth Gwyn

My yu pollat yowynk fol,
    Dhe'm syans-oll ow-synsy:
Kyn whythaf-vy an gwaneth gwyn.
    Aral a-vyn y vyjy.
Prag na-wreta myres orth
    An gwas a-th-worth bynary?
Pup ur y'n jeth, a vowes whek,
    Y-th-whelaf tecca tevy.

It's a translation from Welsh of the first verse of Wil Hopcyn's 'Bugeilio'r Gwenith Gwyn' (Watching the Wheat).

> I am a lad both young and mad
> The dreams I've had I hold to.
> But though I watch the ripening wheat
> Another reaps its gold through.
> Why dost thou never look upon
> The one that loves thee ever?
> Each hour, each day, my dearest one,
> I see thee grow yet fairer.

Being essentially a modest man, Nance seems to have felt that Cornish needed to regain a traditional literature before creating a new literature. At that time it was a fairly general feeling that Cornish was most appropriately used for stories set in periods when Cornish was spoken as a matter of course which led to many tales of saints and monks and Dark Age and Mediaeval people.

Morton Nance's co-worker A.S.D. Smith (*Caradar*) was also involved in compiling grammars, lesson-books and dictionaries and he was a professional teacher. He was also a fluent writer of verse and prose. He prepared books like 'Nebes Whethlow Ber' (Some Short Stories) – a collection of anecdotes – to provide for his students reading material with a wider range than Nance's folk tales. Smith's verse covered a wider compass, from humorous pieces to the epic of 'Trystan'

> **An Gwlascarer gans Caradar**
>
> Ny-allaf-vy kewsel Kernewek,
> Ny-allaf y scryfa na-whath,
> Re gales yu tavas mar uthek,
> Predery anodho a-m lath!
>
> Na-gows dhem a hynwyn tylleryow,
> Tevys kynth-of war an tyr,
> Na-lavar ow bosa-vy Kernow,
> Ow devedhyans Keltek ny-m dur.
>
> Pyth a-dal traow a'n par-ma?
> An Tavas ny-vern dhemmo-vy,
> Un slogan a-garaf hy garma,
> Ha "Kernow bys vyken" yu hy.

In 1934 Smith started *Kernow* (*Cornwall*), a duplicated magazine wholly in Cornish and appearing monthly. Some classical texts were published in the newly standardised spelling as well as the original form but his main intention was to encourage the new generation of Cornish users to write poems, stories, articles and letters in the new magazine, which also acted as a link publication for Tyr ha Tavas, the young Cornish movement of those days.

Smith certainly published many of the younger writers – Edwin Chirgwin (*Map Melyn*), Michael Cardew (*Myghal an Pry*), Francis Cargeeg (*Tan Dyvarow*), E.G. Retallack Hooper (*Talek*), A. St V. Allin-Collins (*Hal Wyn*), Phoebe Nance (*Morwennol*), Henry Trefusis (*Map Mor*) – many of whom became prominent members in the Gorsedd in the 1950s when I met most of them. Probably the best and most prolific poet was Edwin Chirgwin. He wrote mainly nature poetry or poems of place, rather like the Neo-Georgian poets in England of the same or slightly earlier period.

Dhe'n Kensa Bryallen gans Edwin Chirgwin

Cannas an Gwaynten,
Arweth a Dhew,
Gwaytyans y'n bys-ma
Arta a-vew.

Blejen wan melen
Gwrydhyes y'n ke.
Cref agas colon
Yn agas tre.

Ladher an Gwaf yeyn
Fether yn-whyr,
Syn y'n tewolgow,
Steren an tyr.

Ro dhem dha bowes
Pan dheffo nos,
Tryk yn oll hovyon
Dre oll ow os.

Allin-Collins was a raconteur, especially when describing his experiences in Czarist Russia, while Retallack Hooper described his more recent experiences in pre-Franco Spain.

Kernow continued until Smith returned to England in 1936 and the war in 1939 scattered the group of Cornish writers *Kernow* had developed. The number of copies produced was small and complete runs of *Kernow* are now quite rare. The title *Kernow* has been used in more recent times by two different political magazines, mainly written in English.

After the war the survivors came together again and were joined by a younger generation of writers. In 1952 Richard Gendall (*Gelvynak*) started *An Lef* (*The Voice*) as a duplicated magazine for users and learners of Cornish. He passed this over in 1953 to Retallack Hooper who later renamed it *An Lef Kernewek* (*The Cornish Voice*) and redesigned it as a magazine of literary and linguistic interest, developing the tradition of Smith's *Kernow*. Richard Gendall went on to produce a beginners' magazine in Cornish called *Hedhyu* (*Today*) from 1956 to 1958. He later became the most influential writer of songs in Cornish – 'Kemer ow Ro' (Take my Gift) etc. – popularised by the records of the late Brenda Wootton. Later songwriters following this lead were Brian Webb (*Brythennek*), Anthony Snell (*Gwas Kevardhu*), Julyan Holmes (*Blew Melen*), Graham Sandercock (*Gwas Conoc*), Ken George (*Profus an Mortyd*) and Jon Mills.

An Lef Kernewek continued until 1982 and was invaluable in giving Cornish poets and writers the opportunity to see their work in print. It included some of the older writers: Retallack Hooper himself, F. Macdowell (*Map Estren Du*), posthumous works of Smith and Chirgwin. Over the years it brought in a whole range of newer writers: Richard Gendall, N.J.A. Williams (*Golvan*), Anthony Snell, M.C.V. Stephens (*Keybalhens*), R.G. Jenkin (*Map Dyvroeth*), W. Brown (*Crenner*), John Page (*Gwas Kenethlow*), John King (*Yowann Byghan*), Tim Saunders, Julyan Holmes, among others.

This led to a widening of subject from poems of place, folktale and pseudo-mediaeval stories to more immediate concerns and modern subjects, though good work continued to be done in the older genres. Though wide in range of subjects, *An Lef Kernewek* was not wide in readership, its market being normally under fifty. So again copies are scarce nowadays.

Between 1976 and 1980 Anthony Snell and Tim Saunders produced a satirical magazine *Eythen* (*Gorse*). This was a new departure in Cornish and though it was often clever and appealing to younger writers, it was seen by some as directing its fire not at the anti-Cornish nor the indifferent, but at those who had long worked for Cornish, but not in ways approved by *Eythen*, or to the standards it wished to see. It was around this time that Tim developed his idiosyncratic spelling of Cornish which, fortunately, was not adopted by any other writers as that would have made a fourth spelling system.

In 1977 *An Gannas* (*The Messenger*) appeared, edited by Graham Sandercock. This monthly magazine in Cornish was designed to give news of current activities, help to beginners, short, simple articles and stories, but it does give the opportunity from time to time for more literary writings. This has brought in other writers like Ken George (*Profus an Mortyd*), Jowan Richards (*Map*

Roswern), Ray Edwards (*Map Mercya*), Philip Knight (*Tan Golowan*) with a broad mix of subjects. *An Gannas* has produced over 200 issues and is still appearing monthly.

In 1988 *Delyow Derow* (*Oak Leaves*), edited by Richard G. Jenkin, began as a twice-yearly literary magazine containing mainly verse and short stories. While it publishes good examples of the poetry of place and stories in early settings, it encourages modern settings and subjects. It tries to publish the winning entries in the annual Gorsedd and triennial Esethvos literary competitions, which themselves aim to widen the scope of Cornish literature by the choice of specific themes. So, science fiction, murder, love and hate have been represented in 20th century literature. Some of the writers in *Delyow Derow* are Michael Palmer (*Pergheryn*), who always seems to have at least two dead bodies in his stories; Stephen Amos from Australia (*Nans Melyn*); Hilary Shaw (*Myrgh Dumnonya*); Marjorie Trevanion (*Rosen Wyn Evrok*); Garfield Richardson; Barbara Davies (*Gwrek Kembro*); Julia Allard (*Myrgh Fenten Peran*); Rod Lyon (*Tewennow*); Richard G. Jenkin. The standard has remained remarkably high. Its circulation, though small, is roughly twice that reached by *An Lef Kernewek* earlier, so it shows an increasing market for Cornish writing.

In addition to the specialist Cornish-language magazines, short pieces in Cornish have been printed occasionally in *Cornish Life*, *Cornish Scene*, *New Cornwall*, all now ceased publication, *Cornwall World Wide*, *Kernow* (the third) and more regularly in *The Western Morning News*.

The growing number of readers of Cornish today can be judged by the increasing number of books published in Cornish. Often the printings are small, but there are many more books with different themes published now than there were before and just after the war.

The earlier books tended to be on traditional themes like Nance's 'Lyver an Pymp Mathus Selevan' (1939); Rev. D.R. Evans' (*Gwas Cadoc*) book 'Hen Whethlow' (Ancient Stories – fables from La Fontaine and elsewhere); 'Bewnans Alysaryn' (Life of Alizarin) by Peggy Pollard (*Arlodhes Ywerdhon*), a skit in the form of a mediaeval miracle play; Smith's 'Whethlow an Seyth Den Fur a Rom' (The Tales of the Seven Sages of Rome) and his greatest work, the posthumously published version of 'Trystan hag Ysolt' based on Bedier's version.

Nowadays the themes are often more up to date like 'An Gurun Wosek a

Geltya' (The Bloody Crown of Celtia) by Melvyn Bennetto (*Abransek*) which was the first full length novel in Cornish and deals with Celtic resistance to present day conditions. It is full of incident and action but probably not quite up to John Buchan. Other long stories are 'An Wedhowes' (The Widow) by Graham Sandercock; 'Jory' (George) and 'Enys Ancow' (Island of Death) by Michael Palmer; 'Kernow A'gas Dynargh gans Flowrys Tek' (Cornwall Welcomes You with Beautiful Blooms) by Mary Mills (*Morgelyn*); 'Kellys' (Lost) by Ken George; 'George ha Samantha', modern radio playlets by Julia Allard and Rod Lyon. The main criticism one could make of stories in Cornish is that they are essentially tales of events and do not show character or character development.

Children's books are represented by 'Ple 'ma Spot?' (Where's Spot?); 'Orvil an Morvil' (Orvil the Whale); 'Kyrsty ha Mamwyn' (Kirstie and Granny); 'Wella Ha'n Vorvoren' (Billy and the Mermaids) among others.

Traditional themes continue in use. Examples are 'Devedhyans St Pol yn Bro Leon' (Arrival of St Pol in Leon) by Ken George and 'Whethlow Tus Huvel' (Stories of Humble Folk) by Dorothy Richards (*Lelder*).

There still remain unpublished works from all periods in this century and some, like writings of earlier times, have been lost forever. Most books have been published at the authors' own cost though a few have been produced by organisations like Cowethas an Yeth Kernewek or 'Dalleth' or Dyllansow Truran. The initial sale of a book in Cornish is usually less than a hundred and several years are needed to sell 300 copies. The situation is aggravated by the different spelling systems now in use. There are some who will buy a Cornish book whatever its system and others who will only buy books in their preferred system. As a result no book now will be bought by more than 65% of buyers of Cornish books. This is a situation which is going to persist through our lifetime and probably longer. (How do they manage in Brittany where they have had three or more spelling systems in use for more than 40 years? It would be interesting to know).

In spite of the difficulties, the actual production of literature in Cornwall has increased considerably during the century and looks set to go on increasing in quantity and general quality.

[A paper presented at the International Celtic Congress annual conference held in Bangor, north Wales, in August 1996 and published by the Congress in *Celtic Literature and Culture in the Twentieth Century*, 1997]

The Haunting Voice – the English-language poetry of Richard Jenkin

Bert Biscoe

Realising the inner Cornish man

Richard Jenkin wrote poems throughout his adult life. As a young man he used poems to incite and rouse his readership to reach into themselves to find the intrinsic, passionate, justice-denied Cornish patriot that he found in himself. He recognised, as a politician, that this persona needed to be realised in the Cornish people, both collectively and individually. His best poems are those in which he works inwardly to articulate the instinctive moment when he realised his identity and found his true place – as a Cornish man.

> The tough old wild heart is tamed at last
> And beauty for strength is a bargain, maybe,
> But I think of the life of Cornwall past
> And weigh the worth of what will be.[1]

In his poetic life Richard Jenkin stalled the flood of youthful loneliness, of vacuum, when, in seeking the places and culture of his forebears, he opened his inner doors to the opportunity of being Cornish – for him this was a moment of religious intensity, a coming home, a discovery of the potential for fulfilment.

> Always my thoughts would turn towards my home;

> To Cornwall, and my family, and one
> For whom I daily built my dreams anew
> I longed to break the cocoon of inaction;
> Reach steady life, the ultimate imago.[2]

He immersed himself in Cornwall and came to shape perceptions of, and direction for, that land. His poetry was often the place where, garbed in the language and form of a romantic, he worked at his thinking, at the conciliation of intellect and emotion.

As a politician he needed to be certain, convinced, persuasively easy with his case. His poems illustrate both a romantic, and a man assailed with doubt. Perhaps, to some extent, the adoption of identity may have been more of an intellectual exercise than an expression of inevitability. In a poem such as 'A Bird in the Room' he discovers a trapped young crow, fearful – 'a shapeless mound of terror…'. His efforts to free the bird are to no avail and he is afraid himself that if he leaves the room it may escape, or might die – 'Filled with its own fears.' He turns the narrative inwards, having closed the door to leave for work.

> … Do I so beat my wings,
> Unavailing against unyielding glass,
> Or do I seek the dark to die of fear
> When lies escape across the unknown room?[3]

Escape or death, freedom or fear? The doubt here could be taken to evoke the inner doubt he felt that the adoption of a trenchant nationalism, a Cornish man in an increasingly worldly, connected and cosmopolitan world, might lead those who heard and shared his vision to a trap like that the young crow found itself in. Throughout his work, doubt and loneliness are rarely far from the lines. As he plumbed the inner pool and the world around him for metaphor to describe it, so the work became easier with itself – less embroidered with poetique, with archaisms that, for many, tend to feel like poetry and to jar the poem.

'Bird in the Room' was written in the 1970s, when Richard was at his political peak. He stood for Mebyon Kernow in the first European Parliamentary

There's a little harbour in the bay
Where once a fishing fleet would lie by day
Before it sailed to ~~sea~~ work a weary night
With mile-long drift nets near the lug ships lights.
I can recall the harbour packed with boats,
Their holds were stowed with fishing nets and floats,
On deck each rope was ~~took~~ wound in a neat coil,
They smelt of fish and salt, barked nets and oil
And so did Uncle Tom ~~Padyle~~ Guernsey boy,
And all the other members of ~~his~~ crew.
Now the ~~harbour~~ port has lost its working boats,
~~The little harbour is almost empty now~~
Except one drifter that so lonely floats
Between two cabin cruisers and a ~~ferry~~
Crabbers, pleasure boats that need no crew;
Boats for ~~trolling~~ ~~sailing~~ ~~rowing~~ whiffling on the evening tide,
With two ~~long~~ hand lines, just trailing on each side
And catching fish for supper, not for sale,
Old fishermen lean on the harbour rail
And see the phantom fleet that sails no more
To ~~bring the harvest of the sea to shore~~
To bring the ocean's harvest to the shore

Manuscript of Richard's poem 'Cornish Harbour' or 'Past and Present'

election. He brought conviction, excellent communication and a physical presence to the candidacy, and created a sensation by winning about 10,000 votes. Perhaps the weight of leadership settled uneasily on his shoulder or perhaps success, should it have led to him assuming public office, might also have led him to discover how powerless the small nation can be in a union of great states. However it worked in his mind, there is no doubt that he was working through the situation to find a way – closing the door to go to work. What lies did he suspect might lurk there – across the unknown room, the Parliament he sought access to?

Noms de plume
Richard Jenkin was a complex man. Poetry was an arena in which he articulated the turmoil of his inner life. It is often difficult to place his work in relation to actual events – his annotation of dates is haphazard. He clearly maintained a fairly constant file of work, and revisited it from time to time. In his personal file we find many poems entered for Gorsedh competitions. He had a range of noms de plume (as per the rules) and occasionally, in the manner of a laureate, stumbled into clumsy public verse. These forays are amongst his least successful pieces.

The adoption of noms de plume might suggest a complexity in the poet – that he may have sought anonymity so that the poem might find its just place in competition. I'm not sure that Richard Jenkin would have felt so assured of his leadership as to wish to baffle sycophancy – he seemed too shyly modest for such egotistical conceit. He may have instinctively wished to be distanced from his work when it was appearing in public. This may have been less for protection of himself, or even as a means of making his poems stand alone. It is more likely that he wished to overcome a degree of innate, self-imagined inadequacy in the face of his poetic romanticism. How, with such revelations of open emotion and sensibility, could he square up to the tasks and challenges of political leadership? It was cleaner and simpler for his public to see and experience the cerebral, *conviction* politician and leader, and to not have that image complicated by notions of self-doubt. His motive must remain obscure. He was a man calculated in his public life, and aware of the symbolisms of his position, and possibly felt that poetry and politics were best kept apart, at least as far as

Gorsedh competitions and other publications were concerned.

That he chose to enter many pieces under noms de plume[4] indicates possibly that he was aware of the poem as well as the power of the poem, and was sufficient enough of a poet to want his work to live in its own right. Therefore, he strove to disguise authorship whilst working through the dilemmas and wisdom-making of leadership – for those who read these poems closely, and who may have spoken to others about them, it is difficult to see how the adoption of the noms de plume actually served the purpose of disguise.[5] The rhythm, language and argument of much of Jenkin's work betrays its author, for those who knew him, heard his voice or read his prose.

Overcoming the shortcomings of laureateship
In 1980 he entered 'Joseph was a Tin Man' in the English Verse section. The poem is a well measured ballad, and we strongly sense the influence of Charles Causley, both in the chosen form and in the subject matter. He wraps Cornish history, a love of narrative and the Christian mythology together to evoke Cornwall and the effect that the Cornish environment exerts on sorrowful minds and hearts. The narrative draws on the folklore tale that Joseph of Arimathea came to Cornwall to trade tin, perhaps bringing with him the boy, Jesus Christ, whose enduring presence even today is in

> The sound that hushes weeping
> And fills the heart with peace,
> That soothes the hurt of sorrow
> And causes cares to cease.[6]

He speculates that, as the sorrows of Messiah-ship later bore down on him, his few moments when he 'shared the children's play' will have brought Christ comfort – that Cornwall had played the role which very many attribute to it all the time – a spiritual nurture and healing – and in that way, self-effacing and unrecognised, provided a significant contribution to the evolution of Christianity. Behind the fanciful ballad lies a truth which many Cornish people fix at the core of their appreciation and expression of Cornish values – namely, that Cornwall is a place which has a part to play in big affairs, and it does so by celebrating and openly offering the joy and belonging of small communities, the freedom of unconstrained play, by influence rather than rhetoric or action.

Richard Jenkin was deeply immersed in the Christian story, and he finds, even in this most public of verse exercises, an opportunity to celebrate the way in which Cornwall and Christianity have seemed to absorb each other – the culture and the myth reinforce each other. Is it possible that, as the child Jesus played freely with Cornish children during his visit, so Cornish values informed the development of Christian thinking as it spread north out of the Mediterranean, through the Celtic world and towards the Teutons and Slavs? 'Joseph was a Tin-Man' raises a debate, and reaches out to Cornish people to take pride in their story and their contributions to the world.

Stanza by stanza he explores the possibility in quite prosaic terms that Cornwall affected Christ.

> And surely He remembered
> On many a sadder day
> How long ago in Cornwall
> He shared the children's play.

There is, of course, no record of Christ having played with Cornish children. The myth that he visited Cornwall is intensely held and of long standing in Cornish folklore, just as it is amongst South American tribes who characterised him as Quetzalcoatl.[7] Richard Jenkin's purpose, we sense, is less to speculate historically, and more to build a tradition of involvement in the world, of shaping events – if Christ played with Cornish kids, then his request 'Suffer the children to come unto me' is, at least playfully, grounded in a Cornish experience. The poem resolves itself by becoming a celebration of a typical Richard Jenkin theme – the healing and inspirational effect of nature on the human spirit:

> And sure the King of Sorrows
> When all was dark around,
> Remembered days in Cornwall
> And heard the soft sea sound.

> The sound that hushes weeping
> And fills the heart with peace,
> That soothes the hurt of sorrow
> And causes cares to cease.

It is in this relationship, more so perhaps than any other, that the modern Celtic personification finds its truest and most accessible foundation. The Cornish, through their folklore, their art, their religious evolution and approach to the gathering of their physical and cultural inheritance about them, offer the world around them something special – increasingly, compellingly persuasive and rewarding – and it is the realisation of this at an early stage in the post-war Celtic Cornish revival that Jenkin explores, advocates and develops in his poetry. His work as an animateur, politician and teacher embodies this. The results of his energy and intelligent insight abound in modern Cornish society, and in the perceptions of Cornwall held by others worldwide.

Richard Jenkin would have vehemently denied sole responsibility for this celebration, and would have picked out many others throughout history. He was, however, a driving force through the period 1950 – 1990. His work as a poet, although mostly unpublished, reflects this. He entered many competitions regularly and, we must assume, felt that this was sufficient dissemination of his work.

Death's motivation
Richard Jenkin emanated from a securely Anglican tradition. Evidence for this abounds in his poetry. As he immersed himself more deeply in the Cornish experience he, like many others, discovered an evolutionary thread of spiritual expression, reaching back into pre-history, beyond Christianity, personified in the Stones, and forward to a baffling diversity in the modern period. The physical evidence of this evolution is all around us. In 'The Old Stones', an otherwise less than successful entry to the Eisteddfod of Cornwall 1986, he declares:

> The old stones stand as monuments to men
> And their unending quest for life beyond
> The limits of their time and local fame.[8]

It was 'life beyond' that he settled upon in his personal quest, driven no doubt by the less than optimistic life within which speaks out so often, the doubt seeking comfort in the song of nature and in the

> ... mysteries like ruined lanns
> Buried deep in shifting sands of time.

In 'The Holy Well', his 1992 entry to the Gorsedh (English Verse on a Cornish subject), Richard Jenkin again found poetic success. The strict versification is a vestige perhaps of the circumscribed familiarity with Anglican mores that informed (and possibly frustrated) him. The poem opens by drawing the reader inside a well – 'Stoop beneath the granite arch'. As eyes accustom to the interior he picks out 'Where water slowly oozes and rock bleeds' and, alighting on evocative detail, '....a few pale water-weeds.'

He turns to the historical picture and, with ease, gives us the saint 'knelt here', the free availability to one and all of 'God's gift of living water'. He celebrates 'simple piety'. In the third stanza 'officials' – a fine choice of language which jars the reader from medieval simplicity, perhaps hinting at a time before schism, reformation, inter-denominational rivalry and all the clutter of modern Christianity – erect 'A board – "Unfit for Drinking"' – thus 'custom's broken by a new-born dread.' The clash between a time of simple piety and officious intervention, as far as the poem is concerned, resolves to explain why, in this time:

> The body's thirst and soul's baptismal grace
> Have lost their satisfaction and their source.[9]

The poem concludes with a weary lament for the loss of faith which characterises modernity, and which, increasingly, left those imbued with a strong sense of the bond between good society and clear faith in a sense of inner distress. In his deceptively quiet way, Richard Jenkin marshals both his intellectual preoccupations and his poetic gift to produce a memorable poem which manages anger, infers rage and demands remediation.

Earlier, in 1984, Richard Jenkin, in 'Elegy', examines the aridity of modernity, the machine age, and considers the remains of life:

> ... A name in record books;
> Bare statistics on a census form;
> A granite tombstone in a churchyard row;
> At best a foot-note in a history book.[10]

Are these evidence of a lack of a God? The desolation of life without faith finds expression in an extended metaphor:

> The heat-pump stopped; the body growing cold;
> The automaton run down, its clockwork broken;
> The plug pulled out; computer de-programmed,
> Tape wiped, memory gone, connection cut.
> The store of knowledge lost; a live wire earthed.
> Where is he now? – Above the bright blue sky
> Or bubble burst, dispersed? Bio-degraded?

The machine, the body, ceases to operate and that's that – 'The store of knowledge lost'. He casts about amongst the mechanical world – clockwork, electricity (the plug pulled out), computers, tapes, a live wire earthed – even a degradation from romantic metaphor for the heart to 'the heat pump'. The poem is fast, its rhythm bumpy, almost staccato, and it is, again, asking 'What's the point?' 'Elegy' is not dedicated to anybody, and can easily be taken as an elegy for self whilst alive, anticipating death. Faith emerges to save the day, and the poem, from its malaise:

> Does some fragmentary consciousness
> Watch and feel success or failure still,
> Impotent to intervene but yet
> Glad or grieved as generations pass?

At a celebratory AGM of Mebyon Kernow when Richard last addressed the Party before his death, he sternly warned that, if electoral success did not occur, and if independence were not obtained with alacrity, then he would haunt the Party. In 'Elegy' we can find an origin for the image which he chose to leave his

Party with as he slipped away. A thirty year gap between poem and speech suggests a resolution of the doubt of the poem's concluding pleas:

> O God, if there is a God, would that I knew.

The avuncular joke with which he concluded his valedictory speech included a strong hint that he had every intention of doing just what he said, if he had the chance. We can derive, I think, from this that the great question of whether there is a form of life after death – and if not, how does the strong individual reconcile the drive to shape history with the anonymity of death – played on Richard Jenkin's mind. It is a key theme which, in one way or another, he alludes to and tries to tease out in many of his poems.

He asks:

> What remains of the love and care he gave
> To all those causes that he made his own?

The compulsion to adopt the causes is a source of early wonder, the strength needed to sustain momentum and commitment requires constant revitalization, and the purpose remains elusive and compromised by doubt. These are not original dilemmas, nor do they challenge philosophically the common experience of very many individuals – but Richard Jenkin chose to portray them, to publish his work to his peers, and to continue, despite his doubt, to secure and manage the authority of leadership within his culture and society. This is not the behavior of a ruthless or dictatorial man, but rather the preoccupations of one whose convictions led him to lead, and whose vulnerability represents the aspect of his character which followers and supporters found attractive. In this rather complicated manner, it is possible to suggest that Richard Jenkin's poetry played a role in shaping perceptions of himself and served a 'political' purpose.

A lament to inner life

In the body of work which Richard Jenkin has left us, we find two or three voices – the narrator of tales, the political romantic and the lyrical poet. The forms range from tight free verse to well-formed ballads, and are fairly conservative. Much of his appreciation of poetic form and function derives from the hymnal, from the vocal celebration of things, of landscapes, places, nations, sometimes people. The poet himself is a constant brooding presence, torn between leadership and self-doubt, bound to raise spirits with statements of intent, securing the sliding self-confidence of his people, bound to a course of his own choice. He would probably have proclaimed, though, that the choice was made for him because his ancestral loyalties, his sense of belonging and his strongly developed awareness of the injustice in the cultural eclipse of the Cornish in the age of the media determined his path, making it inevitable. The burden of destiny rests in the hold of his poetic craft, perhaps preventing a wider exploration of poetic potential, of inner dimensions of feeling and dimension. This leaves the reader sensing that there is a body of poetry in this dutiful, vocational and dedicated activist which never found the page – a body of insight, exploration, of lyricism and passion which remained frustratedly unexpressed, a humour and an invention, even a playfulness and possibly an anger which infers, presses between the written lines, but never cracks.

The internalized voice which one suspects narrated a different interpretation of many events in his life, rarely surfaces:

> I feel the ageless wind more keenly blow,
>   The sun has lost his strength;
> The blaze of blossom burns more dimly now
>   Throughout the long day's length.
> The distant hills have vanished from my sight,
>   The world's horizon shrunk;
> The fleecy clouds are now no longer bright
>   And my high hopes have sunk.[11]

This sombre and disappointed poem could easily pass for a lament to his inner life, frustrated by the distractions of the material world. It concludes:

> The dark, within, without, has deeper grown
>   As eyes and spirit tire.

The resulting legacy of poems, whilst it offers a versified narrative of evolving ideas, of responses to loss, a series of calculated provocations, together with a desire to flex technical muscles by writing within tightly structured forms – especially the ballad – does not, sadly, present the full inner life of a man, a poet, who could, given time, less distraction and some freedom, have offered to his culture and his cause a lasting lyrical and philosophical body of art.

It must be one of the pitfalls of leadership, perhaps a lack of generosity on the part of the led, and a testament to the inward drive required, that such an original and forceful mind and a motivational and sometimes fiery passion could not break free of the hymn, of the prosaic and the pressure of material compulsion to make the art of which, from the evidence of his published and private poems, he was capable, or, at least, promised to be. The events and preoccupations of everyday life took him away from his internal discourse, which must have nurtured frustration and possibly even anger. The occasions for writing, the many competitions and platforms he felt he had to enter or stand upon sometimes, between his lines, in the potential of the subject matter and the approach, hints at a depth of regret which often sat gauntly in his eyes.

Sometimes he does 'open the hatch', as in 'Garden Thoughts':

> Buttercups and dandelion heads
>   Glow in garden green,
> Gatecrashers of the formal flower beds,
>   Shameless to be seen.
>
> In ambush lie the lurking nettles
>   That wound unwary Eves,
> But spare the butterfly that settles
>   On their resentful leaves.
>
> The apple blossom gently tumbles down
>   Like snowflakes out of time.
> The garden arch the rambling roses crown
>   Helps the woodbine climb.

> Among sweet williams, pinks and scented stocks
> Intruders elbow in –
> Bramble, butterbur, deep-rooted docks –
> Eden soiled by sin.[12]

Here, he is subtle and ironic. The blend of tranquility established by plants and gardener, the intrusions of shameless gatecrashers, resentful nettles, docks and brambles (the wide-boys of the garden!), and the final crushing line – 'Eden soiled by sin' – seems to embody the perfection he saw for himself, the Cornwall he strove for, as he embarked on his life, constantly corrupted and overridden – all this inferred in an image that, with the clarity of vision and lyricism of a poet in full control of his art, strikes at the heart. This is an unforced poem, lacking the polemic which renders many other pieces prosaic. Denied the time and space to hone and shape his poems we can see however in such occasional glimpses that Richard could have achieved a finer body of poetic work than he did.

A political eclipse of the poet

Richard Jenkin discovered Cornwall through discovering his family history. His constant reference to forebears guides us towards this in his work. He also derived from a professionally Christian background, and this structured narrative provided him with much of his experience of form, of narrative and of ethics. When he arrived, his innate romanticism and his appreciation of social conditions – derived in part from his experience as a schoolteacher – will have quickly opened his eyes. It led him to evolve an analysis of the Cornish situation which drove him towards a politicization of the cultural expressions already familiar in the Gorsedh, the Old Cornwall movement and in the emerging popular literature of the day, where Daphne du Maurier's Cornwall was, in the post-war period, gaining a tight grip on the public imagination. Richard's first task on arriving was to find things out, to adopt the mythologies of being Cornish. He had no trouble igniting a passion for places and landscape, and found the galloping decay evident in the mining areas a rich source of fuel for his melancholy. He also found like-minded people and the politicization transformed itself quickly into Mebyon Kernow.

It is interesting to find in reading his poetry that, whilst the personal tribulations of assuming political leadership weighed heavily on him, Richard did not use the poem as a platform for expounding or exploring the developing body of political thought in which he was such a key player. Through his competition entries he often asked his reader to look, but rarely to interpret or to conclude – and despite his clerical background, he did not lead his reader towards judgments. Thus, in artistic intent, if not necessarily in execution, his craft was motivated by the impulse to share and to raise questions, to ask people to look a second time at familiar things and to ask themselves what lay there for them in constructing their new, modern mythology.

We might ask if Richard Jenkin consciously subjugated his poetic impulse and its resultant outpouring to the worldly objectives he set himself. In doing so he may have found it important to edit out of his writings those avenues and gateways of inner exploration which sought to distract him from his chosen Cornish path. He was a busy man with many responsibilities, coupled with a strong drive to achieve. He may have been distracted from poetry by many, competing demands for his attention – whether from schoolchildren, bards, politicians or Old Cornwall Societies. Given time and space, there are hints between many lines of a more profound inner life that could have generated more challenging and insightful poems.

Perhaps the sacrifice of turning aside from the more spiritual journey, a form of expedition for which both his upbringing and intellect prepared him, represents the source of the melancholy which underpins his published work. If we consider this aspect of his poetry – that is, the poems that were not made – then we might conclude this brief reflection with a note of regret. However, the sacrifice of personal artistic and spiritual fulfillment was made to enable the risks to be taken, the thinking to be done, and the graft of foundation-laying to be undertaken that have, in many ways, produced the intellectual, political and cultural climate in which Cornwall finds itself today.

Haunted with poetry
Perhaps we can conclude by suggesting that Richard Jenkin experienced a strong poetic impulse, and he used it occasionally, but rarely did he allow it to flow freely. In doing so, in making what must have been conscious choices –

"Do I use an evening to write a poem or to write an election address?" – he denied himself, but has left a legacy of a culture, a place, a clear sense of direction and identity which is allowing art – Cornish art – to find its feet and to make its mark in the world. The films, books, music, images and thinking which now shape, reflect, motivate and portray modern Cornwall owe as much to the artist in Richard Jenkin as they do to the politician and the animateur – in a real sense we can propose that Richard Jenkin's greatest creative achievement was modern Cornwall, deeply imbued with a strongly rooted yet creative culture.

Of course, it is easy to look at this sheaf of papers, his collected poems, and to consider the reasons why many of his poems were created, and to carp at the clumsiness, the rigidity of form and thought, the inhibition and the reticence to 'open the hatch'. However, we must recognize that Richard Jenkin has bequeathed us a body of poetry that describes his experience, that reflects, cajoles, explores and celebrates; that plots the tribulations, the doubts, the missed footing on Bodmin Moor and the sinking 'ankle deep into a soft green slime'.[13]

In his poems we see him become the character of the place he adopted and whose cause he so nobly and lengthily fought. It is, and should be, for the understanding of the man, rather than for the critical imperfections of his work, that we value these poems. They help to map a very complex man as he shaped a very complex place to meet its very complex future with confidence.

In concluding his final valedictory speech to Mebyon Kernow, Richard Jenkin, in his most schoolmasterly tone, told the Party (and guests) assembled at the Penventon Hotel, Redruth, that if an Assembly and domestic autonomy were not quickly secured for Cornwall, then he would come back to haunt the Party – this poetry is part of that haunting.

Notes

1. 'Wandering Heath' (Lew Dan); Gorsedh competition entry, [1982]. Unless otherwise stated, the poems may be found in the Jenkin family archive.
2. 'Greece – England – Cornwall' (Garfield Richardson); written circa December 1950/January 1951 and Gorsedh competition entry 1981.
3. 'A Bird in the Room' (Garfield Richardson); 'written in the '70s' and Gorsedh competition entry 1980.
4. The footnotes include (in brackets) the noms de plume adopted for each cited poem.
5. For the purveyor of even modest crosswords, the nom de plume, Garfield Richardson, would have been a

simple matter.
6 'Joseph was a Tin-man' (Garfield Richardson); Gorsedh competition entry 1980.
7 The Aztecs thought Cortes was the promised 'Second Coming' of Quetzalcoatl and offered no resistance until the truth dawned, by which time it was too late.
8 'The Old Stones' (Gwythy Segh); Eisteddfod of Cornwall competition entry 1986.
9 'The Holy Well' (Spearsedge); Gorsedh competition entry 1992.
10 'Elegy' (Garfield Richardson); Gorsedh competition entry 1984.
11 'Time Passes'; undated Richard Jenkin poem.
12 'Garden Thoughts' (Scryfer a-Bell); Gorsedh competition entry 1986.
13 'Walking on Bodmin Moor' (Tewolgow Down); Gorsedh competition entry 1988.

Reminiscences

Gawen Jenkin

A very personal family memory
Dad had a heart attack just before [my summer break in Cornwall and Scilly], so there were lots of visits to hospital to see him. Compared to the other men in the ward he was full of life, laughing and telling jokes and rapidly completing every newspapers crossword that we could supply him with. There was talk of a bypass operation being required and everything seemed very positive when he was sent home a couple of weeks later.

Well, it turned out that things were a lot worse than we had been told by the hospital, so when Dad got a chest infection in October, that was enough to give him another heart attack (while I was holding his hand) which took him past the point of no return. He slowly faded away over the next few days. Fortunately, all the family were able to get to Cornwall and spend some precious time with him. He had a great send off, with the church packed with those who knew him through his Cornish cultural and political work. Riwana, my niece, had recorded some beautiful harp music, which of course had everyone in tears. Will Coleman piped a lament at the graveside and then we all went to the village hall for tea, just as such things should properly be done.

He is very much missed, but we have many happy memories to keep. He was such a gentle and modest man, it seems all the more remarkable what he and a small group of others started so long ago now (there were obituaries in all the local papers and some of the British nationals). Nowadays the Cornish flag is seen everywhere in Cornwall and nobody is ashamed to declare that they are

Cornish; a far cry from the situation in the '50s. He revelled in knowledge and no doubt could have won a few quiz shows if he had been bothered to enter. Despite his highbrow side he had a really cheesy sense of humour, which I do my best to continue. Even in those last few days he was remarkably sharp. As I was sitting with him, I read out loud a crossword clue that I was stuck on: 'a small crown (7), 4 blanks, N blank T'. Straight away he opened his eyes and said "coronet, I think boy" with a grin of enjoyment at solving the clue. I tried a couple more, which he answered as quickly, but with his eyes closed. There was much sabre rattling concerning Iraq at the time, and Dad told me something that I had never known – that he had been to Baghdad with the army just after the war. I guess he had never thought it relevant to mention before!

Per Denez

Richard Jenkin (1925-2002)[1]
Two weeks ago I got the message that Richard was in a Truro hospital and there was little hope. I phoned and asked his family to tell him I was thinking of him. Can the kind words of an old friend bring comfort, even a little comfort to someone who is facing death? Maybe, I hope so... Now Richard has left us. I have in front of me some photos taken during the Celtic Congress in Nantes in 1974 when his reputation was at its height; he was not yet 50 years old. As he was in those photos, that's how I want to remember him, that's how I will remember him: twinkling eyes, a smiling face, looking like a leader, both calm and unyielding. That face is the one I will give to my readers to keep.

Richard's destiny was similar to that of many other Celts – he was born in exile and it was here he came to an understanding of his identity. For his bardic name in the Cornish Gorsedh he chose *Map Dyvroeth*, Son of Exile, thus broadcasting the source of his calling. His father, who was studying away from Cornwall to be a vicar, had a great love for Cornwall and his birthplace of Mousehole. He knew how to describe to his children the astonishing picture that one keeps of one's home and childhood. Because of all this, even though Richard Garfield Jenkin came into this world in Ilkeston in Derbyshire on 9 October 1925, Cornwall was in a way from the start alive for him, around him and within him. But it was he who found his own way to the heart of his country through a fortunate event! He was surely lucky when looking in Manchester Town Library to find a book in Cornish. It was an amazing chance that there were any books like that in Manchester. This shows how much influence one book, even an unimportant one, in the language of his country can have. As Richard was a wise man, he made up his mind that because he was Cornish he had to learn Cornish – a language which was known first and foremost for having disappeared with Dolly Pentreath. How happy the linguists must have been for once to be able to give a specific date for the death of a language! Thanks to this chance find in Manchester, Richard became one of the most hard-working people to prove that the linguists had made a great mistake.

As well as being wise, Richard was also hard-working and active throughout his life. In Oxford University where he was studying he set up a Cornish Society. I knew one of these first militants one of his companions, John Legonna. As often as he could, Richard travelled to the old country. He made long-lasting contacts with the movement there after his father had been given parishes there, first in St Gennys, near Bude, and then in St Mewan. The time for his return from exile had arrived. He went to Penzance Grammar School for his period of teaching-practice – it would have been difficult to have gone deeper into Cornwall. He was finally appointed to his first job in Totnes, so even though it was not in Cornwall, he was next door. Cornwall became his main focus. He married Ann Trevenen, who came from Redruth and who was and remained totally behind him in his work for Cornwall. Soon after, they started to publish a duplicated magazine – how many various duplicated works were produced by our different movements, always in need of money – a magazine called "New Cornwall". The name was like the call of the Gorsedh horn. Richard was a member of the [Federation of] Old Cornwall Societies, but his magazine – their joint magazine – looked forward, first and foremost, to the future, even if it respected the fact that the richness of the past should be protected and valued.

Richard and I were friends for more than half a century, from the time of the Celtic Congress in Brest, and I saw him continuously progressing in his involvement for Cornwall. He had chosen a difficult path from the beginning, the language, but he realised early on that the language could not survive if there were no Cornish powers to enable it to live, so he turned towards politics.

Devolution has not so far been achieved, but the fact that there is a movement which has been fighting clearly and openly for it has increased the energy of the language movement. Last year, when the 50th anniversary of Mebyon Kernow was celebrated, Richard, one of the three remaining founder members, announced rather sadly but with humour that he would come back to haunt them if devolution was not obtained in the next 50 years.

However, there has been a strong language movement and Richard worked with Agan Tavas and with Kowethas an Yeth in order to participate in the discussions about the place of Cornish in education and in the Church through the Bishop's Advisory Group on Services in Cornish. He stood as a parliamentary candidate for Mebyon Kernow in 1970 and won 940 votes, and again in 1983 when he gained 500 votes. His greatest success was in the European elections in 1979 where he gained 10,209 votes for the Cornish seat (We can notice that Cornwall had its own seat[2] while Brittany has none in the state that claims to protect human rights!) Two of Richard's children, Loveday and Conan, both work for Mebyon Kernow and have both stood in elections.

Richard was at the head of the Cornish Gorsedh for nine years; only Morton Nance, one of the Cornish revivalists, had that responsibility for longer and Ann Trevenen was also Grand Bard after him. In Wales the Gorsedd is a well-known and generally-respected national institution. It is respected for its work for Welsh culture and for honouring the language. Following the Welsh example, a Gorsedh was set up in Cornwall similar to the Welsh one. It would be an idea to study why the Gorsedd did not develop in a similar way in Brittany. I think some of the responsibility can be put on the Church and on the pro-French attitude of some of the Breton bards.

Richard had an important role in the International Celtic Congress and I believe that the Congress was an important part of his life. It is my opinion that he found solace and support for the struggle in Cornwall through his contact with the Celtic Congress where he was International Secretary, then Vice-President and then President for several years. He was the International President when the Congress met in Nantes in 1974 with over 700 participants, most of them young, and was filmed by the BBC. He had contacts with many Bretons: Ronan and Eleñ Huon, Per Manac'h, R. Loarer, Perig Keraod and his family, where their children went to stay in one another's houses during the holidays, and many others I expect. His daughter Morwenna, who taught Welsh and Cornish in Rennes University for many years, is now a teacher in Diwan. I remember my conversations with Richard, our long exchanges of letters. The Congress has been a place of reflection and creativity for our movements and also a place of mutual aid. One example: I had managed to get a publishing house in Paris to publish beautiful colour books for children and thought it would be good to get my Irish and Welsh friends to take advantage of this project. Books were published in Wales and Ireland – and I think it was done in Cornwall, too[3] – as they were when I was sent to teach in Bergueus (to thank me for teaching Breton in the *lycée* in Quimper, amongst other things!). It was there in the publishing house of my friend from Rennes, Jean Paris, that I had Breton texts printed to stick under the pictures in French books. We've come a long way since then – we can now get the complete Tintin collection translated into Breton. I believe that we have not managed to take as much advantage of the powers of the Congress as we could: for example, we have not publicised enough the Declaration of Cultural Rights which was set up through our joint work in Nantes. Too much work and not enough workers, I expect. Now that our way of life has changed, there are many different opportunities for contacts between the countries in many different fields and things are all the better for it, although the importance of the Congress in Brittany as a great event in the past has been forgotten a bit. There is no point regretting it now. The Celtic Congress is still needed, but it needs to find a new role. I have one regret, a personal one, when I think of the Congress – that I have never visited Cornwall, not even for the Celtic Congress. I know Richard would have liked it. Now it's over, I never will.

Richard was a steadfast worker; a leader, excellent at creating. He knew how to win the hearts and the agreement of people, how to bring them together to work together. He had many responsibilities in many organisations and he always knew how to open wide the door, go towards people and persuade them to participate. He created the St Piran's Day march, named after the patron saint of Cornwall within the Cornish Esedhvos. He was at the forefront of many ceremonies, even if he could not take part in the great march to London in honour of An Gof, the rebel who led an army from Cornwall to London to uphold the freedom of the country. Richard shared with him the same engagement and love for his language and country.

The language for him was not something to be talked nicely about and forgotten after. It was the language of his life, of his people. He was a prolific writer in Cornish, both in poetry and prose. I would like to make a suggestion for something to be done under the auspices of the Celtic Congress to honour their past president. When Richard's family announced his death, they asked us in a fine and moving way 'not to mourn and weep but to remember a great Cornish man'. A wonderful way for us to remember him, to keep alive his memory, to keep him with us even though he is gone, a source of life, of reflection, of culture, would be to publish a collection of his works both prose and poetry, the Cornish text with the Breton translation beside it. Richard could read Breton, as he could also read Welsh. And it was a great pleasure for him to have three Breton-speaking grandchildren in Brittany. Those flowers, put on your grave Richard, would not wither.

Richard left writings after him. The organisations and groups he had participated in, and in which generally he played an important role, will continue along the path he has carved out. The passionate words of his speeches will still echo in people's conscience when his voice has been silenced. But even better, his family will continue with his work, his wife Ann Trevenen who is now working on bringing together the Cornish diaspora, his children Morwenna, Loveday, Gawen and Conan. And the memory of their grandfather will shine for Trystan, Riwana, Mark, Talwyn and Trifina.

Richard Jenkin died on 29 October at the age of 77 in Truro Hospital. His funeral was celebrated in Crowan Parish Church on the 9 November and he is buried in Crowan churchyard. His family did not want flowers, but if you so desire, gifts can be made to Crowan Church or the Richard Jenkin Memorial Fund to work for Cornwall. There is no better way to honour a man who was a tireless worker for Cornwall and Cornish.

"Joy in Death"

Notes
1. This tribute was first published in *Al Liamm* in December 2002. It was translated into English from Breton by Morwenna Jenkin. Per Denez died in July 2011.
2. It was, in fact, a combined Cornwall and Plymouth constituency.
3. The books were, in fact, never published in Cornish because there was no money to do so at the time.

Liz Pritchard

Thinking of Richard when he was teaching with John, I recall images of him in my mind and they all relate to his passion for all things Celtic. Richard was living in digs near our home in Bargoed, without access to radio, no television then. We had a wireless; once a week a programme for Welsh learners was broadcast. Richard came and spent the evening with us. I am not sure how far he progressed with the language after leaving Bargoed, but I like to think that he began the journey listening to our battered old wireless.

The outstanding memory I have is of Richard's passion for Cornwall: end of term and he was away as fast as his car would take him to where he longed to be… Richard said that he could see the road speeding away, through the car floor!

We were very fond of Richard; he was always a welcome visitor, and talking endlessly of Cornwall was no hardship for John and myself; we loved it too.

Noel Carthew

I still regard my time with you both in 1999 as very special, and one of the great highlights of two months travelling around the world, and my first time in Cornwall… Richard had never met me before I arrived at your home to stay for a few days, but he was gracious enough to let me borrow his car one day to drive up to Padstow to meet some relatives of mine – his words as I left were "Look after my car, won't you!"

A much more 'special' memory, though, is that one evening you weren't well, and Richard had to entertain this visitor from Australia (and I'm sure he would have much preferred to be by himself in his study!) However, he and I spent three or four hours talking over all sorts of things from the pronunciation of Cornish place names, to Shakespeare, to our respective Cornish family histories. I have always considered myself to have been very honoured (and humbled) at Richard's willingness to share his incredible knowledge and love of Cornwall with such a relative stranger (though I had met you in Australia and Pennsylvania earlier in the year, and he'd probably heard my name mentioned!), and it was one of those situations where 'the time flew' and I could have kept talking for much longer...

What else... one evening, playing "Upwords" with your family and grandchildren, when Richard came last – and I have no doubt at all that he'd deliberately played in such a way as to keep me from coming last instead!

I also remember travelling with Richard to the Gorsedh at Hayle, while you were being interviewed by the BBC, or some such, at home; then travelling home again after the Gorsedh dinner in a thick fog, with you coming behind in your car... I remember the Breton bards were quite interested in this visitor from Australia, but I had no Breton, French or Cornish, and they had no English – they wanted my address, but I never heard from them... I stayed at a B&B in Liskeard on my way back to London; one of the other guests there was a young Japanese man who was fascinated by things Cornish and had travelled to Cornwall especially to attend the Gorsedh ceremony – he was almost bowing to me when he discovered that I not only knew the Grand Bard but had actually been staying with her!! He was another one who wanted my address, despite problems with language and communication, but I never heard from him either.

When I met Richard again at Dehewlans 2002, he greeted me like a long-lost friend, which was very much appreciated, and I was once again 'humbled in the presence of greatness'.

Peter Berresford Ellis

I was in the Celtic League in 1966 when a friend Pádraig Ó Conchúir (chair of the CL in London) asked me to come and meet Robert Dunstone, then leader of Mebyon Kernow, who was visiting London in the hope of setting up a branch of MK. Sadly, he could not find any Cornishmen or women who seemed to have time or inclination or ability to set up the branch and so he designated us 'honorary Cornishmen' and we set to work to set up the branch. Pádraig, in public statements used the name 'Henry Pool' and even today people still think my origins are Cornish. (My father was Irish and my mother was from a Sussex family whose own mother was from a Breton family). I became press officer of the branch and through early 1967 I was turning out articles for various publications on Cornwall, the language and MK. We held meetings in the City

THE HARBOUR AT ST. IVES — Claire White

CORNWALL—
the hidden land

by Richard & Ann Jenkin

Across the Tamar lies a Celtic country, a Royal Duchy, with a tradition, lore, language and continuing vigour all its own. The authors, editors of NEW CORNWALL, and Bards of the Gorsedd tell a fascinating story of the abiding Cornwall, a hidden land which the transient tourist seldom finds.

Ready Summer 1963 **Illustrated** **Price 4s 6d**

WEST COUNTRY HANDBOOK No. 2.

Please send .... copy/ies of **Cornwall—the Hidden Land** *immediately on publication to*

Advertisement and order form for Cornwall: The Hidden Land, New Cornwall, *July 1963*

Institute and finally attracted an active, genuine Cornish membership to take it over. This is... how I, as a Pan Celticist, became interested in Cornwall.

I moved to St Ives in September, 1967, renting a cottage just by 'The Sloop'. I know I attended various meetings – MK and other groups. I have a feeling that Robert Dunstone was addressing a meeting in Truro and it was there I met Richard. He was a local parish councillor at the time, and, of course, he was producing *New Cornwall*. It was impressive, albeit typewritten and roneo produced... He gave me a copy of *The Hidden Land* which he and Ann had written... and, if I remember, he had written a life of Morton Nance...[1]

Richard was usually always ready to help and advise and in June, 1968 I had the effrontery to start writing a series 'Our Language' in *The Cornish Times*. The series ended in December, 1968. That series grew into the Tor Mark Press pamphlet 'The Story of the Cornish language', that I did in 1971. It used to sell regularly to tourists... Of course, the continued research I was doing led to *The Cornish Language and its Literature* (Routledge & Kegan Paul) published in October, 1974. As I say, Richard was usually very helpful, but at this time – while [I was] preparing my book – he had just been elected as leader of MK and had a work load a mile high. So Pawley White and Retallack Hooper were the main ones who advised and read my manuscript.

Something that Richard did suggest to me was to write a political fiction tale. He knew I was a friend of Professor Leopold Kohr (who was the economic adviser to Ronald Webster of Anguilla) and it was the time of the Anguilla 'revolution' when in 1967 the tiny island of Anguilla tried to break away from being controlled by St Kitts-Nevis and set up its own government. Harold Wilson sent a gunboat and Anguilla was incorporated back in 1971! The idea was what if Cornwall elected an MK majority and the same thing happened? I started to write the story which was published in a magazine called *Kernow* (magazine for Cornish youth, as I recall). I wrote it episode by episode but, unfortunately, the magazine only lasted three issues, so only three episodes ever saw light. Alas, I only have two issues – the third one is missing. I can't remember what the story was called.[2] For some reason, I did not carry on with the story – maybe because there was nowhere else to continue it. I can't even remember who ran *Kernow*...

I am sure that Richard lived in Greece for a time because I remember a conversation about Greece as I had Greek friends and knew the country. In fact, I now wonder what he would have thought if he had known that one of my books *Celt and Greek* (about the ancient historic relationship between the Celts and the Greeks, especially in Anatolia) would became a bestseller in Greek translation.

Obviously, Richard was one the most influential and far-sighted Cornishmen of his time. Under his leadership, MK became far more political.

Notes

1 This was Mrs C. Morton Raymont's *The Early Life of Robert Morton Nance*, which was published by *New Cornwall*.
2 It was entitled 'King Arthur is not dead' and appeared in vol. 1 nos. 2 and 3 of *Kernow* which was edited by Michael Bray and published by Mebyon Kernow in the summer and autumn of 1971.

Rosemary Stone

My first encounter with Mr Jenkin was during my third year at Helston Comprehensive School in the mid 1970s, where he taught me Chemistry. However, what had caught my attention and even to this day still stands out very vividly in my mind was what Mr Jenkin was wearing. For I had never seen this lapel badge before; it was a white cross on a black background [and] I knew it was not the Communist badge. Later I was to learn that it represented Mebyon Kernow the Cornish National Party and it is the colours of the Cornish National flag.

For me one could say that it had sown the seed of curiosity, for every time I would pass Mr Jenkin in the school corridors at the change of lessons, this black and white badge would give off a very strong and eminent aura.

Mr Jenkin's character: from what I can recall he was a quiet man although he had an imposing presence about him. If my memory serves me correctly he would wear a tie defiantly, a tweed-type jacket sometimes with leather elbow patches and the striking black and white lapel badge, black rimmed spectacles and [had] a shock of white hair.

One has to remember that at that period in time we were taught the standard English Curriculum and one was denied everything to do with Cornwall and all things Cornish!

Yowann Byghan [John King]

It was Richard Jenkin, as Grand Bard *Map Dyvroeth*, who took my hands in his in 1978 and gave me my bardic name of Yowann Byghan. He had expressed concern about my choice, thinking that it might be frivolous, but I believe I convinced him. I agreed that Little John was ironic in view of the impressive physical bulk which I have maintained all my life, but he seemed to understand my explanation that Behan was the name of my mother's Irish ancestors, so my purpose was at least partly respectful. In fact, I changed my legal name to Yowann Byghan in 2001, and have never thought of myself by any other name for many years now.

A more serious disagreement with Richard was over the spelling of revived Cornish. A committed supporter of Kernewek Kemmyn (I had suggested that name for Ken George's proposed orthography), I was at an early meeting with Richard and many others which John Chesterfield had convened at his house, in a noble but ultimately forlorn hope that a compromise system could be agreed. I used the word "stupid" to describe a point of view that Richard had explained, and I could tell from his anger that he took my remark as a personal insult. In all the decades that have followed, my support for Kernewek Kemmyn has not wavered one iota, but I have long regretted that moment of speaking in heat, and the impression of personal disrespect which I think it must have created for him. Richard Jenkin was worthy of the highest respect at all times. He worked tirelessly for Cornwall and for Kernewek. His outward effect was modest, orderly, even scientific, but his heart was Cornish through and through, filled with poetry and unquenchable passion. His fire and energy were matched by the honesty with which he always conducted himself, true against the world, a bard in every sense and grand in achievement as well as in spirit.

Lambert Truran

Cornish Worthies: Richard Garfield Jenkin

It is my sad duty to include in this column that the above named passed away in his beloved Cornwall just three months ago. There is no doubt, of course, that members will have read of this sad news in the previous *Piskey Post*, but I couldn't help feeling that a few more details concerning his illustrious career would be welcome.

The greatest tribute I can pay him is to state that in my opinion his name stands among the very top of our host of Cornish worthies. Richard spent much of his very early life following his burning interest in things Cornish and soon after leaving school he joined Mebyon Kernow (Sons of Cornwall) as a founder member. Soon afterwards he became a member of Tyr ha Tavas (Land and Language) [Tyr ha Tavas predated Mebyon Kernow by twenty years. Ed.] and with the backing of such organisations he worked very hard to spread Cornwall's image and aspirations among the people of Cornwall and further afield.

In 1947 he was made a bard of the Cornish Gorseth with the title of *Map Dyvroeth* (Son of an exile) and what a worthy son he proved himself to be! One can easily imagine the tremendous joy he must have experienced when he and Ann Trevenen, whose bardic name was *Bryallen* (a primrose), became partners for life!

Richard was later to become the Grand Bard of Cornwall from 1976 to 1982 and Ann rose to become Cornwall's first lady Grand Bard. What a truly wonderful achievement that was by the both of them – a real fairy story ending if ever there was one!

[This tribute appeared in *Piskey Post* [Cornish Association of Western Australia newsletter] 46, February 2003.]

Michael Williams

I only met Richard on four occasions yet he made a great impression. He had considerable presence and in both his speaking and writing this grandson of Mousehole had the aura of a statesman. Like Winston Churchill, but in quite a different style, he had a fine sense of perspective.

Richard was a major player in more Cornish initiatives than anybody else in his era and, importantly, he saw quite a percentage of his dreams become reality.

He would have been an asset to the House of Commons where he would have brought an enlightened Celtic vision to debates.

As it was, Richard Garfield Jenkin was the first MK member to fight an election to the European Parliament. The fact that he polled nearly ten per cent of the Cornish vote reveals his impact and some 'in the know' reckon that with better party organisation he would have achieved an even more impressive result.

As befits a schoolmaster, he had natural communication skills and authority and, like all the best politicians, he was a good listener. Conversation with him was a two-way business. And, of course, Richard and Ann (both Grand Bards) made a powerful combination: two achievers, two people caring about Cornish history – and the future – and understanding the link.

There is a delightful photograph of them at Trethevy Quoit – long ago called Arthur's Quoit – with their lovely dog Brengy in September 2002.

This is, in fact, the back cover illustration of the 2nd edition of *Cornwall: The Hidden Land* which they originally wrote back in 1965. It may be a slim volume, but, like a proper pasty, it's full of good things: the Saints and the Nonconformists, fishing and farming, the festivals and the sports. These are only some of their themes and they hook the readers in the very opening paragraph: 'One holidaymaker said "Here we get the feel of a foreign holiday without the language difficulty."'

A great duo.

Tom Christophers

Before I was married in 1964, I lived at Rosewarne, Chapel Road, Leedstown, with an aunt, uncle and grandmother, next door to Richard and Ann Jenkin who moved here with their two small daughters in the late 1950s.

We were one of the few families in the village to have a television set. When Richard started to teach Cornish at Helston Grammar School, where he was a teacher, BBC television came to interview him and some of his pupils about why they wanted to learn the language.

When the programme was broadcast, Richard came next door to see it on our television, because the Jenkin family did not have one at that time. Richard was very amused when one girl was asked why she wanted to learn Cornish. She said that if she met an old lady who could not speak any English, she would be able to talk with her. Richard was amused because Cornish had not been used as a spoken language for several generations!

From 1976, I also served with Richard on Crowan Parish Council, where both of us represented the Leedstown Ward for many years. We had both been chairmen.

Tributes from the family archive

'I myself first met Richard in the mid-1970s at a language event and he was Grand Bard when I became a bard, so I had to negotiate my bardic name with him…

He was a dogged, determined campaigner but he was not dour. He spoke with passion and inspired the membership [of Mebyon Kernow] and the electorate… The policies he and his colleagues promoted – polices that today are perfectly acceptable and widely supported – were looked on as odd, bizarre and definitely of the fringe. That Cornwall was not part of England but a Celtic country, that it had its own flag and that to revive its social, cultural and economic fortunes it needed devolution and its own university.' (*Jori Ansell*)

'I admired Richard very much… I was delighted, as all who knew him must have been, that he merited a fine obituary in *The Times*… I'm conscious of the role of *The Times* as the journal of record par excellence, so that to have one's obituary in it is to become part of history.' (*Michael Howarth*)

'Cornwall will long remember his work for our culture…' (*Rosalie Armstrong*)

'He was one of the rocks that guided the Gorsedd and all the works it has been built upon for a number of years… He was a reference point of navigation from whom everyone in the Gorsedd took their bearings.' (*John Bolitho*)

'A central and inspiring personality in the resurgence of the Cornish identity, its language and culture, with untiring work over the past half-century…' (*Douglas Williams*)

'He was a sincere ambassador for our small nation, devoting his entire adult life to winning a better deal for Cornwall and its people, while working equally hard to protect and promote all aspects of Cornish culture.' (*Dick Cole*)

'Richard Jenkin was an inspiration to thousands right across the Celtic world who refused to accept the demise of their language and culture… He was an inspirational advocate of self-determination across the Celtic countries. It is a testament to the vision and perseverance of visionaries like Richard Jenkin that Cornwall is awakening and Mebyon Kernow is progressing.' (*Dafydd Trystan*, Plaid Cymru)

'Richard Jenkin dared to aspire on behalf of Cornwall … he may have chaired everything under the sun, but he also breathed, inspired, laughed, roared and was a friend to very many.' (*Bert Biscoe*)

'It was an honour to serve as a bearer at Richard's funeral and despite the sadness, I know that I was not the only person to come away strengthened in their resolve to pursue the cause of Cornish identity.' (*Merv Davey*)

'Richard was indeed an outstanding gentleman, one in the front row of our greatest Cornish patriots.' (*Vivian Pryor*)

'He will be greatly missed for wise judgment and guidance for the [Cornish] Gorseth and his poetry and propagation of the [Cornish] language.' (*Marjorie Trevanion*)

'We were privileged to have met him and had the benefit, as has all Cornwall (everywhere), of his kindness and his great skills and knowledge.' (*Chris, Joy, Lowenna, Owen and Kerensa Dunkerley/* Cornish Association of New South Wales)

'Richard's passing will be a great loss to Cornwall, but will also be felt far beyond Cornwall, throughout the Celtic world. His contribution to the revival of Cornish language and culture is immense.' (*Eurwen and Hugh Price*)

'… [H]e… played an invaluable part in my research over the years. More importantly I'll remember his genuine warmth, good humour, dedication and real passion for Cornwall. I am honoured to have known him.' (*Amy Hale*)

'Richard will be severely missed in Cornish organizations and events; as Anthony Richards said at a recent 'An Gof' commemoration, he was "Mr Cornwall".' (*Don Houghton*)

'Richard contributed so much to the Federation [of Old Cornwall Societies] with his love and knowledge of Cornwall. He will be much missed on the executive committee and by all his many friends in the Federation.' (*Joan Rendell*)

'… a wonderfully well-informed and wise presence as a pillar of his family, Richard was always interesting to be with – even though his ability at crosswords was most definitely speedier than ours!' (*Elizabeth Alms*, née Trevenen, Whitley, Warrington)

'It is over 50 years ago that we first met in the early days of MK; since then we had often worked together, often in different fields. Always his sheer kindness and friendship have been there (*Brian Coombes*)

'I have a lasting memory of him with utter conviction in his eyes, but in manner always gentle.' (*Eric and Deirdre Dare*, Truro)

'Cornwall has lost a great Cornishman. A quiet, determined, hard working, devoted man… I fear we shall not see his like again… However, Richard does have a memorial – his life long devotion to, and inspiration for, the Cornish people is a wonderful legacy!' (*Ann Crichton-Harris and Prof. John Senders*, Toronto Cornish)

'What can one say of Richard within the framework of a single letter? The fact is he did so much for Cornwall and Cornish causes on so many fronts. We salute him.' (*Michael and Sonia Williams*)

'I still remember his little Cornish sayings and anecdotes, as well as his habit of honking the car horn before every winding turn of road…, and his bright-eyed enthusiasm whenever anyone asked him about anything remotely historical.' (*Karen Sim*, née Trevenen)

'Being a bard has meant more to me than words can ever express. Richard was a role model for me and for many others. The Grand Bard becomes a symbolic father (or mother) for the rest of us. He was a parfit gentle knight, a poet, a scholar, a true leader, and a good, good man, sincere and compassionate, as true as they come.' (*Yowann Byghan* [John King])

'… I know that Richard had a profound effect on Cornwall's cultural life, not only through his work as a teacher in Helston, but through his contributions to the Cornish language and politics.' (*Peter Stethridge*, former Chief Executive, Cornwall County Council)

'… one of the great Cornishmen, but also… a truly lovely person who we will all miss.' (*Dr Rhys ap Delwyn Phillips*)

'We will remember Richard with all his kind smiles, and that slightly mischievous twinkle in his eye whenever he quietly spoke to you. He would focus his attention on you and make you feel quite special.' (*Martin, Janet and Julie Trevenen*)

'What a lot has happened since we were all young and raring to go, and what a splendidly full and rich contribution Richard made…' (*Prof. Charles Thomas*)

'One of my first reactions [on hearing of Richard's death] was to re-read *Cornwall: the hidden land*. It's a super little book, and as I read it I could hear Richard's voice.' (*Nicholas Armfelt*, Secretary Helston Old Cornwall Society)

'He shall be remembered both for his personal qualities and as a stalwart of all things Celtic. (*Dónall Ó Cuill*, Secretary, Irish Branch, Celtic Congress)

'... a modest self-effacing gentleman who... made an outstanding contribution to the promotion of Cornish culture and language as well as to the Celtic Congress. (*Murdo MacLeod*, Celtic Congress, Scotland)

'Every day when I look in that dictionary [Robert Morton Nance's] and think of his work with it, then I think of Leedstown and all that it means... I cannot imagine that cottage [An Gernyk] without Richard in it, working away on some major project. For me he will always be there. (*Alan Trevarthen*, Brittany)

'He was unquestionably the best preacher of the Word in 20th century Cornish.' (*Canon Richard Rutt*, Bishop's Advisory Group, Truro)

'In these days when so much of our national culture seems increasingly trite and vacuous, it is good to remind ourselves from time to time that there are those who treasure the unique place that Cornwall has on the greater tapestry of life in Britain. Richard was one such, and his contribution will be missed.' (*Christopher M. Willis*, Secretary, Cornwall Music Festival)

'He was a gentleman. In full-blooded Cornish circles I'm always very conscious of being the non-Cornish person present but dear Richard always made me feel included, belonging. I loved his gentle smile.' (*Moira Tangye*)

'I knew of all his work for Cornwall, of all his writing, speaking, editing, organizing, and so much more. I knew of all his work for Cornish, which he did not just write about or struggle for, but used in his life, in his work, in his family, and transmitted to his children. And I knew how much he and his wife worked together for everything Cornish. Cornwall, for him, was one in a family of nations, and that is why he contributed so much, so intently, so strongly to the Celtic Congress.' (*Per Denez*, Brittany)

'... for nearly 40 years we have striven for the same ends and I think the changes in the Cornish scene over that period are quite remarkable. Richard... take[s] a large part of the credit for this... He [has] been [a] beacon to inspire and example to follow by all who carry the torch.' (*Roger Holmes*, Liskeard)

'Samhaim is the most perfect time for a Celt to pass from this world to the next. A time when the veil between the worlds is very thin. I valued Richard's Christian example and he was an inspiration to me. (*Elaine Gill*, Newlyn)

'Paul always held Richard in high esteem, regarding him as one of the now sadly lacking Cornish honourables. He was always pleased to meet up with Richard on brief visits to his homeland…' (*Joan Laity*, Somerset)

'I am certain that Cornwall owes him a tremendous debt for his work and service to our beloved land. The progress that has been made in seeing that the Cornish language, culture, history and identity are recognized and given due worth is due to people like Richard who over a long period of time have striven tirelessly to see this happen.' (*Barry Kinsmen*, President, Federation of Old Cornwall Societies)

'I think he was outstanding in the intellectual as well as the emotional strength of his convictions, and the balance and good humour with which he conducted an argument, so that one really enjoyed taking part, even if one was suggesting an [opposite?] view.' (*Veronica Chesher*, Looe)

'I always thought of Richard as epitomizing a grand and proper Cornishman. Since being made a bard in 1982 and being welcomed so kindly by him, he seemed to me to symbolize all that was good and genuine about the Gorsedd.' (*Mary Martin*, Callington)

'There will not be a true Cornishman anywhere in the world who will not be deeply saddened by the news that I read in yesterday's *Cornish Guardian*… There are many great names in the long history of our county of whom we can all be proud, and Mr Jenkin's name must surely be added to that important list.' (*Peter Browning*, St Austell)

'I remember him giving a talk to my old Rotary Club many years ago and someone asked me what was the point in someone devoting so much time to and love for the Cornish language. I replied that such a person preserves a flame which

Crowan church tower flying the Cornish flag purchased from the Richard Jenkin memorial fund

when the time comes is there for everyone.' (*David Peters*, Falmouth)

'Be assured that love never ends. Richard lives on in the hearts of those who love him. He also lives on in the enduring mark he has made in the life of his beloved Cornwall.' (*Liz Pritchard*, Glan Aber, Dyserth)

'I always understood, perhaps in a way that I could not fathom during our brief meetings, that Richard was a little detached from the outside world, following up his own interests, not in a selfish way, but that these interests especially concerning Cornwall were a quite fundamental part of his personality.' (*Chris Rodda*)

'It was always so special to be in his company at Council meetings or at Gorsedds: he always had time and thought for one. (*Audrey Hosier*, Tavistock)

'Richard's achievements for Cornwall – and in so many ways – were enormous, and his tireless dedication will remain as an example to us all. He was a great Cornishman, and will not be forgotten.' (*John Fleet*, CERES – Centre for European Research within Cornwall)

'Richard was a truly great Grand Bard – I feel fortunate to have received my bardship, as it were, from his fair hands – a fine poet, a sensitive and gentle man in every sense, Cornwall will have to wait a long while before it again gets such a good friend as Richard has been to "one and all".' (*Roger and Lois Hebbes*, Calgary)

'A great poet and politician has passed on. I will miss Richard's wisdom and words.' (*Alan Kent*)

'To me, he seemed a very living link between Kernow's past and present!' (*Barry Smith*, Abergavenny)

'The struggle for recognition, justice and independence for Cornwall is made easier with such huge footsteps to follow.' (*Jane Acton*, St Ives Constituency, Mebyon Kernow)

'For the Cornish Language Movement this is an irreparable loss. Richard had a greater store and wealth of knowledge than anyone else. He was always so generous with his help and advice.' (*Hilary Shaw*, Port Navas, Falmouth)

'My own contacts with Richard… go back to my distant schooldays with *The Hidden Land* and *New Cornwall*, and for me and no doubt for many others this is truly the end of an era – and Cornwall is so much the poorer for its passing.'

(*Philip and Dee Payton*/Institute of Cornish Studies)

'The [*Times*] obituary itself was compelling and, indeed, uplifting – one man's dedication to a minority cause. There is a glory which shines through tears...' (*Norman Gallagher*, Cockermouth)

'He was a lovely, lovely man and so erudite and yet unassuming about his vast knowledge.' (*Shelagh and Paul Garrard*, Maidenhead)

'None of us who have known Richard will ever forget the tireless and wise support that he has given to all things Cornish. In particular his place in History as the first M.K. Candidate for Parliament, his voice as Ysak on the Language record, as a loyal committee member of so many organizations, or his place in the history of the Cornish Gorsedd: a quiet voice of reason during and after the split in the language movement or as editor of *Delyow Derow*. Not many people achieve as much in a lifetime.' (*Laurie Climo*)

'Richard certainly deserves his place amongst the great pillars of the Cornish revival.' (*Bill Harris*, London)

'... someone whom we all admired for his unfailing loyalty and support to our common heritage. We shall certainly miss his gentle, unassuming presence at any future [Celtic] Congresses... and we shall recall with pleasure and respect his dignity, his sensitivity and his outstanding strength of character!' (*Murdo and Catherine Macleod*, Inverness)

'I shall always remember Richard as a long-standing friend who loved his Kernow, and who sacrificed much in his desire to serve his country.' (*Gwyn Williams*, Bangor)

'He was an inspiration to so many in the struggle for continued survival of Cornish.' (*Mair Piette*, Bow Street, Wales)

Freedom

Richard G. Jenkin

In August we were all horrified by the invasion of Czechoslovakia by Russia and her client states. Their so-called justification was that any deviation from the Communist Revelation [Revolution?] was mortal sin. Their fear was that the free thoughts of Czechs and Slovaks might penetrate the minds of others and create a desire for change. Their action was a blow to the freedom and dignity of individuals and nations. Let those who have looked leftwards for a lead towards the brotherhood of nations now take warning.

Even if the Russians had believed the Czech reforms were a retrograde step, they had no moral justification for interference. The most precious freedom, because the least understood, is the right to be wrong; to make one's own mistakes and not have to accept those of others – and this freedom to choose is God-given. Men and nations cannot be made good by coercion. Those who advocate coercion, whether Puritan divines, anarchist "students", socialist "comrades", fascist thugs, or plain bully boys, merely show that their case is too weak to persuade the people.

The second important freedom is the freedom to persuade; to put a case to the public and to bring about changes by convincing the majority of the need for them. This is the essence of a real democracy, but this evidently cannot be allowed in a "people's Democracy" where an anti-communist opinion is regarded as a crime against humanity! A true democracy provides the mechanism by which change can occur and is the stronger for it. Those who will not

Richard Jenkin's gravestone in Crowan churchyard

use that mechanism and who advance violence in the streets instead of constitutional action demonstrate that in power they would be tyrants.

Conversely, a fossilized regime of the left, or right, or centre, with no capacity for change, eventually provokes violent revolutions and is ultimately less stable than a democracy. Great Britain is more fortunate than many states in that much needed reforms can be brought about by rational discussion and constitutional action. While this remains possible, any who turn to violence are traitors to the cause of democracy, reform and freedom. Those who wish for a better Britain must beware of advocates of unconstitutional short-cuts in the streets of London or elsewhere. Freedom's false-friends are its greatest enemies.

In Cornwall, many changes are needed and they can and will be brought about by the democratic method of persuading the electorate that they are essential.

[*New Cornwall*, vol. 16, no. 2, October-November 1968]

Richard G. Jenkin: a chronology

Derek R. Williams

1925
9 October — Birth of Richard Garfield Jenkin in Ilkeston, Derbyshire
1934-1936 — Attends primary schools in Bolsover, Derbyshire; Eaton Bray, Bedfordshire; and Castleton and Middleton, Lancashire.
1936-1943 — Attends William Hulme's Grammar School, Manchester
1943-1944
Oct-June — Attends Exeter College, Oxford; forms Young Cornwall Movement with fellow students.
1944-1948 — Military service, mainly with the Forces Broadcasting Service in the Middle East and the British Military Mission to Greece
1947
30 August — Made a bard of Gorsedh Kernow – by examination in Cornish – at Launceston, taking the name *Map Dyvroeth* (Son of Exile)
Winter — Family returns to Cornwall (St Gennys)
1948 — Spends summer term teaching at Bude Grammar School prior to going up to Manchester University
1950
28 Aug-3 Sept — Attends International Celtic Congress at the Royal

	Institution of Cornwall, Truro
1951	Obtains a B.Sc. Hons in chemistry at Manchester University
6 January	Present at the official launch of Mebyon Kernow at Oates' Temperance Hotel, Redruth
September	Undertakes teaching practice at St Austell Grammar School before going to Exeter
1952	
Spring/Easter	Teaching practice at Penzance Grammar School. Attends Welsh League of Youth Inter Celtic Conference in Borth
August	Obtains a Diploma of Education at the University College of the South-West of England, Exeter
Autumn	Takes up teaching post at Devonport High School for Boys
1953	
Easter	Arranges Cornish-themed photographic exhibition for Welsh League of Youth Inter Celtic Conference in Borth
Summer	Sends telegram in Cornish to International Celtic Congress in Glasgow
Autumn	Takes up teaching post at Bedwellty Grammar School, Aberbargoed, Caerphilly
1954	
Spring	Attends Welsh League of Youth Inter Celtic Conference in Borth
20-27 July	Attends International Celtic Congress in Dublin
1955	
23-30 April	Chosen at Cornish Celtic Congress in Truro as one of four delegates to attend International Celtic Congress in Brittany
5-7 May	Attends Congress of the Federal Union of European Nationalities (FUEN) in Cardiff as part of the MK delegation
20-27 August	Elected General Secretary of the International Celtic Congress at Brest; delivers lecture on 'National Life in Cornwall'

1956

Easter	Leaves Aberbargoed for a teaching post at King Edward VI Grammar School, Totnes
9 August	Marries Ann Trevenen at St Euny Parish Church, Redruth
27 Aug-3 Sept	Attends International Celtic Congress in Truro
1956-1973	Co-edits the Cornish-issues magazine *New Cornwall* with Ann Trevenen Jenkin, taking over from Helena Charles
1957	Becomes member of the Royal Institution of Cornwall
August	Attends Welsh National Eisteddfod at Llangefni, Anglesey.
September	Wins 2nd prize for Cornish poetry in Cornish Gorsedh competitions
Christmas Day	Birth of Morwenna Ann Trevenen Jenkin
1958	
7-12 April	Attends International Celtic Congress at Peel, Isle of Man and speaks on the Cornish language in Cornish schools
1959	
11 April	Birth of Loveday Elizabeth Trevenen Jenkin
10-14 Aug	Attends International Celtic Congress in Edinburgh
September	Wins 2nd prize for both Cornish and English verse in Cornish Gorsedh competitions
December	Leaves teaching post at Totnes and moves to 'An Gernyk', Leedstown
1960	Joins Helston Old Cornwall Society
	Acting Herald Bard of Gorsedh Kernow
January	Takes up teaching post at Helston Grammar School
8-12 August	Attends International Celtic Congress at Aberystwyth
1961	Is succeeded as Secretary of the International Celtic Congress by Eluned Bebb
September	Leads Crying the Neck ceremony at Gunwalloe
1961-1965	Secretary of Gorsedh Kernow
1962	Co-edits, with Ann Trevenen Jenkin, *The Early Life of Robert Morton Nance*, a *New Cornwall* publication
18-22 Aug	Attends International Celtic Congress at Landreger, Brittany; chairs meeting on 'Celtic languages in education

	and publishing' and speaks for Cornwall on 'Social and official position of Celtic languages'
September	Wins equal 2nd prize for English verse on Cornish subject, 1st for Cornish prose, and commendation for Cornish verse in Cornish Gorsedh competitions
1963	Achieves distinction in 3rd grade Cornish exam
16-20 April	Attends International Celtic Congress at Carbis Bay
3 August	Birth of Gawen Richard Trevenen Jenkin
September	Leads Crying the Neck ceremony at Crowan
1963-1972	Herald Bard of Gorsedh Kernow
c. 1963-1969	Serves as joint vice-chairman of the Cornish branch of the International Celtic Congress
1964	Recording of *Deu Whethel* (*Two stories*) by Miss J.E. Petchey, Truro
31 March-4 April	Attends International Celtic Congress on the Isle of Man
Christmas	Reads a lesson at carol service for Cornish speakers and students at Camborne Community Centre
1964-1995	Member of Crowan Parish Council, sitting for some years on Helston Museum Management Committee
1965	Co-authors, with Ann Trevenen Jenkin, *Cornwall: the Hidden Land*
16-20 Aug	One of six people representing Cornwall at the International Celtic Congress in Glasgow; speaks for Cornwall at the symposium on 'Modernising Vocabulary'
5 September	Reads a lesson at the annual Gorsedh Cornish Evensong at Kenwyn Parish Church
1965-1967	Sits on Federation of Old Cornwall Societies Publications Committee and Editorial Board
1966	
July	Interviewed about the Cornish language by team collecting material about Cornwall for the Welsh-language programme *Heddiw*
24 Aug-2 Sept	Speaks in Cornish on the political scene in Cornwall at the

	4th Annual Summer School (Scol Haf Kernewek) in Truro
4 September	Reads a lesson at the annual Gorsedh Cornish Evensong at St Ives Parish Church
22 October	Attends unveiling of memorial to Michael Joseph 'An Gof' at St Keverne
1967	
3 June	Is an opening speaker at Closed Gorsedh discussion on 'The Gorsedh in the Community Life of Cornwall'; is elected to Gorsedh Council
26-31 July	Attends International Celtic Congress in Cardiff
28 October	Is a main speaker on 'The Way Ahead' at Mebyon Kernow's annual conference
1968	Elected Deputy Chairman of Mebyon Kernow
20-25 August	Attends International Celtic Congress in Fougères, Brittany; speaks for Cornwall on 'Present situation in the Celtic countries'
8 September	Conducts Gorsedh Cornish Evensong in St Just Parish Church
1968-1970	Vice-chairman of Crowan Parish Council
1968-1973	Vice-chairman of Mebyon Kernow
1969	
7-12 April	Attends International Celtic Congress at the Kenegie Hotel, Gulval; opens discussion on 'Economic situation and its social effects in the Celtic countries'; takes Cornish language service at Gulval Parish Church
27 April	Birth of Conan James Trevenen Jenkin
8 May	Acts as Town Crier for the Hal an Tow at Helston Flora
June	Chosen as Mebyon Kernow's first prospective parliamentary candidate, to contest Falmouth-Camborne in next General Election
August	Attends Plaid Cymru Summer Schoool in Wrexham, and Welsh National Eisteddfod in Flint as representative of Gorsedh Kernow
7 September	Reads prayers at Gorsedh Cornish Evensong at Liskeard

	Parish Church
1969-1971	Vice-president of the International Celtic Congress
1970	
18 June	Contests Falmouth-Camborne for MK, polling 960 votes or 2% of vote
1970-1972	Chairman of Crowan Parish Council
1970-1991	Sits on Federation of Old Cornwall Societies Executive Committee
1971	
5 March	Gives short address at St Piran's Day Dinner in Truro
27 June	Speaks at the annual homage to Michael Joseph 'An Gof' at St Keverne
16-21 August	Attends International Celtic Congress in Stirling; contributes to symposium on Celtic art; elected president
1971-1972	Chairman of Cornish Branch of International Celtic Congress
1971-1976	President of the International Celtic Congress
1972	
14-19 August	Attends International Celtic Congress at Bangor, north Wales
1972-1976	Deputy Grand Bard of Gorsedh Kernow
1973	Stands as independent candidate for Kerrier District Council
1 September	Highly commended for English verse in Cornish Gorsedh competitions
1973-1983	Chairman of Mebyon Kernow, succeeding Leonard Truran
1974	
August	Attends International Celtic Congress in Nantes, Brittany; Declaration of Cultural Rights on agenda
7 September	Wins 1st prize and Jack Evan's Cup for English verse in Cornish Gorsedh competitions
1975	
31 March-5 April	Attends International Celtic Congress at Carlyon Bay, St Austell

6 September	Wins 3rd prize for English verse/Cornish subject in Cornish Gorsedh competitions
Autumn?	Involved in TV feature about Cornwall on BBC's Pebble Mill
1976	
Spring	Adopted as Mebyon Kernow's prospective parliamentary candidate for Falmouth-Camborne
April	Attends International Celtic Congress at Port Erin, Isle of Man
July	Attends Welsh National Eisteddfod in Cardigan as official Cornish delegate
4 September	Installed as Grand Bard of Gorsedh Kernow at Hayle
1976-1982	Grand Bard of Gorsedh Kernow
1976-2002	Honorary life vice-president of the International Celtic Congress
1977	Resigns as Mebyon Kernow prospective parliamentary candidate for Falmouth-Camborne
1979	
7 June	Polls over 10,000 votes as Mebyon Kernow candidate in the European Parliament election, standing on a separate seat for Cornwall ticket
1 September	Wins 2nd prize for both Cornish and English verse in Cornish Gorsedh competitions. Initiates daughter Morwenna as bard
1980	
August	Leads a Cornish delegation to the Welsh National Eisteddfod in Lliw Valley, west Glamorgan
7 Sept	Wins 2nd prize for Cornish verse in Cornish Gorsedh competitions; preaches sermon at the Gorsedh Cornish Evensong at Saltash Parish Church
1981	
23 June	Reads prayers in Cornish at Helston Old Cornwall Society midsummer bonfire at Manhay Beacon.
27 June	Conducts service at St Keverne organized by Mebyon

	Kernow to mark An Gof Day
August	Attends Welsh National Eisteddfod at Machynlleth as Grand Bard of Gorsedh Kernow
5 September	Gorsedh Kernow at Nance, Illogan; wins 2nd prize for English verse/Cornish subject, 3rd prize for Cornish prose and commendation for Cornish verse
6 September	Preaches sermon at Gorsedh Cornish Evensong at Camborne Parish Church
December	Retires from teaching at Helston Comprehensive
1982	Appears on Clive Gunnell's TSW programme *3 Cornish Characters*
7 March	Leads the annual Cowethas An Yeth (Cornish Language Fellowship) Cornish-language service at Trelowarren Street Methodist Church, Camborne
12-17 April	Attends International Celtic Congress in Penzance
16 April	Cornish Gorsedh Proclamation at Penlee Park
27 June	Conducts service at An Gof commemoration at St Keverne
July	Attends Breton Gorsedd as Grand Bard of Gorsedh Kernow
4 September	Gorsedh Kernow at St Just-in-Penwith; initiates daughter Loveday; wins 3rd prize for Cornish prose and 2nd for Cornish verse
1982-2002	Serves on Bishop of Truro's Advisory Group on services in Cornish
1983	Publication of *Naw Pregoth* (*Nine Sermons*) by *New Cornwall* Publications
5 March	Organizes first St Piran's Day procession
5-12 March	Chairman of 1st Esedhvos Kernow (Eisteddfod of Cornwall); wins a number of prizes in competitions
9 June	Contests Falmouth-Camborne for MK in General Election, polling 582 votes or 1.18% of vote
September	Highly commended for Cornish verse in Cornish Gorsedh competitions
15 November	Attends Boundary Commission public inquiry into call for Cornwall to have its own European Parliamentary seat

27 November	Elected vice-chairman of Cowethas an Yeth Kernewek (Cornish Language Fellowship)
1983-1984	Vice-chairman of Mebyon Kernow
1984	
18 October	Preaches in Cornish at Illogan Parish Church on the Feast of St Illogan
1985	
August	Attends International Celtic Congress in Cork
7 September	Installed as Grand Bard of Gorsedh Kernow at Perran Round
1985-1988	Grand Bard of Gorsedh Kernow
1986	
March	Chairman of 2nd Esedhvos Kernow; wins 2nd prize for Cornish verse in competitions
6 September	Gorsedh Kernow at the Merry Maidens, St Buryan; commended for Cornish verse in competitions
1987	Member of the Cornish Film Committee, Skeusow
August	Attends International Celtic Congress in Inverness
5 September	Gorsedh Kernow at Anthony, Torpoint
1988	
April	Attends International Celtic Congress in Newquay; welcomes delegates to Cornwall
July	Attends Welsh National Eisteddfod at Newport as Grand Bard of Gorsedh Kernow
3 September	Gorsedh Kernow at Poldhu; installs Dr John Chesterfield as his successor
1988-1996	Publication of *Delyow Derow* (*Oak Leaves*), duplicated Cornish-language literary magazine, by *New Cornwall* Publications
1989	
4-18 March	Chairman of 3rd Esedhvos Kernow
1990	
21 April	Attends emergency meeting of Mebyon Kernow at Redruth, where party members vote against party's dissolution

July	Gives Cornish version of prayers at service following An Gof commemoration at St Keverne
August	Attends International Celtic Congress at Swansea
1991	Publication of *40 Years of Mebyon Kernow* by MK
1991-1992	President of Federation of Old Cornwall Societies
1992	
5-21 March	Awarded Edith Warmington cup for English verse and commended for Cornish language verse in 4th Esedhvos Kernow competitions
1995	
March	Awarded Esedhvos Kernow cup for Cornish-language verse in 5th Eisteddfod competitions
2 September	Gorsedh Kernow at Marazion; awarded Cornish Crystal for Cornish-language prose and 3rd for Cornish-language verse in competitions
1996	
5 March	As chairman of Esedhvos Kernow organizes St Piran's Day procession in Truro
August	Attends International Celtic Congress in Bangor, north Wales; delivers lecture on 'Cornish literature in the Twentieth Century'
1997	
24 May	Attends start of Keskerdh Kernow march at St Keverne and is present at Launceston and Blackheath
6 September	Gorsedh Kernow at Bodmin; receives an award in appreciation of 50 years' service
1998	
5-21 March	Deputy chairman of 6th Esedhvos Kernow (Eisteddfod of Cornwall)
Summer	Attends Breton Gorsedd; attends International Celtic Congress at Port Erin, Isle of Man
10 October	Made Life President of Mebyon Kernow at Party's Fraddon conference in recognition of 45 years of service
1999	

September	Wins joint 3rd prize for Cornish verse in Cornish Gorsedh competitions
2000	
19 February	Participates in Cornish Language Focus Group (Unys/Unified Revised) at Lostwithiel
April	Attends International Celtic Congress in Bude
September	Leads Crying the Neck ceremony in Cornish and English at Crowan
29 October	Presents public poetry reading in Leedstown Village Hall to celebrate his 75th birthday
2001	Made honorary life member of Esedhvos Kernow on retirement as founder member from Council
2002	
June	Attends Midsummer Bonfire at Helston
August	Attends International Celtic Congress in Carmarthen
7 September	Gorsedh Kernow at Pensilva, St Austell; wins Jack Evans Cup for English verse by a Cornish poet in competitions
9 September	Suffers a heart attack
29 October	Death of Richard Garfield Jenkin at Treliske Hospital, Truro
9 November	Bilingual funeral service in Cornish and English at Crowan Parish Church

Select bibliography of the writings of Richard G. Jenkin

Derek R. Williams and Ann Trevenen Jenkin

Cornish books, monographs, edited magazines and contributions to the works of other authors

New Cornwall (as co-editor with Ann Trevenen Jenkin), New Cornwall Publications, 1956-1973.
'County Grammar Schools' (with Ann Jenkin), in *The Teenage Mind*, The Industrial Christian Fellowship, [late 1950s].
Deu Whethel (Two short humorous tales in Cornish...), audio cassette recording, Miss J.E. Petchey, 1964.
Cornwall: the Hidden Land (with Ann Trevenen Jenkin), West Country Publications, 1965; facsimile reprint with a new introduction..., Noonvares Press, 2005.
'The Lean Year', 'Night', and 'Miranda', in *The Meneage Book* (ed. Anthony Langdon), Bentley Rivers, [c. 1981].
'Words' and 'Spring's Approach', in *Bentley Rivers Book of Mawgan*, Bentley Rivers, [1982].
Naw Pregoth (Nine Sermons), New Cornwall Publications, [c. 1983].
'The Fellows' Garden' and 'Cleave, North Cornwall', in *Gorsedd Poems* (ed. William A. Morris), Dyllansow Truran, [c. 1983].
Cornish sermon for Illogan Feast, New Cornwall Publications, 1984.
Foreword to *The Saints' Way/Forth an Syns* (comp. Michael Gill and Stephen Colwill, Quintrell and Co., 1986.
'Cornwall Recalled (at Volos, Greece)', 'The Irish Lady' [as Garfield Richardson],

and 'The Mermaid', in *Kernow Ha'n Mor* (ed. E.T. Jenkin), An Gresen Gernewek, 1988.
Delyow Derow [Oak Leaves] (as editor and contributor), New Cornwall Publications, 1988-1996.
40 Years of Mebyon Kernow, Mebyon Kernow, 1991.
'Some Cornish place-names around Leedstown', in *Leedstown in our Lifetime: the story of a Cornish village* (comp. Ann Trevenen Jenkin), Leedstown W.I., 1994.
'Cornish Literature in the Twentieth Century', in *Celtic Literature and Culture in the Twentieth Century*, International Celtic Congress, 1997.
'An Gour Tullys/The Deceived Husband', 'Brythennek/For Brian Webb', 'An Dynas/The Hill-fort', 'Yet I Have Hope' [as Garfield Richardson], 'There Is A Shower Threatening' [as Garfield Richardson], and 'An Als/The Cliff' [as Garfield Richardson], in *Writing the Wind: A Celtic Resurgence*, Thomas Rain Crowe (ed.), New Native Press, 1997.
'Pask/Easter', in *The Wheel: An Anthology of Modern Poetry in Cornish, 1850-1980*, (ed. Tim Saunders), Francis Boutle, 1999.
'Our choughs' [poem], in *The Spirit of the King: an illustrated collection of prose and poetry to honour The Cornish Chough*, (comp. and ed. Les Merton), Palores Publications, 2001.
The Cornish Ordinalia: first play: Origo Mundi... (as co-editor with Ray Chubb and Graham Sandercock), Agan Tavas, 2001.
'Langarrow', 'Tregeagle and the Wind', 'Where I Live Now', 'Hurrah for the Tourist Trade', and 'Cleave, North Cornwall', in *The Dreamt Sea: An Anthology of Anglo-Cornish Poetry 1928-2004* (ed. Alan M. Kent), Francis Boutle, 2004.

Contributions to journals and magazines

[Richard Jenkin's own writings for *New Cornwall* – under his own name, as Pasco Trevy(g)han, and unsigned – were substantial, but a full listing has yet to be made. He also wrote extensively for *Cornish Nation* and contributed to *An Lef Kernewek*, *An Gannas*, and other magazines and local newspapers.

An Aimsir Cheilteach (The Celtic Pen): 'Merlin by the shore' [poem], [n.d., but c. 1949-1954].

Carn: A link between the Celtic nations: Letter in support of Unified Cornish and critical of 'Phoemic Cornish' and 'Cornoack Tithiack', No. 61, Spring, 1988, p. 18.

The Celtic Pen: 'Modern Cornish Literature in the 20th Century', 'Gyllys Dheves/Gone Away' and 'An Lavar Coth/The Old Saying' [poems as Garfield Richardson], vol. 1, issue 3, Spring 1994, pp. 3-5 and p. 19.

Cornish Magazine: 'Cornwall Recalled – Volos, Greece' [poem], vol. 5, no. 1, May 1962, p. 28.

The Cornish Review: 'Langarrow' [poem], No. 4, Spring 1950, p. 24. 'Tregeagle and the Wind' [poem], No. 6, Winter, 1950, p. 75. 'The Mermaid' [poem], No. 9, Winter, 1951, pp. 18-19. 'Self-Government for Cornwall? The case for', 2nd series, No. 1, Spring, 1966, pp. 13-16. 'Hand' [poem], 2nd series, No. 4, New Year, 1967, p. 17. 'Mebyon Kernow and the future of Cornwall', 2nd series, No. 9, Summer, 1968, pp. 5-9.

Cornish Scene:
'The House on the Moor' [short story, as Garfield Richardson], No. 7 (New Series), Winter, 1989, pp. 89-91.

Merlin [West Wales Writers Umbrella publication]:
'The Valleys' [poem], [no. 3], 1997, p. 24.

Old Cornwall: Review [unacknowledged] of *Cornish Crystal* by Gladys Hunkin, vol. v, no. 2, Summer 1952, p. 64. 'A Lullaby/Lull ha Lay' [poem], vol. v, no. 11, 1960, pp. 465-466. 'Old Cornwall Remembers... Talek – Ernest George Retallack Hooper (1907-1998), vol. 12, no. 4, Spring 1999, pp. 51-52.

Poetry Cornwall/Bardhonyeth Kernow: 'Picture of boats in the harbour', vol. 1, no. 1, March, 2002, p. 9. 'Gwers an mor/Sea Piece', vol. 1, no. 2, July, 2002, p. 36. 'Granny's Gift', vol. 1, no. 3, 2003, p. 51. 'Can Fleghes dhe Dykky Dew/Children's Song to a Butterfly', 'Pask/Easter' and 'Whegh Bro, Un Enef/Six Lands, One Soul', vol. 1, no. 7, 2004, pp. 29-31.

The Poetry Review: 'For Margaret', vol. 44, no. 2, April-June, 1953, p. 320.

Notes on contributors

Jori Ansell (*Caradok*) is a retired freelance translator (French, German and Cornish). He learnt Cornish with Len Orme at Camborne in the 1970s, is a Member of the Chartered Institute of Linguists and holder of the Institute's Diploma in Translation. Elected Deputy Grand Bard of Gorsedh Kernow (1988-1991), Grand Bard (1991-1994), represents the Gorsedh on the Cornish Language Board and was the Board's Publications Officer (1990-2013). Chairman of the Strategy Committee for the Cornish Language Partnership (2003-2004) and member of the 'Treyarnon' working party (2007-2008) which negotiated the Standard Written Form.

Bert Biscoe lives in Truro. He is a poet, songwriter, performer and politician. During the 1970s and '80s he toured with a variety of rock bands until, after an epiphanic moment, he returned to immerse himself in Cornish life and culture. He spearheaded the campaign to achieve recognition of the Cornish as a cultural group recorded by the UK Census, and continues to campaign to gain recognition for the Cornish as a British cultural minority under the Council of Europe's Framework Convention for the Protection of National Minorities. He is a Bard (*Vyajor gans Geryow*) and has published several volumes of poetry, including *Meditations on Carn Brea*, *White Crusted Eyes* and *TRURRA*. A compilation album, *An Kynsa*, was released in 2004, and *Feast of Worms* – a collaboration with The Moontones (producer: Tony Lamb). In 2010 he featured in *Waterwheels or Bust*, a short film by Brett Harvey. He is a member of Cornwall Council and Truro City Council.

Dick Cole is the leader of Mebyon Kernow – the Party for Cornwall. Formerly a farm worker, he studied archaeology and history at St David's University College, Lampeter, from 1988-1995, where he also gained vital political experience with Plaid Cymru. Upon his return to Cornwall, he worked for the Cornwall Archaeological Unit and helped to orchestrate an upsurge in MK's electoral activity. Dick was elected to serve his home parish of St Enoder on Restormel Borough Council from 1999 to 2009, when it was abolished. He is presently a full-time councillor on Cornwall Council, where he leads the MK Group.

Ann Trevenen Jenkin (*Bryallen*) is a mother and grandmother, writer, former teacher/librarian, Cornish Studies for Schools initiator, founder member of Mebyon Kernow and publisher. A Cornish speaker who started learning the language with Robert Morton Nance in 1949, she became the first woman Grand Bard of Gorsedh Kernow (1997-2000). She has taken part in Gorsedh ceremonies in Wales and Brittany, and has addressed Cornish Gatherings in many parts of the world. In 1997, she was one of the main organisers of and took part in the Keskerdh Kernow Commemorative March for Mikael Joseph An Gof from Cornwall to Blackheath. She also chaired the organisation for the first Dehwelans/Cornish Homecoming of exiles to Falmouth in 2002. She has held most positions in the Cornish Branch of the Celtic Congress and is now Life President. She has lectured or taken part in activities in all the Celtic countries, but has particularly close links with Brittany where she has three Breton-speaking grandchildren. She is also an active committee member of Helston Old Cornwall Society. Publications include two books about Leedstown, two collections of poetry, *Cornwall: the Hidden Land* (with Richard Jenkin) (1965 and 2005), *The Dog who Walked to London* (2003), and *Steren an Kolyn Kernow/Steren the Cornish Puppy*, (2008). She has also steered through and often contributed to at least nine Gorsedh Kernow publications since 2000. Her final work for the Gorsedh lies in her research and contribution to this seminal book on her late husband, which has been a pleasure.

Conan James Trevenen Jenkin is the fourth child of Richard Garfield Jenkin and Ann Trevenen. Born in Redruth in 1969 and raised in the parish of Crowan. He was educated at Leedstown Primary School, Camborne School, University of Wales Aberystwyth and University of Wales Cardiff. Achieving a CSE grade 1 in Cornish, he also has degrees in History and Computer Science. He has worked since 1997 as a Lecturer in Computer Science at Truro College. Living in Truro with his Truro-born wife Emma, he has three children with whom he speaks Cornish: Elowenn, Kelyn Briallenn and Davey Talwyn Trevenen. He has represented Mebyon Kernow in two general elections and has been elected to serve a second term as a MK councillor on Truro City Council.

Colin Murley joined the Royal Air Force in 1954 for five years. He worked in office management in Germany, Saudi Arabia, Papua New Guinea and London where he registered the Cornish Heritage Company Limited in 1984. He was elected as a Mebyon Kernow county councillor at St Day in 1966 and later lost at Penzance and St Just. He joined the Cornish Stannary Parliament in 1993 and retired, at seventy-five, in 2011. While in the forces, he visited the United Nations at Geneva to learn about Human Rights as a constitutional right to control people in power and protect indigenous and national minorities.

Donald R. Rawe began his writing career in 1950 with a story in the first series of *The Cornish Review*. Since then he has written novels, short stories, folklore studies, plays and poetry in both Cornish and English, being made a bard of Gorsedh Kernow in 1970 for his services to Cornish drama. His plays include *Hawker of Morwenstow* and *The Last Voyage of Alfred Wallis*. *Petroc of Cornwall*, *The Trials of St Piran* and a modern acting version of *Gwryans an Bys* (the Creation of the World) have all been produced at Piran Round. His poetry collection *Eglosow Kernow* (*Cornish Church Poems*) was published in 2005 and his most recent books include *Spargo's Confession: A Novel of Cornwall 1810-1822* (2010).

Peter W. Thomas was born and brought up in St Agnes, where he has returned to live. He is an academic/rare books librarian by profession. His publications include (as co-editor) *Setting Cornwall on its Feet: Robert Morton Nance, 1873-1959* (2007), the entry for Henry Jenner in the *Oxford Dictionary of National Biography* and an article on 'R.M. Nance's spirituality and the Cornish Gorsedd' in the 2008 *Journal of the Royal Institution of Cornwall*. He was made a bard in 1980, has worked on the Gorsedh Archives and is a member of the Archives Committee and the Holyer an Gof Committee.

Derek R. Williams was born and brought up near Camborne and has retained close links with his Cornish homeland, despite working in the Welsh Marches as a librarian for many years. A bard of Gorsedh Kernow, he has written, edited or co-edited a number of books, including *Henry and Katharine Jenner* (2004), *Setting Cornwall on its Feet: Robert Morton Nance, 1873-1959* (2007), *A Strange and Unquenchable Race: Cornwall and the Cornish in Quotations* (2007), *Cornubia's Son* (2008) and *The Francis Boutle Book of Cornish Short Stories* (2010). His latest book, *Williams, the Llawnt*, a study of the life and work of the Welsh scholar the Rev. Robert Williams, was published by Y Lolfa in 2013.